The Collected Poems of Jared Smith

1971-2011

The Collected Poems of Jared Smith

1971-2011

Jared Smith

The New York Quarterly Foundation, Inc.
New York, New York

NYQ Books™ is an imprint of The New York Quarterly Foundation, Inc.

The New York Quarterly Foundation, Inc.
P. O. Box 2015
Old Chelsea Station
New York, NY 10113

www.nyqbooks.org

Copyright © 2012 by Jared Smith

All rights reserved. No part of this book may be used or reproduced in any manner whatsoever without written permission of the author except in the case of brief quotations embodied in critical articles and reviews.

First Edition

Set in New Baskerville

Layout and Design by Raymond P. Hammond
Cover Photo by Deborah Parriott Smith

Library of Congress Control Number: 2012930700

ISBN: 978-1-935520-51-1

The Collected Poems of Jared Smith

1971-2011

for

My wife, Deborah Parriott Smith,

My son and daughter, Russell and Heather,

*My late parents, Russell and Wiltrude,
who read me Housman and Auden as a child,*

And all those I have loved throughout life.

Contents

The Uncovered Poems: The Early 1970s to Early 1980s

The Wolf Shadow / 23
Estuary / 24
Watching / 25
Death by Drowning / 26
Letter to H. S. Mauberly / 27
The Corridor / 28
Underneath / 29
Violins / 30
Promontory / 31
Searching the Horizon / 32
The Dover Gas Garage / 33
A Marriage / 34
Across a Continent / 35
Animus / 38
Destination: Hunting / 41
The Insomniac Groom / 42
The Wedding Night / 44
The Beehive / 45
The Tower / 46
Evening's Song / 47
4/26/72 and God / 48
There Is Something Soft in This / 49
The Blood of Wolves / 50
Eternal / 51
The Last Nightmare / 52
Solitudes / 54
Silence / 55
Dead Stalk Watercolor / 56
Within the Garden / 57
A Recurring Particular Day / 58

After Midnight / 59
The American Museum of Neutral History / 60
Departing From Portland / 61
Expectation of Six P.M. / 62
Looking Back on Having Left / 63
Meditation on Old Movies / 65
The Glass Forest / 66
The Spellweaver's Workshop / 67
The Young Success / 69
The Last Wedding / 70
A Silence of Wings / 71
A Time of Looking / 72
Dallas / 73
Only One / 75
Annelid / 76
The Turning Off of Lights / 77
They Did / 78
Where Nothing Gentle Survives / 79
Saturday Evening / 80
Coming on New Mexico / 81
Autumnal / 83
The Street of the Little Sun / 84
Elegy to a Beetfield / 93
The Only Man Who Lives / 95
Saturday / 97
Of Fire / 98
In the Dark of the Station / 99
Another Time / 100
Because No Space Is Now Mine / 101
Datamatatrons / 102
And All the Day / 103

Song of the Blood: An Epic

Song of the Blood / 107

Dark Wing: Book Two of Song of the Blood

Dark Wing: / 151

Keeping the Outlaw Alive

From the Rigging / 177
Keeping the Outlaw Alive / 178
A Man Screaming / 189
Fast-Food Lunch: NY / 191
The Wall / 192
Sitting Dark in Life / 193
So Far Descending / 194
This Town Is Young / 195
An Essay on Illuminations / 196
Impossibly a Businessman / 198
Give Our People / 199
The Mind / 200
If...but No / 201
This, Really, Is This / 202
When October Comes and the Wind Blows / 203
What Makes the Man Different / 205
The Wind in Winter / 206
As Evening Draws / 207
The Company We Keep / 208
Evening in the Heartland / 209
Autumn Is a Red Deer / 211
Nobody Writes about Children / 212
It Takes a Man / 213
Finding Love / 214
A Day in August / 215
The Incident / 216
Visions of a Pencil / 218
Morning Owls / 220
Exultance / 221

A Response to a Conversation with William Packard Where We Tried to
   Define Poetic Craft as Practiced by All Schools of Poets / 222
We Are the Poets. We Live / 223
Hibernation / 224
Beach at Oceanside / 225
The Interview / 226
One / 227
Face of the Phoenix / 228
They've a Kind of Patronage / 229
Model for a Romance / 230
The Eyes Too Walls / 231
Evening Coming in the East / 232
Invisible / 233
Commuting / 234
In Memory of Strain / 235
You Cannot Write a Poem / 237
The Penitent Voyeur / 239
From Your Flesh / 240
For a Woman Dead in Grand Central / 241
The Paycheck / 242
For My Daughter in Moonlight / 243
Greenwich / 244
On the Official 40th Anniversary of the Dignitaries at the U.N. / 247
Modern Man, Artificial Intelligence, and Humanity / 248

Walking the Perimeters of the Plate Glass Window Factory

Lines Written in a Waiting Room / 253
Remembering the Union Dead at My Door / 254
Walking the Perimeters / 256
He Who Says the Name of God Will Perish / 259
In the Plate Glass Window Factory / 261
Not the Lone Ranger's Horse / 262
Then Gone / 263
Wondering What It Takes / 264

Some Primal Memory / 265
Believing That You Understand / 266
Pebbles in a Stream / 267
On Mr. Peabody's Estate / 268
The Reservoir in Drought / 270
In the Year of the Comets / 271
Ode to a Goose / 272
Walking the Shore / 274
Putting the Passengers Off in Small Boats / 275
Where Wind Shakes Our Bones / 276
Putting Your Money In / 277
And the Beat in His Chest Goes On / 278
The Board Meets in November / 279
Something Natural Happening in an Office / 280
Between Meetings / 281
A Memo Torn Along the Dotted Line / 282
Another Saturday Night with Cassandra / 283
Tales of Silent Men / 284
The Eyes on the Coin / 285
At Evening / 286
The Sun Finding Your Hands… / 287
It Has Started / 288
Sound of Late Moonlight / 289
I Wish That You Were Here in Spring / 290
Returning Home / 291
The Last Trip We Took Together / 292
Our Last Walk / 293
An Apology / 294
Andrea / 296
At Home / 297
Before the Fire / 298
In the Parking Lot / 299
Turtles / 300
Information Superhighway of Death / 301

Lake Michigan and Other Poems

Getting Ready to Move On / 307
Passage from Home / 308
Mood in Grays / 309
Lake Michigan / 310
Controlled by Ghosts / 319
Seven Minutes Before the Bombs Drop / 321
Finding Oneself in an American Fairy Tale / 323
A Quantum Species / 324
In Our Attraction to Electronic Media / 325
Picking Up the Empty Packages / 326
Driving Small Town America / 327
Evening Along the Outer Banks / 329
An Erosion / 331
Erie / 333
Talking to My Son / 334
Eyes, / 335
Having Passed the Solstice / 336
Imagination and the Man / 337
It Is Time / 338
Reflecting on the Visions / 340
The Lessons of Millennia / 341
So Much Growing / 342
Within the Islands of Solitude / 343
Witnessing the Writer Who Tried to Raise a Family; Dark Matter at the Beginning of the 21st Century / 345
The Endless Chairs / 349
Tossing Jobs Around Like Manhole Covers / 350
When All Is Said / 351
To Remember US By / 352
Wait / 353
When It's Time to Go / 354
Unhinged at Last / 355
Your Room by Candlelight / 356

The Perfect Mirror / 357
Trout Fishing Along the Allagash / 358
A Space Between Time / 359
Things to Remember / 360
Of Moons / 362
Coming of Age / 363
The Last Snow Fell / 364
Hollowman / 365
So, Here's, Then, to the People / 366
Brain Creature / 368

Where Images Become Imbued with Time

The Word That Had Many Voices / 379
Storm King Mountain / 380
Father, / 382
The Alchemist's Stone / 384
Why Put Up with This Anymore? / 385
A Mountain in a Suitcase / 386
Symmetries / 388
A Matter of Degrees / 393
—Twenty Years of Empty Spaces in the Rolodex— / 395
Unforgiving / 396
At Christmas, Just Before Midnight / 397
In Age / 398
Snowball, Gregory Corso, and a Village Stoop / 399
Translucence / 400
Dead People / 401
Being Born of Bone / 402
Fossil / 403
Full Moon Above Main Street / 404
Ka-ching! / 405
Stroke! / 406
Leaves and Spit / 407
Ramses Visits the Cradle of Democracy / 408

Masks and Carved Animals / 409
Wallpaper Memories / 410
Rivers in the Ocean / 411
An Arborist's Taxonomy / 412
The Hand-off / 413
The Intensity of Light / 414
Proud Ilium, / 416
Nationbuilding / 417
The Gates Are Set to Close / 418
Little Cowboy Geniuses / 419
Fine Bone China / 420
Not Time / 421
The Little Things / 422
With No Return Addresses / 424
Helios / 425
What Light? / 426
Nanotechnology Man / 427
Roadhouse Restaurant & Grill / 428
Where Colors End, / 429
Observing the Constellations in Grand Central Station / 430
Asking Forgiveness / 432
Along Back Roads from Illinois to Pennsylvania / 433
After Sundown at Rye Beach / 434
Where the Farthest Galaxies Roar into Nothingness / 435
Best Not to Know a Town Too Well / 441
In the Beginning / 442

The Graves Grow Bigger Between Generations

A Silver Zipper / 447
Tea Leaves in a Chamber Pot / 448
Evening, Yes, but a Man Is Still a Man / 449
The Graves Grow Bigger Between Generations / 450
Tracings / 454

Life at the Margins / 455
Of Little Things That Carry Weight / 456
Having Never Wanted to Own the Business, / 458
Human Kindness / 460
Symphony / 461
To Be Alive / 462
Coping with Technology / 464
So You Say You Got a Job? / 465
Dark Machinery of Maybe / 467
Communing with the Dead / 468
Transparency among Ghosts / 469
Lowered Expectations in the Lower 48 / 471
Whatever Happened to Johnny Rebel? / 472
The Dirty Smelly Mess / 473
Poets / 474
Who Carries the Message? / 475
Fortress / 476
Learning to Breathe / 479
Looking into the Machinery / 480
Something There Is / 483
What the Gardener Knows / 485
The Renter / 486
After a Woman Is Removed from a Rome Necropolis / 488
For a Woman Minding the Store / 489
Finishing Work, / 490
Where We Lived / 491
Becoming Another / 492
Wafting Through Trees / 493
A Prayer in the Teeth of Time / 494
Pondfield Road / 495
Unsheathed and in Pain / 496
In Grief / 498
After Twenty-five Years / 499
With Sunsets / 500

What I Take to My Grave / 501
Night Heron / 502
We Are the Dawn People / 503
At Breakfast with All the King's Men / 504
Watering the Lawn / 505
Something New Is Hunting / 506
Poetry and Baseball and Pay-As-You-Go / 507

from Looking into the Machinery: The Selected Longer Poems of Jared Smith

A Trout in the Pick-up on Papago / 511

Grassroots

This Poem / 519
Not One Homogenous / 520
Knowing What Grows / 521
Grassroots / 522
Soaring on the Tectonic Waves of Time / 527
Living What the Mind Can Hold / 528
Monsoon / 529
Keeping Watch Over the Dead / 530
Camelback / 533
Do the Fish Drain Out? / 535
The Science of Expanded Understanding / 536
Petroglyphs Above *Mesa Verde* / 537
Among the Mystic Mountain Men / 539
American Hero / 541
The Eye of the Cyclops / 542
If You Squeeze a People / 543
Societal Psychosis / 545
What's in That Great Steel Belly? / 546
Wanna Be an Executive / 547
Perhaps That Too the Shadow / 548

Retaining an Empty Cell / 549
Not Cutting Too Close to the Root / 550
The Girl in the Coffee Shop / 551
In the Rooms the Motels Match / 552
Cold as a Politician's Tit / 553
People, Not So Much / 555
Know in Your Absence / 556
Flight 539 / 557
Mementos / 558
Inside the Municipal Building / 559
The Majority of His Life He Could Reduce to Movie of the Week / 560
What You Do When You Cannot Fly / 563
Why Real Men Don't Read Poetry Anymore / 564
If You Want to Write / 565
When You Stop Stroking the Machine / 566
One of Our Own / 567
The Making of Language / 568
Looking for the Foundations of Poetry / 569
Not Letting the Form Go On Another Generation / 571
The Things That Happen / 572
Things to Say in an Empty Room / 573
Mining Coal in Marshall / 575
Preservation Hall, New Orleans, and Gregory Canyon Beyond Boulder, CO / 576
Remembering the Touch of Stars / 577
Once, Beneath the Moon / 578
The Enterprise Mine / 579
Virtues of the Grassfire / 581

Seeking a Transrational Contemporary Postmodernism

Seeking a Transrational Contemporary Postmodernism / 585

Alphabetical Index of Titles

Index / 587

The Uncovered Poems: The Early 1970s to Early 1980s

Poems in this section are "uncovered poems" that have never appeared in a book, but have been published in the following magazines and journals. The years of their publication range from 1971 to 1987.

Acknowledgments

Attention Please; Bitterroot; Cafeteria; Changes; Coe Review; Colorado North Review; Colorado Review; Connecticut Fireside Magazine; Connections; CrossCountry; Dekalb Literary Arts Journal; Dacotah Territory; Green's Magazine; Grub Street; Inlet; Northwoods Journal; Pembroke Magazine; Poet Lore; Poetry Windsor Poesie; PULPSMITH; Road Apple Review; Second Coming; Stone Country; Tamarack; The Greenfield Review; The Lamp in the Spine; The New York Quarterly; The Remington Review; The Smith; The White Elephant; Telephone; Vagabond; Wind Magazine; Write On; Xanadu.

1971

The Wolf Shadow

When the wolf flew his voice and shadow
Hanging, vibrating out over the cliff
Unmeasured miles from home
Wherever that may be
It may have been a chance that John died then
With napalm flaming through his bones
And his last cry a long vibration
Signifying finality.
It may have been a chance that shadows crossed
    for that one instant
That wolf shadow flowed into shadow pines
Which flowed as smoothly into shadow hills
    and rocks and miles
And flowed at last into shadowed death
A long, strange chain of chance.
Or just one shadow which somehow traveled
    just that far
Before its outer boundaries were reached.

1972

Estuary

Dawn is starting to exist again
Growing pinkly from behind a dozen trees and rocks
And sending purple shoots into the air
Which rise upon the sky and float apart as smoke.
A gentle prolongation of the game of death.

The mountain cat looks up from her meal
And tasting the rocks beneath her feet
With her warmly sticky paws
She melts back toward the night
And leaves the bones to scare the timid eye.

Your dreams and mine are scattered;
Our separate worlds are brought together
By the spreading, soft delusion of light
And we forget again what we are—
Strangers to each other,
Just partners for a day…a life…who knows?

Down by the shore it doesn't change much
For the small fish in the estuary
With night or day; their lives live on the tide,
   not light.
The gull from up above, however, can see them now
And swoop upon their backs to kill.

Watching

Looking down from the grass
I watched the killifish
Spilling rainbow-colored flashes
Quickly, smoothly through the water,
Kaleidoscoping just beneath my eyes,
Fading out to different shades of warm
Within their silver medium.
They slipped between each other briefly
And were then gone in darkness
Until, finning by another,
They briefly burst in flame again.

They weaved smoothly through the grass
And swam and leaped and laughed
But didn't really touch each other's sides.
I watched from shadows as they shone
And I coveted their twisting backs and naked thighs
And wished to stroke translucent dresses,
Perhaps to find the mind beneath
as well as love.

As my fingers touched the water
It broke and scattered like thunderclouds
Torn apart by opposing winds,
I could not see the fishes disappear
But they were gone.

1973

Death by Drowning

A dead man's finger rests upon the bone,
And the quiet clink of metal in a lock is ignored
On the façade of a front town street.
The fog blows off a high river tonight
Where levees toss their heads, and break away,
And the smell of mud is rich in the air.

Fishermen's nets, abandoned in the first rush of tide,
Circle and crash in tangled webs
Around the trunks of sinking trees.
The metal beams of useless bridges,
The white flash of swimming bodies
Rolled through sieves beneath the moon.

That house—
I watched a woman weaving on its porch
Twenty days ago, or was it ten,
And she leaned out above the railing
And, cramping her dress, she spat
into the dust of a long dead land.
She smiled in my direction
Without teeth
And I shuddered then,
Knowing who would be among my dreams—
It was that night the bed was broken,
The crystalled beads were torn away
And I sang of country roads.
The house was small upon the flood.

The keyboard flashes white
In a staccato drumbeat.
The skull of the calf,
The eye of the dog,
The ear of the pig
Are placed upon a plate.
And, without rearrangement,
A wavering shape recites
The future of the bones.

Letter to H. S. Mauberly

Unbearded
Counting fearful Jesuits,
Unconcealed by flowing yellow robe,
A mullet turned—departed down the street.
In frostbit unbelieving eyes—
That so many men have died
Would not seem reasonable or in conjunction with
The many men who do still live,
He mused upon a peach.

Good morning, Hugh.
  (Three faces returned from underground)
Not bad—and you?
Not bad—and you?
Not bad—and you?
Not bad.
I like your pant-legs up that way—
I too have counted cats
And seen them sleep that way
And curled myself before a stove.

Surely some revelation is at hand.
The crickets sing of chamber-music dolphin songs
And the emperor is stretched sprouting on his bough
Singing words that are not songs, more songs than words,
And playing them upon the ears of old men who do not live here.
They all walked on beneath the dome
And as something caught his eye
He smiled.
A lady raised her skirt.
Orion bowed.
That is not what I meant—
He counted statues in his dreams.
Repress sometimes the images of books—
It will not matter if they are not all read.
And tho the hills are shifting high
There are miles to go before I rest,
And books are for the scholar's idle time.

The Corridor

Come, we shall pace this carpet together.
The length is limited
But we will turn, return, and pace its length again;
We will lose our toes in the luxury of wooly places
And will stub them where they wander under furniture;
They will wriggle with delight when straying onto the
    coolness of the hardwood floor.
Our eyes will cleanse and re-cleanse these walls,
Discover cracks and imperfections.
We will make pictures in our minds of those imperfections
While our lips murmur of their beauty—
We may talk…they will not change.
we will walk, return, grow dizzy, laugh cruelly at each other's
    stumbling—
And at the far end of the corridor when we grow tired or bored
There is a chair,
There is a bed,
And we will sleep.

Underneath

Dark trains are moving through the northern suburbs
heading south into the era of a long lost war not lost,
soft as windowpanes through burned-down mansions.
A breathing from the marrow of the bones is going, weaving
itself out along buried mountain passes moving west—
stretching like the dead sea grass along its tracks,
gray as six a.m. in Carolina winters;
torn between the wooden ties of deserted Arizona mining towns
    going west meaning nothing:
meaning only the sun bright on polished steel.

Violins

Outside dead leaves are rustling
Under the feet of searching things
That can't be seen.
I am warm.
I have found a place to listen to violins.

The moon is higher than the clouds
And the willow grows in mysterious ways
Where it looms over the bottomless river.

1974

Promontory

You go out onto the sand,
and the sand is the sand
and the water is the water;
and the faces looking up at you are calling
your name from the fragile bones of stars
burning tiny, silent holes in the skull.

You raise one arm above the waves
and laugh the full laugh,
the wind a part of you as it empties from your coat
filling the lengthening of shoreline shallows,
dropping in crystalline grains upon us all.

Searching the Horizon

The air is filled with birds
      wheeling on hollow cries.
The wind blows clouds horizontal,
and roads are closed across America.

Eyelashes brush distances beneath the old rail tracks,
and a laughing couple die within his breast.
The wanderer from northern Oregon wears a red scarf—
    nothing else:
he is thinking into the tin cup between his knees.

Home is where the last mallard flew
or where its webs became the glue of rivers, bays, tunnels.
Home is where the carpet went red on Sundays when his
    brothers drank,
or where the one green plant grew toward death in the living-
    room.

He is an announcer's voice
and rattles pebbles along his tongue and laughs.
He cried in the singing of the meadowlark between the weeds,
and catches his scarf across the last locomotive north.

The Dover Gas Garage

On Charles Street
lies open on three sides
across the street from where a dog lies
counting cars, wagging his tail,
remembering tooth-marked fenders.
The first thing I did returning from L.A. was piss
in the middle of black-coppered railing sidewalks
  in the park—
the blood of my groin unwrapped itself into the wail
of naked bodies before iron-grilled cathedral gates.

Like duck-webbed feet
over whitened clamshells in the desert
with feathers tucked behind my arms I count
   the steps
gathered around behind the back
of a screaming-son-of-a-knife blade shaft
poured through an ink indelible.

The earliest hours luminescing
the concrete towers of my city
looking more their like than any other time of day
while cardboard boxes are shunted down tunnels
into the post office of a politician's mind
in a teacup in the window
in an apartment
where houseplants grow silently without care.

The painting of the pavement cracks beneath
  too many feet.
A startled dog looks up and speaks from behind a
  white board fence.
Circling around I approach the gas garage from all sides.
It pushes its furry-feathered breast into my lips
            Two blocks down
Until the White Horse Tavern
and the biting of another dark back alleyway.

1975

A Marriage

She sits in a room of orchids
and wonders at the green filtering through the blinds.
Music paints slow circles across the sheets
and her fingers move lonely when beyond her reach.

Across the hall angry insects move into the plaster
and it crumbles down across her bookcases and her love,
and it sifts across the light shafts from her window
making her bed an isolated spire
as the orchids pant with dripping leaves
along the floorboards toward the center of the room.

Somehow her fingers far away
curl around the smoothness of the lock
   and in the green slip
falling away into the corners until they try again
and the record catches in its groove.

She listens
as light footsteps move outside the door
  pause
    and move on again
with her eyes connected to their laces.

And at times she sees him look in at her
fearing that her wings will catch in his hair and smother him
as he dives away into his better wishes.

Somewhere a camera snaps
and two smiling faces whirl off into a void
with handshakes, champagne, and tin can rides,
while the real bride and groom watch in fear from the shadows
and, tightening their fingers, begin to pray for love.

Across a Continent

for Mary Ann Stone

A black cat comes in by the window.
Silently...She presses white paws around my naked breast
and the pins of young teeth make my body hard as the night,
swelling and sweating along its rigid muscles.
For years we have been hurling ourselves
into a deep hole which faintly smells of death.
No longer are there memories.
No longer are there plans, except to stay alive.
No longer are there clouds to place our feet upon.
For the first time we have become one upon a bed
where there would be no reason to speak, or think, or exist,
                or
                     cease
                          existing.
Minister of the Supreme Court,
there is a dry locust tree growing outside a window in New York.
On Twelfth Street, beside St. Vincent's Hospital,
a whitened man can be seen digging among the rocks of the planet,
planting tulips grasses Christmas trees
in a long attempt to hunt for friends.
And he finds them.
The dogs have never passed that corner once
without pissing
                on
                    his
                        hands.

Old ladies
in their neon nightgowns,
electric needles humming
also try here to recall a time.
Their eyes are roaches
rushing into lights-off rooms
where food is left prepared;
a giant foot is stomping madly
to the sway of hard rock love
trying to remember deserted truck town stops
and coffee cups floating miles down country roads.

A stranger has stood by the railroad tracks
somewhere Upstate or in California
and watched the snow wrap about his coat from Barneys.
         (Seventh Avenue and Seventeenth)
He has wrapped his fingers along the howling freight cars
         from Colorado to New Orleans
until they caught upon the bone of some freight man
         standing in an open doorway
and tore themselves apart above the endless road of ties.
He has been that freight man, without a job or pay,
without a destination,
and has leaned out over small Nebraska Kansas Iowa towns
watching young girls lightened by their kitchen fires
or riding horses over roads which have no edges,
and has not been able to speak their names.
He is a stranger
in a California
                Upstate
                     town.
His eyes turn the corners of the wind
and in the stars his ears are elongated.
The breathing of the train becomes his body
and his dreams are loosed upon its wheels.
Every yard from across the country
appears the same in its darkness after the moon goes down
and the light is the light of the watchman sleeping by his
         empty luggage rack.
The warehouses with their broken windows are the same.
But they are the vital source of life, and it is what begins
growing outward from their closest shadows
that makes all
              the
                 differences.
Three blocks from the warehouses
there are couples lying in the night intensely aware
of the spaces extending through the rumble of city trucks
         beneath their windows.
It is there, in loving,
a young man pauses to be carried away upon a long and moaning
   sound

and begins to feel the happy crying of his own existence
passing miles and years along a night
                                    wet
                                                continent.
In the space before the city sounds its advertisements,
before the polished buildings where men go to drink
   medicines into their bodies,
a silent music fulfills its night-felt rites...unexplained.
Two bodies close in a quiet summer rain,
and in closing are released—
having ceased to search among the signs for what they
                     heard
                            was
                                    here.

Animus

Born to shorten nature quicken cheapen
enrich, and for every word to find one syllable
        one
but not coordinate with the face—
the sounds were more than half the word.
Vaguely aware of other footsteps in the room
        of the eyes looking over shoulders
but watching the trees outside
  caught silent through nicotine windowpanes.
Looking indifferent, but scared—
  that being the best defense;
having returned to childhood, but with a literary
  reference point.
Loving the silence for its words
and knowing if the prophets speak on subway walls,
the scrawls have blocked the plate-glass map.
The honeysuckle burns the air.

Why not do it now!
He shoots pigeons off from towers
captivating the sleeves of his desires
  with metal crumbs
and watches them spill their feathers in slow motion
to the stream below and the red horses
packing rubber tubing on their sides.
Indifference.

    Holding a conch shell to the ear,
    it tells of the world being blue, but,
      unfortunately,
    there being nothing dead in it.
    Those were the words;
    we were the scream of a sandpiper's eye
    turning in the currents above our heads
    like last meals set for the dancing girls of 14th
    or the pinball slot at a favorite bar.

    In the entire scene only the transport planes
    flew a precision with their maker in their womb
    and a noise great enough to interrupt the day.

So then supposing
                all the roads are crossed
and it is done. It is
bored into the corners of a punch-card mind
    as small as the diameter of its parts;
and we were all to come together upon one corner
        in Flushing maybe (forgetting all the non-obscene jokes)
and find the metal neon ceramic tubing had drawn us
   somewhere we did not know
or in a turgid mass where we could not see each other
  but saw the black-cloaked preacher scrabbling in the dark
  not saying masses but hunting candles,
  flooding the whole of his aisles with anxiety.

We would know
the lights above each factory are neon bulbs, or they are
   escaping gas.
They are the minds of prepubescent dreamers of autoexhaust;
and it is more than once we have caught ourselves dipping
   fingers deep inside.

Or if perhaps to please either you or me
or some of us or some of one
we were to learn to speak in brighter ways;
if it were not to feed the greater greed
what way would there be for all to begin?
This has nothing to do with roads converged
  but never met—
and both taken.

      An old moon maker bends over his bench
      fingers moving among the tools of his dreams
      shaping silent nights from blond and dark-haired virgins
      filtering lost and careless along the lashes of their eyes.

      He collects the pieces unlabelled in boxes—
            storage words for tomorrow—
      but wishes now to think with nothing but his finger pads
      and the scent of sun warmed earth as it moves into his mind
      with the search of the lover who never had to ask.

> *Light moves in the circles of leaves across his floor,*
> *and he does not watch the slack-jawed locusts building.*

Well, then, supposing all the fields
should sprout their grain and run on spider feet
down into the silos of the country's armaments
and across and through the telephone chains which fail to
   tie her mind.
Would they come to place themselves upon the doormat of
   the breakfast-eater of champions
without even a token struggle of resistance for the forgotten man
who after all had planted them each time with the thought
   of life?
But there is no energy too little passion
for the magnitude of the time we live outside of;
the golden chalices that have been raised
to catch the rain for tomorrow's mouths have rusted
        (gold does not)
or are spread too far apart beneath the crevices of mountains,
and gaunt alley cats pave the counters of our kitchen
circling the jars of dried desserts
digging their claws deeply into the strings of apricots
until no longer fit to eat;
but they eat, and the teeth grow gummed together in the skulls
   of fetuses—
they carve their way to freedom through the lamb of flesh,
growing old beneath the weight of its own eyes.

But it knows.
And I, I know that I will never know.
Eyes do not speak directly now, if ever,
and the web of Hercules is bound into the man
   circled by buzzards in the sun,
as all but empty barges move down dark rivers from the city
leaving the living to tear their handkerchiefs upon the waiting
   breeze.
And no one understands.

Destination: Hunting

He is a man on a platform
who cannot control his body: (yours)
the shaking of his muscles.
His eyes are pale
      soaked in pumpkin wine,
and he drinks coffee cups without lifting them
      from the table.

Lamp-sheen woman
      of the geese packs of dogs howling
          across wilderness ponds,
there will be something hiding in your suitcase;
      hidden among the blond hairs of your trinkets
      or bedded-down along the creases of your flesh.
No, do not leave your arm along its top
      studding diamonds of the time-rush—
the lock cannot be kept.
Bring your children with you to
the rendezvous you keep tonight.

There is a corner of your city (big city!)
where the elevated ends,
plunging into the concrete hands of the derelict,
      exposing its underside to the gulls
          bombing with packaged rations from the sea.

Sunshot contrails are the threads
you have read since THEN,
squeezing the corners of your master plan
until it bleeds   (cough, cough)
from raccoon collars in department stores.
(Do not forget the pocket in your pants
with its madly clutching hands.)
I am tired.
It has been a day of wall posters
of men brewing beer from their sewage
hearing the bottle caps fermenting through their eyes;
you miss nothing,
I might have told you from among the boards
      your husband built:
they were designed with your flesh—no more.

The Insomniac Groom

Alert in his bed
he thinks of animals
which move quickly   silently
                and once.

Tobacco shops and magazine racks
play crossword puzzles across his pillow.
Rumpled by the hours of a half-formed machine,
the mattress remains ready to fully accept
the first weaknesses of an unconscious body—
he watches all walls in turn, and wills them back.

Beyond the one where the bedpost is outlined
    by a passing car,
a female lies who smells much the same as he.
She sweats his sweat from an unknown mind
and wears cold cream when not awake.
Tigers pass through the plaster and pry his
    eyes from a swollen head.
A banshee catches in his throat.
There is nothing more to give—the game moves away
and a rough hand pulls him backward.

After the wedding ceremony birds circled above
    the church
and tin cans rattled halfway across a nightmare.
Neither person knew what to do, having thought in
    wet silk-prints
and suddenly finding the canvas torn across its center;
they moved into separate rooms and stayed there, even
    when lying together.
There was no rain for fourteen summers
and when the window ledge perspired it was someone else's window.
The dew on their grass appeared mysteriously each morning.

Still there was the fascination
of camels moving through the flower beds
and the eels lying beneath the kitchen drainage.
He saw them only with his glasses off,

and spent too much time trying to see.
His Oriental watercolorings repeatedly descended
into Egyptian walls, and the ceiling grew narrower.

He sways on his bed,
trying to regain a lost balance
above the light-headedness escaping him in all directions.
He is a spire with the ground pressing his forehead
and a needle pulling back his skin to show the wires.
There is breathing on the far side of the wall,
    and it does not concern him any longer.

The Wedding Night

Tonight dogs grow restless in their dens,
and my bones are washed at the bottom of distant oceans.
This winter was not created for our survival,
    if for any purpose;
no cars are moving through the distance of trees.

Being used to the snow along your fingers
and the deep pull of the Niagara River along our arteries
it is hard to see the fragile understanding of the child
    who walks beside us.

The white horse of night is distant,
but when he is wanted there is no need to point in his direction;
his mane blows outward to all points in the compass,
and so you sit everywhere.

The door is slowly closing
and there is pain, but no source.
There are many understandings which will not be remembered
but there will be explanations for them all.

The Beehive

Above this grass, these flowers shining,
Below the monstrous energy of summer winds,
These walls stand like naked bones against the sun—
   melting, being built, and eaten—
Spit out again in perfect geometric form.
Blank cells of white with pallid, leaking interiors
   which grow impure with the changing seasons,
Are trampled upon by angry feet,
   and are fed to irresistible machines.
This beehive—
It has grown from two deranged animals
   who flew upon this pasture and multiplied to one
And there are many.

Small children used to come to pick the purple flowers
   to test the too-weak thorns between their fingers,
But they are dead and their blond nectar has filled our
   bones and hairy bellies
So that our tower still may grow—
Expand like the mountains which are its birth,
   until the earth is only flowers and the roar of hungry wings...

Winter ice we laugh at you—
What is our death when we have spent our lives
   in the perfection of our bloated creator?
When we have torn our wings and minds to build those walls
   which will protect her misshapen creative organs
And will build another world from those.

The Tower

The skytower aerials point steel singing fingers toward
   sunset clouds
And a long drawn echo of pine trees holds the city
Beneath the arms of a bearded child.
Windows, broken beer cans, plaster walls
   vibrate to the sound
With the gentle hope of alcoholic eyes,
Park Avenue breeze trees above the flowers repeat the words—

I repeat—
More than steel, than steel-wool soap,
There are hands being held
By mountain rivers and rocks and grass,
Feeling every day the wood smoke of the Catskills
Rolling under the ground in the bitterness of joy...
Repeat
Repeat
Repeat
Meaningless words without the wind...
A child is lifting eyes, and the long veins of silver vibrate
   in an eternal fire.
And the smell of melting tarmac whispers with the pines.

Evening's Song

    1.

Evening collapsed about the city
With its quiet fingers probing, smoothing
The soreness from the woman's mind
And lifting the wall from her eyes
With gentle patience.

Her clothes slipped gently away
And the depth of solitude remained
To hold deep within their arms
And allow her face to warm
With the breezes of the night

    2.

Through the open window
The shadows held her song,
Talking, laughing it aloft
Through the darker corners of the city,
The sweet, off-key melody
Of the aching body's joy.

Without the clarity of a singer's voice
But much more filled with joy
And the pain that is its birth.
It touched the sleeping birds
That light the daytime
And brought them deeper dreams
While day and night suffused
In perfect harmony

4/26/72 and God

for Paula

Blue midnight glows under the stars
And a large, black fish swallows
   beautifully
before rolling into a white foam…
A lonely fisherman shivers…
The night is warm.

Fire shivers over rocks, hills, and ponds
Smooth and as bottomless as yesterday
With sadness growing out of them…
And the ripples roll into silk.

There Is Something Soft in This

The seed flowers have already fallen from the maples
And are pasted together solid in the gutters
   and along the corners of house roofs,
Flowing down along the sides in rain,
And being walked upon and sticking to the shoes.

They are building the tower apartments where the graveyard was—
Tossing through old bones hunting for a firm foundation
On broken children
Through old men
Between the sleeping sides of lovers...
All eyes are vacant
And everything that grows becomes cement.

An anteater wanders along between rows of high sand homes...

I would swear the ground shivers when the wind blows—
The pendulum I live in is counting time in the number of rotting teeth
   it sways beneath the clouds
And the people who disappear abruptly clutching at anything
   sticky and warm.
There is something soft in this.

The Blood of Wolves

Brown grass beneath a brown-mud sinking moon
And the memories of tomorrow are impressed upon sand grit
 under leather feet.
Willow branches whipping through the twilight make thirsty
 swallowing noises
And I think of long, long dark hair.
Gentle lips are the same which tore the marrow from cow bones
And I myself have splashed the blood of wolves.

Eternal

I crawl under the rocks of the stream
   like the salamander
And smooth myself against his smoothness
And slip within his slipperiness
And taste the liquid life between my gills
And I flow between my gills
   and warm myself.
I breath deeply
And I feel my toes wallow sleepily
Into the ooze of my back.
I feel the rocks shift
And I am pounded into them
And incorporated into them.
I breathe the shape of crystals,
Multiplying within,
And I achieve a perfect balance
   which I never knew before.
Then wasting away I keep my perfect shape
Until green of life surrounds me
And becomes me.
I rise and bloom more quickly
And spreading my soul upward toward the light
I fold into decay again
And growth toward what I am.

The Last Nightmare

for Galway Kinnell

The moon becomes unsheathed
From its mold-rusted growth of clouds.
Somewhere the darkened surface of Loch Ness
Is cut by an unknown animal
Which has long ago become extinct
And no one hears it breathe.

There is not time enough in this one afternoon
To make a record of the world,
To think or even listen to its sounds:
The sounds of active, vital mountains
Surging upward at half an inch per year;
The sound of evergreen needles
Falling brown upon the ground;
The sound of love transforming
Into flesh;
Of flesh transforming into bone;
The sound of bone blowing away in dust.
The horror is that we can close our ears
But we cannot close our eyes.

Last night we lay upon the smooth hardness
Of a level patch of dirt,
And we made love upon that dirt
And upon a billion microscopic forms of life
Which make love and were crushed beneath the beauty
   of your back and legs
And we did not hear them die.
We made that spot of dust and rock the center of the universe,
Of all the trillions of stars of dust and rock,
And in Vermont Galway Kinnell did the same,
And in Pakistan a dying baby in his mother's arms
   also was the center of all things,
And William Shakespeare was speaking his first words,
And a lonely microbe drifting off through space
And the grinning camel bones wandering
Somewhere in the deserts of the United States
   of Mr. Roosevelt

Also made the center of all things
And whispered softly of their power.

The walls of the burning hotel
Come falling in and roaring down upon their tenant,
And the last nightmare written in his book
Comes peeping out of shadows.

Solitudes

It becomes visible in the cone of early light
Funneling into an evening room
Where the frightened bride removes her shell
And starts to feel cold with fear
And is lifted by hot hands from dreams of sweat.
The dust settles upon the farmer in the field
And it settles in the humid soil and breathes.
Money rustles in a lonely hand
And the evening moves toward over-brightness.

Silence

Beer turns golden chandelier darker in the evening—
Whispered, maybe partly drunken down the throat
Or just sun setting heavy over New York dust.
Dust river memory of distortions.
It is time for darknesses:
dresses, legs, Socrates, and spring...

Dead Stalk Watercolor

Deep blood-river
Carrier of silicates
As one, as sand,
Boiling up from sand.
Flowers drink of river—
One blooming and then death.
I drink.

Last year's moss
Turned sometime into this year's moss—
Green to brown and brown to green
Somewhere—
Somewhere under snow,
I think.

Empty tigerlily stalks
Do not bend as well
When all laughter has passed,
They crack and split beneath my fingers
And they do not bleed
As my last seeds blow away.

Within the Garden

It is this window that I spoke of...
(Old men rock with a vengeance on their porches—
What is it then?
Why have we come this far?)
I could not tell you how to look.
I spoke. You listened. I waited
and the pearly cat of fear drew curled around.
What more was there—
They cut the furniture and built the fire:
The night was cold and the flame was good.
The night is cold and the flame goes low.
The sputtering of rusty leaves enclose
The handles of our purple-cushioned home—
The whistling sounds may be only thoughts entangled,
Lost and mazed among themselves a hundred years.
Or a generation of the youngest lifetime.

Where were we then
When they spared the ax
Upon the mountain?
Not here: I should have shook my fist
And would have counted grains of sand
Until they too grew purple at last
Contrasting with the whiteness of ancient frames
Deserted by the homes which once were there—
Until those frames too were dim.

Be silent in the presence of the plants;
The flowers listen in their stillness.
The phlox, now hidden,
Grows anyway.
Trips unseeing feet
And draws us still—
The stillness of the earth,
Lost in its momentum
And traveling far.

1976

A Recurring Particular Day

Sanity is small:
the prairie-dog watching from the mountain of his burrow
is one of many in his village—
nobody appears to bring the food...a plague spreads
  and thousands are exterminated.
He knows the eastern relatives are doing well.
But in Germany, they celebrate Badger Day...
and in England, All Candles Day
                    (Something more in this?)
shadows are relatively meaningless.

Tunnels are not remembered except as dark escapes
where roots clutch downward at the eyes
and the flesh seeps into impossible positions.
They are not inhabited by families of television sets,
and Chet Huntley is a nightmare seldom explored.

The jet ports through desert
do not concern the mangled strips of flesh which remain;
only the range of the condor is impaired:
we hold these truths, from pre-smoked pipes, to be
  self-evident
at least to those who are initiates—and for the others...
  well, well come.
There is nothing as sterile as sand, or as a lack of light,
unless it is their absence.

After Midnight

In New York
in the bars at one a.m.
they do not speak of the buildings.
They talk quietly of the girls with long, blond legs
and trace their fortunes through the peanut shells
   and sawdust floors.

They do not speak of people in New York
as closing slips down the rafters
or as the last quarter plays out its time
   to a wandering candle flame.

And it is time for closing—
somehow they all know and start to disappear—
when they do not speak any longer in New York.
No women walk the streets
     except for one far away
hurrying to catch a cab before her face is seen.

New York
becomes a silent light above a theater
upon a corner
and bends both ways into the night.

The American Museum of Neutral History

It all amounted to nothing.
People stopped driving their cars
      suddenly
and got out, walking into the wail of Styrofoam sirens
hanging senselessly over Washington—
and they disappeared. Just that.

The dust of blinking neon signs circled slowly hovered
scattered around the corners of the cities several weeks
and, only a few at the beginning,
                    spread off a last time into the dark.
They were not missed, and the wind moved as always
   through strands of cherry blossoms.

The caretaker with plastic eyes
folded off at last into the land
and his fingers were no longer the guardrails of the legitimate.
The buttons of his coat blew away and filled the air
     with birds,
and sheaves of grain fell from his shirt.

Strange rodents came to nest in the abandoned upholstery,
and the bright eyes which watched from under dashboards
   knew nothing of what had disappeared:
their children grew and died with eyes to their own.

Departing from Portland

Outside the window a bird takes shape
   from the tremolo of your lips.
It leaps erratic from tree to tree in ascending lines
neck twitched and turned
eye cocked
it swallows the sun
drifting as a feather's spiral to ground.

I give you tea and cookies
and am unaware of where your eyes go
in taking mine.
Its beak fills my pocket
shaping a spear to impale time…
already thirty miles an hour   forty   fifty   sixty
and my eyes cannot follow,
   growing fat and heavy as the moment—
it is hard to even care anymore that not all things
   (myself being hard to mention)
are either graceful or even of one piece,
or begin to know what the other wing is doing next or why.

I insinuate myself beneath the springs of your seat
creaking   creaking
warmed around your legs and bathed in words we have
   agreed upon—
I do not take you out too far.

Expectation of Six P.M.

Outside my door in evening
I can hear the excitement of peeper frogs
   spreading their eggs among weeds;
I live as far from her fingers as time allows.
There are leaves to be sewn to the earth.

Being too rare to be named,
   it is not sold—
hardly promulgated, never advertised.
And my friends, well, each in his way,
and they often write of her to me;
each one gives a different name.
They don't know.

She has no name, no face;
and my arms are filled with autumn.

Looking Back on Having Left

Sleek down by the riverside
she lies a flame of flesh
yellow petals wound around her head
      her breasts
and then whitens down
  to the first pubic hairs.
Her favorite flowers are the grass;
the game is nothing, is waiting.
She is the hidden part which no man comes near;
stirs in the June heat
   a rising of mayflies off the stream
           cadence
swiveling without meaning and short.
She watches for rain in the drone of wings;
and who could catch her lips with his?

The currents carry out
     carry out
the fingers of the body toward the city.

Trees left behind
     Homes
         Birds buried where they fell unfledged from nests;
a corner in the city in a shaded room.
Light is in the expectation of the stars at night,
the secrets opened with the scent of polished floors and beer
with a knickknack on each table to say it can be given away
         but given harder
than the glass which fronts the door, at least;
and this is much.
The currents carry out
     carry out
the darkened shapes, the twisting lines.

Rain across the contours of a face
where something grows
is unknown and it takes two at least to say.
Nothing young:
nothing which is born of moon or wind,
although these are needed too:
and who could catch her lips with his?

The currents carry out
     carry out

Something wild
   the roots of the violet plant strain
in unmoving webs against the side of their glass container
in the window box
   watered and fed and closed and grown
where the light is only a luxury, being there;
where they are tangled in complexities
   which no eyes have totally seen
     which could not be without the hands that do not touch.

Meditation on Old Movies

I wish to propose a toast to the ghosts
    of the cowpokes of long ago
who left their loves with guitars beneath the trees
    just to stink and shoot the breeze.
I wish to raise my glass to that ass
    who lived with chimpanzees.
Alone   I'll drink to all of those who don't remember me;
and maybe it's just as well they don't—
Cecil B. left me free.

Because

as he knew

If Tarzan did not leap   (for example)
     a
     a
    a
       a a a e e a
     a   a
              a
              a
              a
              A
              E   like us, he would not fall;
but neither would he cleave the air,
nor elephants grow anxious in their damp socks.

The Glass Forest

You have awakened in a glass forest.
The test tubes stretch above you brittle boughs
of commas   splices   syllables
cut crooked to the wind and rattling.
The falling leaves draw blood from your ears,
but it would not be wise to try to stop them with your
   throat.
Your blood is pregnant from the fall
and the pain is the birth of animals which run
   trying to hide among splinters.
The animals curl around your feet and keep you warm.
They chatter in the night.

The Spellweaver's Workshop

Dropping   Dropping
on the roof the rain falls
incapable of communication or of meaning.
Bright yarns dangle from the ceiling
   casing air in reds and blues,
swaying above a bench of perfume bottles—stale candles.

Round as the hollow of the eye
billowing of walks alone on sunlit days
down into the knowing of the blind
and the washing of water with rain:
down into the gaze of water-stains on flesh.

Old father died today,
his beard crawling into the stoplights of his dresser
where it found its mourners in the form of ants
dragging honey to a lasting marriage.
We were locked into our separate rooms;
we were hidden by smoke, pulling rocks from each other's pockets;
we were scribblers in the address books of socks in need of darning.

The holes are meant to be filled,
to be plucked,
to be walked among—
across the green there is a club for drinking slowly
and telling tales of what the woman did today
or of the children on their first trip home alone
   together and unforgiven
or of the grandchildren peering unnoticed from under new felt hats.

The air spun from his mouth is filled with decay:
the feathers of large dead birds
circle windless spirals into tapestries.
His probing, turning fingers ring down upon each other
turning faces so white that they drop to the floor.
Old wood:
caves which grow into flowers from the runner of his desk
bearing on each leaf their fear of life.
Maria Faschin, 21, a visiting nurse,
paid a visit to a patient at home a year ago
and was stabbed:

the music stopped in a room where there would be no
   violation.
Her mouth chews trees now
in its certain waiting.
One of many.

Father
where among the splinters of his nails
dark cities shed their lights—
moon steel of the seventy-two years of aviation history.
All comes back.

Through the skylight there is a blue
of blue mountain cold
wrapping pulsing fingers in steam.
The windshield is a maze of flesh stains
   beneath cumulous;
a flashing chance of light on negatives
transported by secretaries on their way through drugstore photomart
   machines.
The floor is plastered with what remains.

The Young Success

Torn from the eyes of the root-growing tree
where candles waver white between the houses of his home
without direction or internal passport
he looks only for silks or liquor or flesh
to throw into the bleeding hole which is his mind.

He sleeps without dreams at night
catching themselves along the machine carved bedposts of his feet
and lying through the sweat between his nails.
He remembers nothing anymore and collects old rubber bands
to shoot at hummingbirds beyond his window—
there are no hummingbirds in winter; not this far north.
There are not many in the summer.

Torn, and without a place to be,
he shaves a beard which does not grow.
It has no name and twines around the trellises of upper suburbia
   towns
where white moths circle string legs around the leaves
and the wind is there to know that they will be in spring.

the language is too complex—
there is a bowl of soup upon the table.
The table is pine and has nothing else except dark rings.
He remembers eyes in a mirror.
The table used to be the home of raccoons—covered
   with wasps and stinging beetles
back in some dead swamp somewhere maybe—he knows.
The language is too complex—
the soup is the color of water, and he is drunk.
Torn from its roots, the table is dead
   and its power speaks of Easter Island and stone-carved
   gypsy emptiness across the moon.

The Last Wedding

They were married in a white house at the end of a rainbow.
Her mad laughter suppressed itself in desert candles
descending her spinal column like footsteps into caves.
Her pillow was smothered from the beginning by small groanings.

In the leaves of oak trees she saw the destination of her
   would-be children;
and the music on her radio made her hair grow white before
   spring had passed.

Her husband polished ebony statuary between meals
and grew uninterested in what he could not shape.
Canaries and fish tanks filled the corners of his passion
as he read his way deep into Ellery Queen or Alfred Hitchcock.
Small, whimpering animals came to disturb the house of his
   working,
and he closed doors across the face of the moon.

When the sun lifted
and lovers walked over lakeshores
he killed himself;
and the day did not begin.

1977

A Silence of Wings

Now silence grows
  an unwinding of meaning
  until nothing is meant;
music of the beer cans after a city rain
like the voice of any man who has not been
 what he might have done best,
who carries the whistle of a locomotive
in his mind
whenever he walks the heated blocks to his livelihood,
who dances off the iron grill working of its final
 platform
raising dust to fill the eyes of rebel troops
  returning home.

Packages bound twice around with string
  of nondescript
are being placed on the doorsteps of a community
  today:
they will fill the mirrors of a cemetery,
and shadow pictures of men will be made on bedroom walls
  to carry them away
without fear of touch, of breath, of change.
Each ribbon is a track of steel which will ride
  only itself into its miles.
Other senses begin to feel themselves
and children spend their days digging beneath earth
curling their fingers around salamanders
  hunting for smoke   rebirth   like their fathers
told about;
but large birds swing down and grab their findings
  disappearing into towers of smoke
until they are not wanted again
  and descend again, never growing old
being born from that.

A silence grows between the webbing of their fingers
entangling the constellations and binding them into the earth—
a net where nothing grows and breathing is difficult.

A Time of Looking

The many graces
   of Washington
  are a needle in the eye of night.

There is at least one woman
  who lives there
in a room of ferns—
who does not know the time of monument,
except as it applies to silence.
She must be living somewhere here.

In this place, dreams are erect
into clouds of corridored luminescence.
It is a dark and heavy man who pulls them
    from their covers
and drags them with the fanfare of his smile
  into her room.
She does not care that they are to be hidden in
  her bureau drawers.

Cognizance
   like the creep of lichens over walls
swells into our minds
and is dropped with other angers of the day.
At times it is best to come to the meeting place
  to be alone.

No man who is not wanted will remain.

Dallas

How do you tell anyone wanting to believe
   platitudes
that you devised a motorcade
and triangulated your positions
and raised an umbrella as a signal on a sunny day
and fired three rifles
       almost simultaneously
and you yourself developed the filming taken of the event
and you sent mud-coated station wagons with Goldwater stickers on each one
   which nevertheless would be denied
that you killed the most powerful man in the world
because he could not be any longer the most powerful man in the world?

And when you are getting older yourself
and all the reporters have asked you and you say
I do not know
   how fifty witnesses of the event all died
   within only ten years' time
and were robbed and killed in their apartments or in plane crashes
which have gone unsolved and are coincidence;
and you yourself are getting older and have maybe made a mistake
   but have tried to absolve it
unconsciously
yourself by speaking as if in your sleep
and telling so many stories so many obvious lies
that they will have to contradict each other, but you make sure
   they will all be told
and cancelled.
How do you tell anyone who is wanting to believe each word
   to take it out of all context of your past
that you killed the President.
That he was only a man like many you might have chosen
and that you yourself are only a man and might have lost but did not
that you planned a trial in a southern city that had to throw the
   bastards off the scent
   but even then would leave the clues you left.
That you then hired yourself to kill yourself and found you were too
   big
   and the men you bought too small
because only one man can be that big and he was dead or dying.

How do you tell anyone, even as you yourself are growing so old
    you cannot think,
because even dying you are afraid of dying
and you have your family still who never understood what they were
    supporting
and you have your home and your country
and you are dying and the most that you can do is kill the country,
so you try to force your way out by lying and letting them discover
    you are lying
but you have never lied, at least they have been told that much;
so it has to be by accident,
And how do you let it slip?
And what if you die before you do,
and none of the lying knows each other?

Only One

The molar smooth eyes of the mask soften
beneath the tracing fingernail
perplexity
of living three thousand years
of untouched sorrow...
used now and thrown away so many times
the original oven-baking now builds the bone
or men never seen who own
blurred and flattened photographs of ancient art.

Humanity in the essence of the adolescent,
hardly shaped by the winds which blow all day
   through the years...
the eyes with their complexity of railroad tracks
etched in the red network of forgotten ties;
neither blurred nor rested in their passing miles,
   and unchanged.

Oh—it is only one on the shelf, you tell me.
Only one.
Yes, I say, Yes...and the solid smile.
I am the collector's idol and close my wings...
and everything becomes so clear.

What would we say now
of the nightmares of passing wheels,
and the distance of the horizon
where everything goes to earth,
and the lapless rides home on stainless steel,
and the love in bedless rooms
and public beneath coats
and Mississippi steamboat philharmonic rides—
such as only they really know—
and the colorblind birds batting out their brains
on windowpanes
                if we could know
I think that we would smile and do it all again
because stone or metal and flesh
have an affinity I told you of
   too long ago.

Annelid

At five years of age
   a moth
would have been forgotten as a god
     long ago.

The new apartment
  is hardly big enough
to contain words of our last moment.
Curtains have flown down
     circling falcons to the men below;
it is only ten o'clock and the beer is gone.

As a failure of species
   we have pictured concrete walks
        or white-clothed women,
watching each other swimming through.
Here and there my palm passes
   where the shadows of its fingers might be.

Sometimes a pair of legs
   will turn and run in an opposite direction
as Old Men knew.
Zeus was afraid of one woman;
     she turned virgins into cows.

The Turning Off of Lights

Hunched up in its cage
the bird is waiting to be covered:
is waiting because it is always covered at night
   even though this night will be different
after you have turned off the lights and are preparing for bed.

It is holding you through its one bright eye,
drawing you deep into the feathers of its skull—
pulling you toward the cage,
forcing you to lift the sheet which serves as cover
and drop it over the cage containing dark.

It is sitting quietly on its perch
  and watching
    shifting sometimes from one foot to the other
  but waiting and knowing you will come
will walk over to the cage
to create the dark
  where it will grow
until it fills the cage,
its heavy beak hooked and sinewy wings pressed tight
  against the bars
as it grows and it grows until nothing can contain it
and a dry throbbing beats itself around the house
   through the empty rooms.

In the same way,
       I wait for you.

They Did

When the meteor fell the people acted together;
they disintegrated into their pockets.

They began to treat squirrels with respect
and every store carried its supply of nuts—not like now—
and small currycombs with maple tree handles with knotholes
   which were the answer.
They looked at the knotholes morbidly and discussed anti-matter
   and misogyny;
and mystery writers became shamans for want
of a better profession when everybody wanted one
and there weren't enough maple trees to go around.

So they noted the way ground squirrels drew up the fragments from
   the ground
and they spaced them out in little ground meat patties in grilling
   them
to find if their teeth were magnetic
   or just their eyes
or if they thought with their asses as they bounced along the
   ground.
And in that way they got an idea at last.

They set out to reassemble
   what had landed
from the nuggets of their teeth;
and they took the slowest, most physical means to their ends
     (like ground squirrel)
and pounded their babies into little casks which filled their days
in order to reassemble
   what it was that landed
into something which towered so far above the ground
   that the ground forgot
and melted away never telling anybody
why there was a hole without bottom but a big top in everything they did.

Where Nothing Gentle Survives

From her chair in an old frame house
a gray-haired woman develops a control over homicide.
When talked to by the doctor, she does not answer
but speaks of thunder with her eyes—
and they are blank as the wall they wish to place her behind.

Who could understand
the deaths of her children
or her younger friends as she grew older;
or how she lives eating little more than memories?
Who could understand that it was planned
or that her mind is tied stronger than steel
  to the mind of any human she sees?

When younger, there was no danger.
She walked the double line of worlds
and spoke for happiness.
but age is the growing of paranoia and a closeness
and a flowing into the half-thought of senility
where time is captured and disposed of
and the dead have never died
  and never can.
There is no responsibility, and the body has failed it
  anyway.

From her chair she causes atomic tests,
and some part of her plans the holocaust.
They feed her sugar in a tube
  and talk as if she could not hear.
But in the night she sinks her teeth into their minds
  and chews
until their flesh ages with the fall of leaves
or they drop from windows with the scream of victory.

It has been said only
that this house lies in a dust-filled field in the country
along one of the many roads going nowhere,
and that cars hunting life pass by it every day
unaware that they have taken on a new passenger who howls
  with laughter at every turn.
Sometimes they notice the weeds growing from
the windowpanes.

1978

Saturday Evening

The snow is falling in a room:
white mice curl in mounds of dusty bone
hanging from broken fingers in the wall,
falling, rattling against the windows.

I have lain here many times
in the canyon of this bed—it is my bed,
and the emptiness of myself is lost in it,
reflected and returned.
The lark turns back upon the mountains
in an anger of burning sun.
Forests explode—there is no room,
not this room. Not now.
She wanted to be kissed—
or was it you who wanted…but not really. She wondered
what the crawling noises were
where the walls disappeared
and were hidden with a mirror—
so much easier than to have it all explained again
by saying I don't know. I do not
want to sleep at night.

Coming on New Mexico

I.

Breeze falling across the sand of evening,
and the loose dirt of aceqia madre rolls beneath your feet
   through the fields of heated adobe.
Coyote looks out from your eyes and moves silently...
the houses flattened cardboard the leftover color of picnics...
   the color of earth...of evening...
   invisible
except where the squares of luminescence float
with the smell of living alone, not knowing where you walk.
Not knowing how the whole town fills your bones...
How the mountains themselves creep down in the desert wind...
And how the dry rivers continue to sweep across the miles of sunset.
Coyote chooses the time and melts into night
leaving the silent marks of turned earth by the garbage pails
and following along the telephone wires into time.

II.

You are seated far above the plains and mountains
sipping the last dregs of ice from your glass.
You look down from the vast scaffolding which supports you...
   over the metal framework which has just begun
   to fall away behind you.
Below are the glowing stadiums...bowl-shaped depressions
entering upon your mind like memories which are lost.
You fasten your seatbelt with the thought that you will not be here.

III.

Turquoise and silver...
   the waiting of motionless fingers;
and of something watching
beneath the ageless roof and the newer stores
   of the palace of the governors...
the well which would always run dry in times of siege
and the changing generations which have been.
You look up, and the eyes of the Indian are hidden,

buried deep and furrowing in old cloth;
until in compassion you ask how old she is.
She sells you a blanket, and you are gone.

IV.

The moon is your reflection…
flowing among the piñon trees over the sage,
filling your throat…
until you too are caught,
   listening to the stars.

Autumnal

Something painful
      like butterflies in late autumn
turning in upon themselves
where the fields have begun to be left in dust—no longer
  irrigated
and the children on their way to school can walk straight lines
out along the furrows of the country's breakfast food.

The time of fashion is passing
    and it is good again to watch the hawk circle in the wind
    and to fill the belly by holding hands with strangers over fires.
The age of the mink has swum its way into another riverbed,
and the spawn of dark fish has returned among the reeds.
Tonight the restless will raise their tangled limbs
and dance beneath the stars.

The Street of the Little Sun

                1.

From cloud straits
   in sunset
   beneath the hill where I live
crows fly
   flock upon flock:
arrow-feathered scythes to cut the green from trees.

Let there be no tipping of the hat
   to pledge amends
in this plain where jet contrails
   spread the distance of highways;
no amends the snail will not make in time,
swirling them along his silent horns.

One foot before the other
let the deck be set
to migrate with the seasons of your feelings.

There is a shaking in the earth beneath my feet,
a far-off roaring indifferent to our stand.
There is nothing in the wells that was planned
to bring together anything that is thought or seen:
they are—and at the same circumference of an eye.

I bring them out upon a street and call it
       the street of the little sun,
and live there playing blindman's buff
with the daughters of the mayor, waiting to be seen.

The street of the little sun,
where our families have left on endless airplane rides
leaving the denizens of the street corner night to leave us food
   and wash it down with day
until, discovered by ourselves,
we die;
but with a little sun that feeds the roots
as like from like grows into like.

The vines have long been gone from the corners of this house;
but their memories whistle into tomorrow
and bloom there
with long, white flowers which breathe loudly
    deep beneath the leaves.

*

If all the young girls
    were petals on a meadow
dancing and rolling and dropping
    with the grass,
then you couldn't touch one
    without the lot of them feeling
and you couldn't see one
    without a lot in the way;
and if it came easy then there's no knowing
    what it is that you've got.

Still
the boys build leaf dams in the gutters
in the rain on sun street
and chase large freighters down among the factories.
Worms roll from beneath debris,
snagging the current in their mouths—
helpless serpents told about by nonexistent men.

They pass beneath
where the lovers with their two-hand grip
drag their crotches across the light…
heavy   obese
    but almost translucent
where the wind cuts across their laughter
scattering it among the leaves so that it cannot be heard
    a block away.

* *

Strangers carrying mirrors and cosmetics in cases
pass from door to door
  noting in their books which houses

    mend their front walks with tricycles
        which with worn cane chairs.

            Open this and you will be relived,
            seeing that all neighbors match my sunglass lenses
                on bright days
            and knot their fingers with my laces.

            This receipt need not be signed…
            smile on the dotted line.
            Your house too will have a need for these;
            they all do on some days. They are all the same—
            whether they cut the grass in spring,
                or scrape the walks of ice.

They offer only what is earned
and help to spread the leaves.
The town is white to soldiers returning from the east
as they drop their webs and, losing traction,
spin into the yards they grew among.

And now as the last latches fall to the dinner call,
the street is filled with an old yellow dog
sauntering toward the river without a head of ideas
belonging to no one
turning the town to dust in his passage,
obliterating the little signs which once designated a map,
raising clouds to be the light of evening,
crawling deep into the eyes.

                2.

Far down   where the road went out to dust
flickers rose in thickets from our tires.
And that was where the girls went for their first affairs
      with rock
         with the waters,
where their dry casings afterward rattled the earth
    as locust wings;
but also where they learned to grow eyes for seeing in the night.

That was where before young
   I used to go to take a boat upon the water
to raise pumpkinseed sunfish from the weeds;
but really to watch for life upon the lake,
to count the red heads of mergansers where they floated
   over rippled backs in waves,
to sit quietly while an old woman's laughter crept up behind
   in the form of a loon
to burst from beneath my mind.

There.   Here.
where the deserted office buildings now stand
row upon circling row
forming natural arenas for the new strips of meadow grass.
There is something sad about this town—
in the ease with which it perches in expectation
   of the coming boom
even when no children return at night to drink their milk
   before the fire.

A little town
formed of the webs of young thought
and abandoned in the granite of time:
a flat stretch beneath the lava flow of stratus clouds
which hold light for many hours
after the first evening news is turned on.

3.

Imagine the psyche
    as a well
imagines water.

NonIndo-European   (like)
the language was hard to decipher
   nonlinear
  thought-impression-instinct;
even then the words were not the grammar,

might mean anything—just sight or sound;
merely finding patterns where the simplest
might be best, or might as well.

When the body died it was young.
Didn't move—no sudden swooping to Hell,
but a sudden stillness   precise   as the earth
moved along its past path farther.
A gentle jingling away of jewels into the soil,
semiprecious stones down among the crumbling ribs
   or silver falling from the finger bones;
and a smile which is a mask saying nothing anymore.

Not moving but in its stillness
flickering through space with the speed of a universe
over distance the living left behind—
nothing mystical: a translation of dimension passed.

Dust blows from all corners
around a house on sun street.
Everything inside is transfixed
in the harshness of a single bulb hanging from the ceiling,
where nothing goes out.   Ever.
Last autumn's leaves shift in the corners,
and the new baby on the street makes requests.

A screeching fills the air of the newborn
cutting across sleep
until her stay-dry pants are changed and washed
     away—
something precious, built from love   (in its way.)

Washed out into the bloating of a landscape…
trees horses hills children dogs birds mice butterflies lilies
          men gazelles
which circles around upon itself;
little gained, but less lost.

Two bodies would strain in the dry reeds of their fields
conscious of a voice they could hardly hear ringing

its way above the wooden rafters of a village,
above the scrabbling animals tunneling beneath their feet.
They would follow their eyesight into the blueing-out of distance;
coupling their arms around each other, pressing their lips
   into the earth—

two antennae transmitting muting magnifying
what flew through the air unobserved.
totally unconscious…but something passed,
and their laughter filled the grain that year
spilling onto tables at truck town stops across a continent,
The hiss of weight upon heavy wheels was almost unknown
to them—completely then, to them.

It was as if
a plague descended on the silent street of transference;
a plague causing the dead to rise
and melt through building walls;
a plague where communication was easy and there were
no words;
all that was known was not.

4.

The hacienda on sun street
lost among white shingled peace and loud cars
   is owned by an unusual man.
Most odd.
I have never seen him pass
   but in the distance of my childhood
   without a face ever—even then.

Bridge on the train 'til six
   commuting home.
A short drive through blind alleys,
streets no longer there.

Tonight he gets new furniture.
Stripes instead of solids in his living room,
but no one knows.

He comes in the guise of a businessman
drinking pink champagne among the evening's moths.

Until, in sight of his home, he pauses
thinking he is seeing dark cars pulled up
before the driveway where there were never any cars
and heavy-handed men loading his family one by one
   above the other
into a pile which has no height.
Their lips move and mean nothing
he can hear,
and a hollow wind blows through the bottom of his pockets
as he watches the moon drop down its craters upon their silhouettes.

He turns and walks into the night
and walks until the soles of his feet burn through
and walks until he passes through the trees of his property
and walks until his body grows small
     and he slips out into the rungs of darkness.

5.

A pale oblong lies within a tub of water
where the furthest shadows of the sun scrape against tiles.
So much of my body lies out across the landscape
that not even the bombs of seventy-five years of war
   can make a dent.

The framework of a bridge that can't be crossed
has been laid;
that is all, and all of space falls through.

Somewhere in this we may have joined hands
in the hope that one may fall first and shield the other
   with his flesh;
or perhaps the spaces between the equations we do not read
   have seen to this.

Your hair is comfort;

      a rag doll
        turning through my fingers
           crashing out through distance.
Nothing changes
  like the symphony of your breath

              6.

Being the wife of a Spanish man
                  (it is said),
she at one time traveled far
and married her sons to the moonlight off the River Platte.
She is wise
        having been all the way to Omaha and back
        the hard way: on a smile.
No grass will grow upon her grave
        when she dies, they say.

Her house is in a cradle of the hill
        first to ignore the natural shadows of the day.
Imagine   her eyes
   as they look into you   coiled springs;
you who will one day race screaming from the streets
hunting trains whose windows cast your image
   from windows back into the town.

You, who if surviving will be
a fine writer some day,
allowing your thighs to sit naked by the night
   chuckling into time
      oblivious to most of time and too much
              of what surrounds.

You, having swept the x-rays from the gutters,
will join her in her cradle,
have fame for the part of you which cries
   so small
beneath a sky reflecting no city lamps.

This will be tabulated;

   entered into your account,
so that you will be known as the old hag
who chases the young from playing in your trees
waving a black cane and shouting names forgotten
   long before your children died.
This will be entered in the streets of your beliefs
as your image emerging from a dying woman's will.

7.

The first snow begins to fall again:
an operatic curtain wrapping the trees in silence
and swirling into darkened doorways.
I have seen it fall before;
around the bristles of the highest weeds,
upward through the staring eyes of the owl.
A cry which is born of fire
fills my throat and drops in icicles from the air.
The earth grows still
within time.

1979

Elegy to a Beetfield

In the land of vegetables
   there is no language.
Leaves grow independently
heaving away at the small flecks of mica
   which cover their beginnings.

An indistinct form waters fire-hydrants and wags its tail,
   changing its name
until it becomes the quiet man watching it from behind his
   automobile window stopped at traffic lights along countless
   dusty corners.
It brings slippers, old newspapers, and love to skeletons which
   rattle with despair and frustration
and do nothing.
It watches honestly dishonest politicians on television screens
swigging beer from a can and trying to follow baseball scorecards
   while the designated hitters are appointed
to knock the balls off any fan who will not be whitewashed
and wonders why the mercury rushing to its brain through canning
   processes from numerous industries
does not rattle as loudly as the other silver it is accustomed to
and assumes it is because it is not as important.

Out of all this
he came to develop many thinking styles
               all of which were valid to degree.

Sometimes on a dark night when the howling of the wind across
   the boards of his house caused the outside world to almost
   appear to take on the aspects of his most inner and secret
   consciousness, thereby causing a strange state of harmony
   between himself and all of creation, his thoughts grew elongated
   into patterns similar to but not identical with those of the
   great novelist, Henry James.
Other times he took walks with his girlfriend. They always wound
   their way down to the dockside. The nights were hot. The two
   of them would drink cheap beer. They would talk of death and
   have affairs. They compared Hemingway to the moon over the
   water.

Puttering among the plastic bottles and scraps of paper

theories grew haphazardly, but making almost-sense,
and it is discovered that
> Europe = the masses X civilization^2,
>> the meaning of which is relative and inconclusive to
>>> any time—meaning basically that nothing really moves
>>> anywhere when taken with everything

and it is almost discovered that it also holds for the United
  States of (not quite Africa), but unfortunately not quite.

And even each of all the people
> each in all of his three lives
>> each of which should not be given to a dog

restrains himself from not shouting out why "not quite"
from the dancing of angry over the tops of old greyhound buses
> but it's just as well

because they would not be heard or listened to
anyway
probably,
as they attempt to lay out the miles between California
  and the Redwood Forests
or Corpus Christi and the Gulf Stream Waters
where this land was made...well
while mad shapes dash screaming among the wheels
carrying old slippers and new ceramic teeth so that life will
  not be too hard to chew
and be worth living after all;
and there will be no struggle for the exits
and only the fat survive.

And in the land of vegetables
  all things that run are to be envied
and are the enemy
and are, potentially, the enema of the people,
but will in most cases disappear on paper rafts into the curse
  of time
speaking of there being no time, and all things being relative.
And in the cultures they leave behind them
there will continue to be inlaws and outlaws
and a myriad of criminals too timid to steal even for their own
  survival.
And at the very least there will be a plot of beet-greens
growing in the country.

The Only Man Who Lives

Ezra Pound Dies in Venice at Age of 87
That headline in the *New York Times*
one morning. November 2, 1972.
Six years ago, one father, several poets, many friends.
And I was not old enough to know
more than the collective coterie of chroniclers had written
and a few books of a once young man.
But it shocked me even so
and I cut the story out—not
   putting it in a scrapbook
and I cried and was exhilarated
and I wrote a poem "To H. S. Mauberly"
    which was printed in
    The New York Quarterly,
which was the greatest thing
  which had ever happened to me.
And I kept the clipping.

Ezra Pound Dies in Venice at Age of 87
printed victoriously
over the picture of a bitter
and very lonely—though not for himself, ever—
old man who glared beyond the photographer
and looked into the tangled fears of civilization.

It is an old photograph now
(newsprint ages quickly),
Ezra Pound Dies in Venice at Age of 87—
those damned and hopeless book-learners
   scribbling on the backs of paychecks!
while the world itself turns
   slowly within a black void!

and I'm not sure which drunken
night I pulled the yellowed clipping
   out of which forgotten midden,
but tonight as I drink my beer
I stare down at it where it lies
beside some papers on my table.
A yellowed group of columns on a man.
Ezra Pound Dies in Venice at Age 87;

Ezra Pound: A Man of Contradictions
My god, the damned stupidity of the clichés
breaks through even this moment
and I pause, wander in my head, and curse—
an insignificant thing, but I think of all the people
who have hated Jews and Poles and Gypsies and Blacks
   and have not written poetry.
And then there are the pictures of Ford and Joyce and
  Pound and Eliot and then of Pound again
and the agonizing recital of all the others who once were there.
Once. And there died a myriad.
And who else is left,
who now still knows the contradictions
and can make them one?
Yes…perhaps in part…
but he too is now getting very old
and will not be with us long.
We are a people of moveable type and passing time,
and Ezra Pound is dead.

Saturday

The sun people are writing in your room.
(I could say the moon is waiting in
         your room.)
They are fingering your wandering jews,
   are plying the bookcases,
filling out the *Times'* crossword on your floor,
speaking of your hair and your warmth
         by analogy
you might be cradling them in the way you walk.
But we are lying in bed
   and it is the blinds which are talking;
And we are totally fulfilled.

from the early 1980s

Of Fire

Tonight is a night of comets.
A warm wind drops from the leaves of elms
inflating the naked flesh of animals with excitement.
A communication occurs. Silhouettes
fill the sky, passing with moonlight between clouds.
A deer pauses in the clearing out beyond my house.
It is filled with night and lowers it head to graze,
untouched by those things that are close.

Tonight is a night of fires.
In living rooms along highways sparks flare out
and savage faces are softened in the darkness between features.
In the Nevada desert sudden blazes break out between squares.
Owls sail off into time on heavy feathers.
A lone man sits down upon the sand and traces a circle with his finger.
Nothing can disturb this peace.

Tonight is a night of magnesium
flaring outward from our dark wires
and backlighting our cities' negatives.
Something dark moves beyond their light,
defining itself in its settling through air.
It is silent where we sleep,
and the velvet lips of forest spirits close above our heads.

In the Dark of the Station

It has been raining since the trains left,
and the men who remain slouch back
   against the billboards.
They watch the windows grow small
   and shapeless in the cold.

For many years it has been like this:
the men are always the same
   even when the names are not;
the same women are hunting the same lovers
   from beneath nets.
They have no purposes, and the best among them
   know the catch would spoil
      upon the beach.
They are standing there by choice and are
   the envied of the caught
and cry because between trains they forget
   the dark moving
      of the silence bird.

But this time, it has been raining a long time.
The signal lights are red and everything has frozen.
The tracks have not vibrated in so long they are
   forgotten,
and there is just one man alone
   crowded in his corners.
His tongue passes along the hair above his lips
and he draws closer to the earth.

Another Time

I could tell you that these things do not matter:
that your flesh is composed differently than mine.
I could tell you that it may rain tomorrow in our
                southwest
        pointing toward the maps
toward some obscure place far
in some dark canyon fifty miles from man.

We turn to the candle flame
and exchange the time of day,
and laugh deep within our bones;
your lips sealed in the virginal determination
parallel arrows
flaring before the space of space
and the snow falling and falling distant and
                then near
    and gone.

Because No Space Is Now Mine

Because I have gone far from where my father died
I begin to approach him.
The distant country where he was young
and I was never young
is inevitable in this time of jets.
When my father was nearing death men went to the moon.
When he was young he read they might in sci-fi books.
They have not ridden the absence of light for years
and I think they have lost the notes that let them go.
Some man rode to President on that and let it go.

The dark of crickets now fills my life
and lets me go; its caustic rubbing urge of youth
  in timelessness
is the dark of a woman's back curving into time.
It is a girl's eyes.
Snow falling into a western sunrise.
At last I begin to have all things that can be
traced into my space where the cool water of spring runs down.

Datamatatrons

              Big Pieces
     little pieces
          little little bittle
    pieces littler than a breadbox
round pieces fat pieces
       tinkling scats of plaster pleases
   dusting all together pieces
   tearing down and pasting up
fragment dots of data pieces
   microchipped and macramé
all ground out to cause dismay
   all swept up and reapplied
melted down and hung out and dried
   clumped on pedestals as clay accretions.
That is why we know so much more
   without knowing what it's for.
It's data doggerel of blips
      laid out in psycho-social chips
that grind around and disappear
   starting there and heading rear.

And All the Day

The young man in black coat with tails runs
   mad down the avenues
dodging hopefully through barroom doors
   and wobbling out drunkenly seconds later hopelessly
with the jabbering shades of anxiety
   still pursuing and screaming metal thoughts
which cannot be taken home to where his wife sits in blue eyes
      and long white gowns
but must be taken home because they cannot be released without
  the scissors of her hands
which she may take away at any instant she so chooses
to leave him dying of convulsions on a park avenue bowery bench.
        And he sings money money money

His lunch bucket has been left behind dented and useless
    where it was kicked aside by an angry postal clerk,
spewing its raw egg odor into the smog of a hungry city;
it has taken the form of a demented streetcar
     shortcutting over vacant lots to surround him
    at his every exit.
       And he sings money money money

There is no escape—no south to fly to in the winter,
as he has mended all the fences carefully,
having listened dutifully to the lecturers and followed notes
left scribbled on the monuments of stone across his country's
  construction sites.
His silver body folds over into the abyss of everything
melting out into the air below the golden gate above the waters
  of a final harbor,
and the boat he does not have the fare for comes to rest
  beneath his feet.
        And he sings money money money
           and the rain falls all day

Song of the Blood: An Epic

Published by The Smith Press

Distributed by Horizon Press

1983

Acknowledgments

Bitterroot; Coe Review; Mati; Poet Lore; The Smith.

Song of the Blood

Song   catch
          me
                    as
          snow
falling into air……
Song of the blood of this land,
fill these veins.

Song burning in earthen fragments,
filling the granite bonds of city,
building the bones of time,
Sing in the arteries of my mind.

You   insubstantial but emanating source,
pass these individual walls
and course through the pavement we have come to hate,
the plate glass windows of whitecollar bribery,
the sweat in synthetic cloth of the labor force:
Pass through and sing
of night roads
of the cold fire glittering beyond
        imagination
     ………of the unity of solitude.

I stand upon the edge of Redlands California
looking out across the san andreas
and her waters as
evening pulls the separation of industry
in a yellow wall down the valley from los angeles,

this night as many in the year,
the city becoming clear until the sand
      beneath my feet
which city shifts and rubs against itself emitting life
which city in blue horsemen dancing into the sky.

I stand and lean into the wind removed
from the stink of generation and of
      indolence
removed,
placing my hand before me until
this glittering vision is erased.
The sand speaks quietly which city
drawing the distant rattle of coins in phone booth
bars.

mai lai   distant
    which city
a fogged vision of twisted mouths.
I did not know that women would die
   like that;
that sex could dissipate so quickly
in the earth
and remain in its most violent form
a crater in the scaffolding of life
like the metal chassis I build in Detroit
and carry home with their moonless roads
  in my overalls
I no longer see the torn bodies I create
yeah tho I walk through the valley of the shadow of death
lying empty along highways or even gaping
silent across the bottom of a Chappaquiddick pond.
      song Song of the blood of

There are mistakes.

We all make mistakes,
I tell my wife when she burns the toast
or when our child fails
    to come home.
There are mistakes.
The gray mare which parades these streets which city
at night comes riderless jingling
its bridle
as it turns to gaze in windows as
it passes.
It comes alone
and the metronome of my heart swings back
through the desolate space of memory...

the demonstrating in the rain
        back and forth on Pennsylvania Avenue.
And I remember the woman met there
and the fog of love lost into her hair
upon the pillow,
the drinking and the marching and
        the laughter.
I look down the assembly line and the twisted years
     remembering mai lai

Song of the blood of this land

My body lies shattered
in Brooklyn pool halls of the sixties,
the blue chalk of my eyes erased against concrete
a sound of nails along the spine

       and

I hear the horses
heavy on their brains as they come through mist…
sometimes six sometimes seven…inevitable
as gold through Colorado rivers.

We are the light lifting
around clean spring limbs
maidenly in the airy distinction of step
   and the stubbornness of disposition,
a part of sunlight through silhouette—
a solid erasure of solidity
leaving us turning lightly upon a music
pounding within our blood.
Oh, blood of the land,
my body lies shattered.

When I wake it is Sunday.
A gray man without eyes tells me
I am fine…
all of my wishes are increasingly being
       taken care of,
and he has filed papers on my behalf
in some secret corridor where the wind does not blow.
He uses my fingers to create a smile
and the black holes of his compassion draw me in,
oh, Song,

We are going to do something now, he says.
I have seen that the dark horses which surround you
will stay far away upon their sunswept hills
while you sleep.
Come…that is the thing we have time for now…

   rubbery fingers passing across my face;
and, yes, the horsemen are drawing thin

and I see instead a line of numbers printed
white upon the horizon:
and yes they pass insubstantial in and out
          beyond control,
beyond the range of my words or hands.
You have elected them, he says,
they are my guardians if I will have them
when I awake fully taken care of in all
          that matters…

From the distance I see
those shapes now losing form in scattered confusion,
 withdrawing into earth and rocks and trees.
They are no more than trees! I say,
and he takes my hands to make him smile a loose
flapping into eternity.
They are only trees!

They will not ride upon your heels, he says.
They will not bother you, for we have time.

Song of the dust of this land,
Song of the dust…
Out of dust, the thought;
Out of thought first the dust
slowly shaping/settling between the stars
through eons of nonexistence
        drifting—
out of thought, out of energy;
the tiniest specks of matter settling,
drawing together by some spaceless force
   into the seeable; the float evolving and the mineral sediments
the ions, the growth, the settling, the life.

The morning   gray
a heron freezes into shoreline
its stark bone beak poised between clouds
and the silver rattle of scales about its feet;
the eye pinned dark into a static motion.
I draw back into the reeds
too much a part of this, thinking
No, if I wait long enough there will be Words,
dreaming I will touch this thing as it touches me;
watching as the brightness of the moon in brightness
falls into the ocean's growing luminescence,
lost from definition;
thinking, No, a man does not need to think to be a man...

As the Half-king once said
when speaking to Major Washington once said
> *In former days we have eaten*
> *from a silver basin wherein was the leg of the beaver,*
> *and desired of all to come and eat of it.*
> *Now, fathers, it is you who are the disturbers in this Land.*
> *Both the others and you are white, George Washington.*
> *But we live in a country between (which city);*
> *and the Great Being allowed it to be a place of residence*
>   *for us.*
> *I desire you to withdraw, George Washington.*

Song of the blood of this land...
Even as now, I sit at the mouth of the everett claim
looking back from sun-cracked Colorado rock
into earth and dark
stained memories of men who spent their gold
   in Eldorado,
a boomtown just west of here whose name was changed
still booming perhaps in anticipation of deception

   to Eldora:
then a boomtown; then a weathered scattering of shacks; at
   last almost resort
somewhere west along the shaft behind me.
That darkness from 1905, I think,
once mined by the family I have married into,
stretching out beyond me.
But the price of time changes
and I turn so that spencer mountain rolls
heavy to middle boulder creek and Nederland.
The price of time changes, and the heritage of families
cross and swirl. My father's last estate
   for his family:
      built on printed words on careful shelves.
My father-in-law's: a miner's cabin from 1893
   where we sleep at night
      but not tonight,
looking down toward barker dam and its darkness
   hidden water,
sitting here, still sitting with the golden lights
sparking silently on and off
in the tunnel behind me/matching the occasional car
to Eldorado
lighting up its distant road long before it comes in sight.
The cars at night along the road to Eldorado,

              Song

I walk along those dirt tracks
    the ruined buildings
       ELDORADO!
and an old miner swaggers from what once was the general store
and waves. I have seen him teaching math at colorado state…

Here too in the echoing bowl of stone
rippling through aspens

catching the metallic glint
my mind comes around upon itself again.
These shuttered windows upon sand!
These worn boards hiding something
  even here where
    paint does not exist.

Song
Turning
until I too look half back
through the window black now within the tunnel
and her face translucently reflected
hollowing out in shadow as the passing lights
    pass and then
etching her features again into the glass
      in dark
as our train speeds now deeper into Grand Central in
new york among the concrete roof supports.
The passengers seated, forgotten, (whichcity)
she stands there between the cars forgotten,
her eyes/lips detaching my skin
as I raise the *Times,* Forgetting.
And brightness falls into the ocean beyond the east river.

Until half sleeping I am shocked awake
seeing her passing down the aisle of the car,
gray dress passing lightly over hips
and a gold cross hanging down before her
  from the chain belt worn loose about her hips.
And the cars rattle…we are alone:
and I think of my child, and of all my children
and of the miles of time which separate them……

Song of the blood of this land
Song of the dust of this land

you are my death.
You are my birth.

*

Old Edmund Newstart climbed
up to the top of Mayberry Hill
and leaning back against a firm boulder
looked down over the city and counted the lights.
There's one and two and...well, a whole lot more
than there were people living there when I was younger,
he said and tilted his head back so that the moon fell over his lips.
And I guess that most of them living there now
don't have what I have: I own this hill, he said.
I own this hill; and what else; and what do any of them own.
And his hand reached out until it touched a dry stalk
and he pulled it from the sand and sucked it to his mouth
and he closed his eyes and smiled.

Out of all the fear of grabbing an acre of land
and the drinking times with Jim and the other bankers...
well, they're gone now, but after all someone had to live
   and together we lived it well
and maybe better than one man alone might live...
but I've got the money to buy another pair of shoes to climb this hill...
no better than what I had but just as good.
I wonder old friend moon, how do *you* fly without replacing wings.

And he answered himself
You don't need wings on Mayberry Hill.

*

A man is walking toward you wherever you are
the bushes bending back from his raised arms

brushing through evening space toward you
with his mouth open the tears running from his mind
until too soon his hands will curve outward and his feet leave
the earth almost in their speed
until out of the night about the time you rise to walk the streets
he will reach you and clasp your knees,
and he will say nothing
because through this time he is unknown to you.

But you have drunk many times
to the sheltered things which you carry in memory.
I know this,
as I know that now you are sitting in some room
where you do not wholly want to be
and are reading this along with other discarded words
and then pausing to stare outward toward the sheltered things.
And are wondering what this faceless man comes to you for
and what the gaping lips you pass flapping in restaurant windows
   may be meaning;
and why it is that houses and children
                       but never works of art
                                     grow from these
   shapeless patterns.
Or what it is that weighs some men down or makes them
become horses sailing across the moon   or
of a small white bird sitting upon the ice on a lake
which stretches as far into here as you have wished to go.
Perhaps you do not see the horses, or they are not horses…
but only something which travels as swiftly as you. You will know.

And I know you will say
that you have seen this movie one time on the late show
or have suspected the setting some time in Dreiser or in Norris,
   but that it was not poetry.
But you are wrong

because it was never filmed and because
even the word is a hollow cave echoing with massive earth groan
    shifting endlessly on itself.
And because he does not have a face and is approaching silently
until some day when he reaches you and you
will look down and know an overwhelming closeness
and will not know his name.

                              *

My body, like yours, is filled with love,
with hatred.
My mind too, a gray river,
a writhing with patches of light rolling across its surface.
I too have debated the office clock,
have slammed its metal tongue against the floor,
have stalked out with freedom in my lungs
and bad liquor in my belly,
my belly a hairy animal moaning in the night
and going softer in its sides with sedatives.

The animal of hominid
gnashes its teeth along these streets at night,
whispers to itself when the wind blows,
huddles in shaking silence upon the sweat of pain and labor.
The deadly struggle in the alley. The blood.
The hairless paw passed lightly on a face.

                              *

Bending sheet metal
            connecting wires
stringing signs:
HOTDOGS FOR AMERICA
or

CHOPPED MEAT THE WAY TO GO
or
VENUSIAN PLEASURE PALACE
twisting above the concrete cracks.
Light of this light
balancing equal weights upon each other
turning themselves upon themselves turning.
Sometimes one above his head,
sometimes others.
A SOUPCAN FOR THIS CIVILIZATION
A WARM HOTEL
And always the round rubber wheels
bounding across a continent of flesh.
Dressing male and female models radiant
colors of the forest birds;
pale silhouettes twisting against winter.
And the snow of the creator obliterating tracks within his mind.

We sat down together once
at a trucker's stop in Arizona;
he with a map spread between the coffee and
   the saltshaker.
And I drank the coffee and smoked a cigarette
   while we talked.
So, I interrupted,
   THE AMERICAN CANCER SOCIETY will get me.
Yes, he said, the country will be free
     for the clean.
He pushed a pin into the map.
I put fifty cents on the counter
and went out into the night.

Many years from then
when I was standing at the top of Flagstaff Mountain
  in Colorado

leaning into the wind and watching
the stars twisting far back through the space of time,
I looked down to see a set of headlights turning toward me,
drawing up the mountainside from Boulder. And I thought,
Those lights are death coming up an unlit road;
and I will wait.
But they were not death.
And he leaned from his window smiling,
his teeth sparkling beneath stars
and his eyes the blank of moon over desert.
Hi, old friend, he said.
We are both lost here on top of this half-baked wilderness,
and I am thinking of buying it.
I nodded and turned my collar up.

*

We celebrate the little victories.
The meetings.
The money coming into hands.
The salaries.
Some mornings when we rise
the sun is rising over the river.
The wild horses riding along the clouds
cast eyes above us as we move
  inward toward the office.
And weekends…weekends are for sleeping.

*

A visitor without shadow enters the room
pours a glass of liquor and
leans back, smoke pouring from his fingertips.
The phone rings and no one answers.
The body is relaxed.

A light across the street
is a woman writing letters to herself
in the indelible darkness of time on paper.
She does not know that he is watching
or has already walked alone, again, the beach
she writes of
small plants and shells long blown into the sea.

She runs her palm across her forehead,
fingers brushing dust blonde hair from flesh,
talking to herself and shifting weight from one arthritic hip,
feels the milk come down into her breasts
and twists as the baby chases antlers in another room.
She feels the keys beneath her fingers and slips them
in as she has for years in light
in the darkness
     across the way
He waits
remembering memory
as his smoking fills the room
and the shimmer of alcohol glows blue
in its pulsing through his veins;
suffusing the heart and eyes and liver
which make a man who casts no shadow
as the corners of the room
     fade out
the body is relaxed.

       *

Slate house empty in the moonlight:
A woman's footsteps

       *

"Come, have a glass of wine
to celebrate our being here
in this closeness of candles and old tables.
To the darkness beneath the rafters, Friends!"
There he and we lifted our glasses.

There before those sightless orbs
we listened to a tale of time
with each of us removed,
contributing at times.
I could not tell you how.
But it was heavy with smoke
and the bright skirts flew by outside.
Sometimes the trees turning their leaves
      over in the wind.
Sometimes the rain.

Do you remember…
"Yes," we said.
The thunder. The sun.
The love we had within us.

                        *

The simple lives
tinkle from our fingers;
the crazed howl of actors
a wind roaring in the earth's bag.
If there were a way
a way to build these timbers
selected from the hardest pines chiseled from the softest rosewood trees,
if there were a way
then surely we would speak of them;
and your long, salt hair streaked
in the candlelight of coast-to-coast hotels;

your lips curled bitter in the glass.
Nothing spoken. Nothing.

A woman who
is the only one I know who can
bring a name to such a season
passed this way.
You may have seen her.
Not recognized;
for what is to be seen but the eyes
or long flesh legs passing quickly?
What is to be seen,
     or named;
if she were here
who she is the only one
would tell you this.
But I cannot speak her language,
nor do I think she would speak again
though I have moved many times since then.
The simple lives.

We were drinking once
down on university place
to one of us.
Discussing how he was the best writer
  of all of us;
or how he was the best drinker;
or this or that.
And how he had died unpoetically even so
  without warning one morning.
And how he had been more than merely best
    at anything.
And someone said,
someone who had not known him said,
yes, but you are talking only about you

because you say only that he was liked by you
ad infinitum ad nauseam paternoster,
and I said yes, I must agree if we are being polite;
but there is one thing more you should write down
at least if you are going to sit here and drink with me:
He taught me a great deal of the world I write about.

*

arlo and Pete Seeger
singing from the wolf trap.
Not Woody...
No, the younger generation
left surrounded by the older understanding.
The dyed cloth chairs. The
   microphones.
we all fail to carry our sons upon our knees
when we come from the lumber mills
and the long dirt roads their legs
   can't quite keep up with yet.
But the old friends try, Woody.
They keep your children close to the fire,
murmuring the quiet undertones,
and listening to the wind rattle among needles
of old phonographs. This land now
is ours, *Sing goddamn!*

*

barmaids in empty rooms
waiting for the offering
listening to the dust filtering through sunlight

the girls of Washington Square
leading their naked children

to bathe in the fountain
to guitar and bluegrass and smoke.
The old professors sitting between classes
in spring evenings and the drunkards,
the students long and dark haired
with faces serious for the business of The Arts.

Lincoln Center
and the rows of hollow husks
torn by a dreadful ecstasy
which vibrates through minds,
terminating in champagne and subway rides,
decaying piers along the Hudson
with their DO NOT SMOKE signs
and SAFETY FIRST among the rotted roof supports.
The couples hiding in the captain's balcony
of the second floor leaning over water.

*

The lights pale,
the dusty lines of dawn crawling among furniture
when she came over
leaned smoking across the candle.
Everyone's a poet, she said.
How many publications do you have?
I took her home.

I made it up, I said.
Everyone's a poet.
The clothes lying in secret packages of scent
scattered across the unwashed floor.
Her anger taut across my belly,
the fingers pressed tight into my shoulders.
I have been with Gregory Corso, she said.

He said I was a female Rimbaud.
And so have I: we talked
of a baby gorilla in the zoo, the Bronx,
and I recited The Mad Yak from memory.
Rimbaud is dead.
Everyone's a poet, she said,
                      and left.

                    *

When you are dragging your zippy new suit
  jacket over your shoulders
dashing white sun mad to the subway stop
on your way to the gleaming citadels of your destination
in the heartlands of city filled poor
through shrill dust of the urban rush,
You are kicking a can tied to a dead dog's tail.

And

When you are leaving the brightly lit
to walk sage deserted western deserts
rattling the finger bones of past experience
loose in the pockets of your memory
or polishing the stainless hollow tube of
        the equalizer metal
to burst through the comfort of suburban
houses in a flash of blood upon the screen
or are brooding brooding brooding watching dark
   pirate ships fill the sun,
You are kicking a can tied to a dead dog's tail.

And
if you are reading this
or breathing in the silence of your living room

or reading more than one paper or book
   or page a day
or are thinking
         —most of all this—
are thinking of anything other than NOW
You are kicking a can tied to a dead dog's tail.

And
whatever else the possibilities
the tail may break at least
or the dog flip over
if you kick hard enough.

                *

She wakes in the night
crying
Who came through the door?
No one I say I have been here
You were hearing footsteps on the floor
         above us.
She babbles something about money
money money
and rolls off into sleep.
I count the footsteps and listen to the
wind roll by my window.
The air is thick with sirens
drawing me in their northward flight
through winter.

At last I too rise
too certain that some fast and not too silent
momentum has caught in the marrow of my bones,
hurling me at a speed beyond direction
so that my impressions and ours are meaningless

empty bottles set down empty before a barn
and shattering one by one, the targets of a boy
aiming his father's rifle the first time.

And like then or like the evening of that day
I walk into the living room by myself and I sit
and take a slow drink from a glass of milk
looking out upon a brittle landscape of winter.
And like then although the sun is about to rise
          unlike then
I look through a frozen web of ice crystals
thinking although the strangers I live with now
are much less strangers than then,
it is something I have seldom seen and it
is startlingly solid, much more so than the news,
how everything outside that window is more distant
     than this web;
and I think just as I did then, this is something
which must be shared so that I turn toward
the other rooms of the house although the house is new.
And once again I turn back.
Because it is something which cannot be said in words.
There are moments when you too look out the windows
and turn away.

And I sit back looking out through the ice tracks
spreading out across our windows,
the iron straight tracks running forever across space
throughout their lengths crossed at regular
and immediate intervals by shorter iron lengths,
parallel and spaceless tracks of timelessness. Outward
until the lines blur while maintaining their direction.

And I lean forward as each of you has done
while the moon fills each faultless line and the train,

I think of the train even now lurching its heavy metal
sides down canyons toward the city where I carry what I can
in a thin black case to the office where I like you have earned
      my keep.
Or like you, I step back from the automation at times
when the sun is dipping low and sweeping from the day
and walk along those tracks, kicking my feet among
the dark ties and loose rubble which contain our civilization;
through the small fields which arise from lost buildings,
falling with their captured memories upon the earth of their immediate
      path,
past the solitary piles of papers and beer cans which collect
      in such places,
and the dark and boarded windows. Like you, I pass in the dark
the rooms where solitary people sleep or share their visions
with the walls.

Or like you even farther down the road,
I come upon those stretches where great machinery has passed
      for the last time;
and the skeletal remains of empire-building are shattered,
their ties lying like lost teeth scattered among weeds
where there is nothing to slow the wind but the occasional butterfly
or the dry cricket rubbing its legs against itself in celebration.

Perhaps, even, I have watched you or have tried to say some word,
although you thought that I had gone long ago; or have watched
you from that building you passed just yesterday which was coming
down and was being picketed by unions who were losing work as I
wrote while watching from high above the city; for I have watched.
Or perhaps it was I who was picketing, or who called you one night
when the phone rang and rang; for I have done that as well.
No matter.
The early light reveals the trees outside our window are white
      and leafless

except one pine; beyond that pine another, but white and leafless
    in this light.

No, there were no footsteps, but the stars are lifting,
withdrawing; and some great and awesome beast beyond our sight
is riding northward through the clouds.

*

Where the car stops
on this Thursday in late November
when I go down to the river the roads are walls of fog
and the buildings which are summer's amusement park
are white as the bone-gray of winter
are the land
are leaves over dry earth when the candy wrappers are gone.
I am the only walking man
moving toward the riverbank
in this whole man-built façade of cultivated trees and
   hand-carved granite ribs
the only man moving in this place fashioned from the mind
for the family of America.
The oak trees bare brown frames against the sky
   this time of year
to the left not far away the rigid statues of the Detroit dream.
Further out the drying winter cattails. And
the soft wind the closing metal fences the missing radios.
I am the only man who walks here and the only man
who will ever see this thing.
I walk into the grayness of the water
and it surrounds me and fills my eyes
carrying my body a small green crab scuttling over broken stone.
Behind me there are voices calling,
but they have their world.

Do you think of the man as you read this,
wondering what it would be like
to share coffee over a table;

Even now, I am thinking of you
as you sit reading these dry echoes;
perhaps even sitting there with you
building on the words like blocks of ether,
and wishing instead we were walking drunken
examining the autumn weeds growing in some sacred place
or kicking among the rusted remains of where we lived,
our arms across each other's shoulders.

Not talking craft or names
or yours or mine;
since these are meaningless
and since we say only the little we both know;
but walking along the dry gullies together,
collecting the sticky seeds of weed growth
on our socks and on our trouser cuffs.
Thinking if we were the unshucked brilliance of these weeds
we would be poetry, and would not call it anything
and would cry always with the hollow cry
of Life.

The stamps CRANE and ROETHKE and JARRELL
glistening posts entwined within the mind,
and the master scytheman WHITMAN squinting through his sweat
and saying I am this and I like this
and This is me.
And the countless overgrown hummocks,
and the swirling fogs of teaspoon-measured mermaids.

Until we would take these home
and sip dark liquor together long into the night

with so many memories we cannot begin to talk;
drinking a toast to this and a toast to that,
within ourselves
and to our children
who will kill the cows which feed upon our graves
as surely as we are sitting here reading these words.

*

There is a stone within me, smooth and impervious…settled deep
   into my belly. I keep this stone because it was given me by
   time. It grinds my food with the eyes of fragile birds, and
   bears outward on my back until I stand less straight.

There is a stone within me. It grows on nights when the moon
   fills my bedroom window and falls on the white flesh at my
   side. It too is white, but hidden in the dark redness
   rolling from side to side in blind despair.

It grows with the shifting strain of continents. Through years
   with the broken fingers of men's dreams. The rusted anarchy
   of machinery. It bathes itself in the tobacco of the southland.
   The fermented grain of the midwest. The camaraderie of
   isolation.

There is a stone within me. It was given me by time, and time
   will not let it go.

*

Loveliest of trees my family's now
is drunk with dry rot in the bough.
And since to look at things in bloom
takes me into darkened rooms,
about the country I will go
to see my family's urine flow.

Let us go then, you and I,
while there's grease upon the sky.

My son sleeps.
I sit in my den and type a poem
before preparing for work in the morning.
My wife bends over a table downstairs
writing a study for the Navy on where their planes will fall
   when they miss the base.
The house was built in 1870 for studies which were not dreamed of
   then.

Try to remember
how to dismember
this kind of September

Old wood strong enough to hold six generations,
stone soaked with the seepage of one hundred eleven years.
An old car running on three cylinders
     spitting gas fumes into the air
on a three-year guarantee expired.
Why do we build these things to fall apart?
Sometimes I think to meet a man who will live longer than I
is the hardest thing which I can do;
knowing he will drink beer and walk these fog-draped streets
   when I am no longer a part of them.
The movies of dead men. The wet sheets of Marilyn Monroe.

In Samsonite did Kubla Kahn
a shapely broad decree
where all the sinful rivers ran
through taverns measureless to man
you'll wonder where you money went
when you give it to the government

I have never been one to be able
to look at old movies and say I know him That is Errol Flynn
or There is Hitchcock standing in that corner with a shopping bag.
He is the bald man.
nor would I recognize James Dickey if he firebombed me
except by his words.
Something in the way the wind blows.

Oh Chaplin, My Chaplin!
On the burning bible lies...
The Little Tramp!

I remember only the burning blue signs
shouting wordless on and off into neon night.
It is said when a man is my age he is at his most productive
   machinations,
having gathered the nameless in scattered figurines
and building models that cannot fly...heavy bumblebees
descending through time on the needle of their death.

Fuzzy Wuzzy was a bear.
Fuzzy Wuzzy had no hair.
Fuzzy Wuzzy had bursitis.

*

I am the night wing
the steel hawk upon darkness
eye bright ore beneath the damp loose earth.
Separation is the spreading of an oak leaf in autumn
and the silt growing in the estuary of some great river.
I live and the room I live is all I need
beneath a lamp as my father sat beneath a lamp
     thirty revolutions of the earth ago
illumined by past death in the glowing center of his room

    a glass bulb
as I sit straining the dried blood from his skull.
Books. Bitter ladies.
The sour scent of sleeping fills these curtained windows.
The torn clothes belonging perhaps to those who remain
        or those who left
whose names are labels on glass bottles beyond the wall.
This is all I need
battering burning against the incandescent center of my
        universe.

*

Something massively large has slept
these last days in the valley outside my window;
something of unimaginable weight,
along the far banks of the river outside my study;
and yet silent in the ease with which its resting limbs
uprooted trees and boulders, cascading earth and rubble
down to the water's edge, leaving an expanding pattern
of metal frames and the abandoned summer houses
pressed flat into the depression of its presence.
Some thing which I do not have a name for
which has passed the night these recent days
quietly waiting while I slept,
so that when I rose in the gray of morning
the land outside was changed each day,
and the vegetation I remembered further crushed.
So that is why tonight I wait
long after my wife has departed for the bedroom,
and I smoke cigarettes or sip from my drink
as I stare into darkness listening to the wind
as it builds along these valley corridors
and the air inside this room grows heavy with discarded time.

And I listen to the rain in its falling
as it has fallen each of these past days,
rattling along the shingles and sliding off to silence.
And there suddenly I begin to hear
the distant splintering of wood and a heavy settling,
as if the smoke which fills this room were taking solid form
and rolling to a final resting place;
and yet the room is filled with smoke and it is rolling
   without ceasing in the darkness,
moving in or out with the coolness of the partly opened window.

As I write this,
I am staring as intently as I can
out over the valley beneath the distance of the stars
until almost I think there is a less substantial shape
transforming in the valley, or a gathering of gray within the night.
But it is too hard to tell about, and the shape
or shapes if they are shapes too hidden in their form.
The brighter focal points perhaps the flashlight
of some landowner puzzling over forgotten land,
his eyes every now and then reaching out to touch a stone
and glittering there. I do not know,
but only that something there is hidden from the light.
And I know that everything is fading as the morning comes,
and that the earth will slide still farther down its swollen river.

*

We leave for New York at 1 p.m.
light even for this day to the hudson river drive
through yonkers the heavy barrels of winter sand red
   and white along tarmac arteries
through the woods of fort tryon the borders of the cloisters.
And I think, when the body is ill we go into the country.
When the brain is ill we go into the city.

And we drive without notice:
My three-month-old son strapped into the back in a plastic chair
looking out the rear window counting his fingers as they wave
   before his face
leaving the road in long bounds where its surface is torn
   by freezing water:
You know when you enter New York, I think.

Down into the older districts and the hospital
and through the older doorway to the waiting room.
The wait within the waiting room from 2 until 4:30;
and the pacing and the endless fear of parents
and the coughing of the patients waiting for a bed;
the hungry wait for milk from plastic bottles because the breasts
   are dry.
The slipping off into a brain of rivers and trees
and where there is no language
in the city of the concrete word.

At 5:02 we go up to the northern wing,
to a bed,
to the children without motor development and with speech
   impediments,
to the autistic children without words—with rage,
to the lost women smiling to each other
and to me and to my wife,
to the tips of the wing of Hell.

And we sit, my wife and I, beside the crib until the night
and it is time for the father to drive out home.
The drive itself along arrowless roads which somehow
I do not know, lead back into the hills of Westchester.
A descent into my cellar to trip the pump,
drawing underground rivers from my home.
The night. The same long trip by dawn into a maze I cannot
   memorize.

The walk back into a brightly painted room
and the blue eyes beginning now—only now!—to smile.

Yesterday was St. Patrick's Day,
and HAPPY ST. PATRICK'S is written on the windows in green,
and clovers,
and GOOD LUCK!
There are no snakes in New York today as I look through the glass.
The message, as usual in the city, is late;
and there are only two kinds of people alive:
The Irish and those who wish they were:
Ask James Joyce.
And then at 8 a.m. my son is collected
and packed in a steel-barred crib on wheels and we walk away
beneath the hospital and the city in a circling ring of dingy concrete
   tunnels without signs
to an x-ray room where he is wheeled away;
and I return to the upstairs room.

And I sit watching for hours
the crib my son was lying in.
And see the semicircles which 'Graff
                            and Moose
                   and Moosical Squirrel
lay out above my son's pajamas on the mattress;
   foam-stuffed heads solemn in the waiting.
I lay my jacket over the pajamas to keep him warm.
My wife is marking city planning maps on the hospital table
sitting in a children's chair—
a little plastic chair, money for survival,
passing time for sanity. I call the office. I write rituals.
My words cannot find the place
they took my son.

11:00, I am somehow sitting in the upstairs waiting room
looking out over an old city.

For up to three blocks I can see the wood frames of brick
   windows facing us.
At four, the curtain shades…at six.
Beyond that, for another twenty, the dark black eyes.
Then buildings only. And the haze.
Beyond them all, the river; or I say it is the river.
And the vertical shadowed land beyond.
The sky is overcast. It is 11:00 a.m.

At 11:25 the white man wheels my son into the room.
Asleep. Pupils tiny.
Respiration and heartbeat good.
He screams and the moosical squirrel sings my son to sleep.
The sitting into dark. The drive along the unmarked roads.
The drive back into the dawn.

And the brain scan is abnormal;
the head like my own too large for a little body.
But there are no tumors and no arterial bleeding;
just the fluid settling quietly among the growth.

But there is no need to change this yet, perhaps ever,
like father like son,
though it will be measured every day.
And my wife and I embrace and cry. And my son cries for milk.

And we go for the time we have back out into the country,
believing it will be forever or for most of our lives at least.
And we know that we are lucky.

*

When I was eight
I used to fish with an old man sometimes,
and he would talk to me about life

   at sea in the war.
He had written a great book
and was a great general in the war
   against Franco.
But I knew an old man in a red wool coat
who huddled with me by the rail
and talked of death at sea.

When a man dies at sea,
and you cover him with a flag,
you slide him from underneath into the sea.
You fight to keep each other alive
but you slide him out into the sea.
    And if he would have betrayed you?
You keep the flag.
    And if he was your captain?
You keep the flag.
And every ship in the ocean keeps
   the flag.
That means something.
And every ship in the ocean is alone.

I never asked him why he spoke of the sea
when he had fought upon the arid land of Spain,
or what dark secrets he hoped to pull from the mud beneath
   our feet.
But on days like this, I hurl telephones from windows.
All across the city, the dark heavy wires
hanging from broken glass, trailing
loosely down over blanched stone façade,
the dull clicking of receivers in the street
below and disconnected.

               *

Last football player,
      that's me
   spiral into ol' number 31.
Shampoo and hairspray commercials
end over end to the goalpost. Hey
        pretty girls like ice cubes
                on the floor.
Hey, I'm thirty-five selling
        my old man's Brylcreem and punch cards
   already
end over end for a handsome fee going
              to fat
and it's the last thing I want to grease
  my body down…
Toward
      that last kick if they let me have one more season.
They said when they put those pompon girls somewhere
           yeahinmypocket
those papers said number 31 would just keep on coming
back and take the ball all the way.
But what am I going to tell my boy when he says how come
            you're just selling used cars, Dad.
And I'm going to point to all them street lamps
curving up through the back window while we drive,
and I'm going to place his head on my shoulder and say
        Because
I was the last football player, son.

                    *

Twisted with the crazed light of sixties
  viet nam flesh,
I was there fighting the peaceful fight
  of my country
bleeding corridors of worthless Washington.

I walked them all with the force of young.
Or, oh Spirit, the drunken moon-ripped
Greenwich Village scare scenarios—the
burning more much more than alcoholic rage
and the phosphorescent searing of our brains.

But never a battle like this!
The dull and ivory handle of the butter knife
pressed inexorably between the eyes
until the flesh grown fat follows flesh
and the eyes are pulled within
the gray mass of sameness coiled
and fit to strike.

Why, the rank, slimy bile green inertial mass
   of Government!
The bitter despair of rationality marching
in neon façade to the open grave of industry!
And all for the cardboard farm of ownership.
This is the battle now,
Against the impatient pulsing of the blood
in mad circles through humanity.

No wonder the fascination of our time
with the machinery of death.
No wonder the fascination with Nazi dream machines
flooding out across paperback America.
This ivory handle of the butter knife...

This need to let the skull fly in upon a landscape
to walk naked beneath the moon.

*

Song...
Song of my blood...

*

Indian tortoise moon rises heavy over Westchester
   Hudson Valley.
I listen to CONCERTO FOR FIVE KETTLE DRUMS
   AND ORCHESTRA.
Heavy earthen doors slam shut across the wooded hills.

Reddish hued in night
   the trees...
moss hanging from straining limbs
fastened in place the old estates bordering down
spaceless to the fish's belly of the water.
Song of wind through flesh.

Song of borderless division,
of Irvingstown and New York,
of storms which hardly shape the land,
of brackish Tappan Sea crescented by metal road
and the old ones in their bones
counting time by sails upon tide.

Slow tortoise moon upon white frame
wood clap churches of America
long isolate in uncleared land.
The sleeping millionaires and factory workers,
carmakers, papershufflers,
struggling silently upon the edge of some long known
slow moving song of wind.
The television aerials, the wrecking crews
and half-remembered legends written in blood.

Slow tortoise moon upon the eastern passage
to the west.

*

Song

Out of dust the thought
Out of thought first the dust
snow naked woman running toward the village
young breasts high to hand clutched
red flag waving dust clouds from road
bleach dyed pubic thatch rubbed tight
across frontier fence boundaries...
pied piper junky rats dancing the red
immobile stillness in their homes
seductive smile and the rolling smoke dark
filling sodium-lighted city air.

Grammy, will you take us riding now.
Pack your bags. The horses are ready.
Ready.
Small young faces generations
trailing out beyond the green-tipped New York isle,
porcelain doll pressed tight against the flesh.

I think that I will marry him...
Oh, Daddy, be a dear...
Pick up some thread in town.
I think I'll go. I think
I think
Daddy...

No longer home
the gray salt of winter safety roads

piled for dispersal here.
chain clank December night
or rotting auto body condom urban edge
echoechoecho
stream pebble cool
in the furry frenzied mass of tangled limbs.
Well, you pay your coins
and take the cattle crazy ride.

Cotton sterile room
lips useless confusion of foreign language
eyes only printing unspoken
unspeakable
warning
money is the warning
not pronounced
but
the eyes are the medium
not what is being said
fear and little boy in stretched out flesh
useless for control.
A stroke of luck.

Mass plague death fascinates
     the people…
the last ant struggling across cyanide powder
the first bacterium upon a petri dish
the wide wash of tree ribbed muddy waters
perched rooftop spinning along the flood.
You think the dreams and not the bones.
You think the passage beyond the stench.
And you think of what you are…
And out of thought the dust.

Do you think still
it is better

to be
unmalleable encapsuled
limited touch of dead wires on nerve
than loose?
That it is worth thinking of?
I tell you it is not so.

Do you think even that you
        are
encapsuled for time?
It is not so
except for the twisting moment
of stars upon nighttime water.
Do you think you are not your own bars
        and temporary?

When I wake in the morning
to drool over my texts
I do not throw my arms wide.
No...these fleshless appendages heavy
and useless as the arms of my chair
paralyzed upon my sexless form.

Only the words I cannot move my lips to speak
have opened arms and match the colors of
    the dress I wear today
whatever they chose to dress me in
in my sixteen years and 300 pounds
    of broken evening conversation.
My teeth themselves removed
for the straw that draws my food within.
And at sixteen years a girl dreams of ballerinas
and of gods.
And I believe in gods.
And in white swans beating their wings

listlessly across a television sign-off sign,
their feathers choking the air outside my windows.
I believe.

A statue has been constructed within my body:
ticking of metal keys
Selectric words on disposable cassettes
chipping out the stone from blood.
Something white and solid as pigeons in the evening
coming home to roost in Kubla cons.
The weather-woven stone of coffee hours and tv
The money spent.
The chanting silence of trees upon a country plot
        of land.

It comes to this worshipping of leavings
and the drinking of liquors which dissolve the stone;
the arid spaces which have built the flesh,
the feathered thoughts which have become concrete for some.
And from somewhere this icon then has been set aside.
Removed from family and centered in the square.
The years blow against it; and fashion follows form.
The stone becomes itself a feeling unpredictable.

We would walk out into the mountains
when only our feet could be trusted,
and he would say Look to the gnarled and isolate trees…
I will teach you of the trees against evening.
Walk quietly. (and he would speak in whispers)
Stand clear from the moon shadow of that boulder.
(We would sit in sand clearings among piñon effigies,
looking to the trees and the moon shining from beneath their boughs.)

And one night we lit a fire from the dead
beneath a neap tide moon.

Stand close within this ring of silver he said.
Do not leave it ever. (The flame will die
I said) Do not leave it ever.

Or winter
and the vast snow prints we would find
and would not follow.

I stand where she stood
   beneath the trees
watching as evening lights the earth
as I watched her there perhaps three years ago
...or more...
Marriage makes the time run faster or
   the time run slower
or eliminates the time at all
we stood there within the same depressions
flesh so hard against flesh it was not what we expected.

I watched that evening
as wind lifted the dark hair from across her face
and she turned gray eyed to face in my direction
not seeing me
but touching in that way which names do not allow—
as there have been many others who have stood in that depression
looking out among tree limbs over the valley
at that same moment through the years
hobbling crippled only when the limbs began to move
or the broken cacophony of speech intruded
and we were moved away.

Song
Song of the blood

Dark Wing: Book Two of Song of the Blood

Published by Charred Norton Publishing

1984

Dark Wing:

They said you should go into medicine.

They said you should be a lawyer.
>   *the windows pock pock*
>   *the masonry*

why…the real estate you could
  have had
>   *empty as brick dust the ache*
>   *in your legs, Mr. Moreson*

all the white-gowned dark-haired ladies of groupie passion,
the high school sensibility of virtue honest for destruction
>   *black shattered hulls of air*
>   *in walls above your head.*

Broken wing.
Dark crow,
Carry who will carry
my peeled door epitaph
hulking heavy-sided to the moon.
Who's gonna make my deathbed
when I die?

She sang beyond the genius of rubble
who nourished me
in the distant place with mutton-fatted meat
who fed me liquor until I puked the poison out
and we would walk beneath the midnight light
(Aurora Sodiumalis plastic globes!)
but the rubble did not sing.
Dream carefully and practice magic
that will not feed the office clock
          Since I have been there
and the winds whip through my ribs

peeling the dry white of picket fences
sterile seeds across the concrete shore
                        she sang
the torn fiber.

Ligament of passion
  connecting
and so I did not go
far from the unlighted room
until long after she had gone
dreaming of the song and
tasting life stained rock
  in a mockery of lithely settled limbs
pock pock the missionary tile
        the distant place of brain
        stranded column on air
until they had all gone
        to the brighter passageways
        companion of the hollow eyes.

And I set about surviving
        pock pock
the graveyards of my family
scuttling wounded animals to earth
        Burrow! Burrow deeply
        and sleep ragged beast!
In whatever way I could
        You should have been a doctor
        and plunged steel needles beneath flesh.
would not have let me rest
in any way I can. I walk,
Dark Crow. Carry me as you wish.

Random. Random were the notes she sang
creating land

which together we could stand upon.

> *mr. moreson, where are you now?*
> *mr. moreson can't pull a plow.*
> *mr. moreson can't feed the kids.*
> *mr. moreson should call it quits.*

So I got a job like they said
hooking television aerials into telephone wires
from 7 a.m. until so tired my body
  was carried
aloft on white sheets in sirened cars
battling the battling of blood
> *You know*
> *You who connect and drill and patch*
> *the concrete slabs we dance upon*
> *You know*
> > *how we will wonder where you*
> *will dance*

for every day remembering the hidden song
too torn to try the notes; too cold
to hear the swans come in over Erie in the fall.

And my muscles, like they said,
learned to hum the mechanized;
to stretch their ligaments on syntax of absurd.
They learned to hum my time on metal keys
and I to wait until some day
I would smash my way from the metal trap
pawless and bleeding sustenance.
But how can one wait
     or do anything
when dead.

Dark wing,

carry me away,
you ragged bloody beast!

I move heavily

              hips flared sagging of bone,
shoulders hunched on gray wing.
Heavily. There is something that does not speak of youth
whether animal or figurehead as in the wall of china
destroying the creator's mind.
And so I move heavily
       at those times I move
watching this faceless slab of sediment
which closes in the darkness when no one comes.
Sometimes I walk through a sea of limestone,
small calcium deposits sifting through blood.
The great sand mother stirs my oatmeal
  lumpy over rusting silver spoon.

What happens to the man who doesn't return
from the concrete towers of his desolation…
the paperclip missing in action.

          star burner,
          carry salt tongue memories
          relaying parti-colored birds over
          blue phones

From the stone doorways,
the rows of dead along mt. hilltop
moving on the minutes of each other,
I draw no comfort.
From the silken passing over flesh
from the multicolored cloth
from the thin stemmed glass

I have made the choice,
and draw no comfort.
From the survival of the minute
into the endless plain of hours,
learned through pain—as abstract as meaningless—
I draw no comfort...

some say
gray morning he finds himself
down red tunnels

> *eye twinkler*
> *some say he is carried away*
> *beyond dream on the dark wing*
> *beyond isolation*
> *some say*

But move more slowly now
and irresistible—
stone settling into stone;
and the rain the ice cracking in earth vein
such quiet change that it is not noticed
is not pain and is not missed,

> *he forever dials phones*
> *writes letters*
> *flooding open-ended obituaries to us all*
> *perfectly*
> *on schedule in perpetuity*

I have made my choice
on measured particles that do not mix.

They sit on a ledge surrounding our city
    Out just beyond the last walls

      gauze hand to hand encircling
    mouths the sweet mouths of brittle candy
cracking through their wrappings
Singing words no sound
        no monotone
    humming of the bone
     the caged white particles of life erected high
      driving through the marrow-
          hollow bone

She reaches out her hand.
She settles night in motion
          Turn the instant soup higher,
          Review the day. Read the funnies. Turn on
          the news and do the dishes.
Another on the distant ledge reaches out
its hand.
And the others. They form
        a circle
        and they dance
the ancient hills.

Whatever useless information
you can feed the young
Whatever black terror you can use
        to fill the void
encompasses   comes back
   to paint ring
of bone flat auto shops,
comes back in the half-drained beer
   the drab lit country barroom.

Nothing fills your life
   like the flat glass eyes of bedtime shelves

                    or slowly opening closets…
as a soothing hissing in the night,
the white maiden red lipped as autumn
　　　sleeping uneasy
　　　cannot be controlled.

When every woman disappears
　when every man breathes
　　the pungent earth into his lungs
　　　collapses on his bones in horror,
what is it that remains playing long tuned
　reeds into marshes along the river?

"Tell me how she died and I will tell you how
　she lived."
Tell me if she died
or if she looks out upon us now
from the gold wrought cavern of our fears
　　　—from any one of them—
shriveling in some never answered question
posed in a quiet walk among buildings.
Whatever useless information you can feed.
Whatever terror you can use to fill the void.

A priest comes into the room.
Makes a wish.
Blows the candles out.

Today it rains across dry towns.
Cars dragging their paper chains
　five hundred feet behind them.
Fish dragging their aquatic eyes from muddy fields
pelted with supra-aquatic life,
　chilled within metallic sides.

Drunken men filling the wells of overhanging roofs.
Dried urine
     bedsores
          disease
huddled feathers in the eyes of night

Marcia in her room
takes off her shoes
looks in the mirror
drops the dress from her shoulders
steps back to sit upon a bed
one hand drawing back gray-dusted hair
the other fumbling for a radio.

Disjointed music.
Disjointed as it fills the folds of her flesh,
some lightness not meant to breathe
     caress, I like the word "caress"
     from college probably
     from frightened lovers,
a nine-to-lifer wanting dreams.
Broken wings
   tired arches of polished floors.
Dark breasts sore with time.
I could have had the child
  like Lois
  or Suzanne
     more like Helen
     in her razed years of wooden horses and death;
     taught him little except excuses
     for why one-eyed men grow large and die
     and those with vision are never home except in war.
The sun is an eye of evil
painting handles on the world.
I suppose I could have taught him this.

The earth remembers life
as a river of obsidian
flashing the distant heat of stars.
It remembers slowly
  ! such distinctness!
the falling off of each motion
  in infinitesimal amounts
    the fly ball frozen
    in the catcher's hand...
    the light clad foot upon the stair...
    the stray hair upon your breast
      in the white sweat of being.

Slowly...
the farthest ancestors
  cell by cell
in the lightless rock of mind
struggling upward to remember
      US.

What does it mean to be a father
What is it in the gray ebbing
that shoots off to time
  beyond our time
evident in the first hospital photographs
          the candles
  hidden shadows across your life
dark wing of flight

My cerebral sweetheart,
the fish are rising to the fly back home;
you do not belong thinned out upon concrete...
      they told you
you should put your money in your future
from deep within whatever lost room you choose.

man in the walls
               light through cracks
                       up
                       and
                           down
                      stair
                         wells
                  passages
                           never
                             built
pressed flat behind the closet behind your back
  screams OUT soundless in condensed air
man watches
               flesh shifting patterns
hollow-eyed wild-haired man
mouthing fear.

blueprints
       why
       don't'
       they
       read where I am
                buried
seeing them without faces
their feet their ankles the mirrors
in their rooms the bottoms of doors
man in walls
never dying the generations pass

The murderer comes home

eyes bright buttons in a lacquer box
creased photographs of smiles
svelte dresses liquor laugh evening life
the gala music folk strung life

comes home on dark exuberance
sucking starlight from the bricks around him
dust granule digesting marrow.

In California you can see him
In Colorado
In New York the winding foyer stair
The Great Plains swilling sunlight heat
the open throated breathing of night
soft unending jangle of television
        aerial
mass communication of the candled vault

and nothing happens here.
Nothing. The rattle of dead fingers
in the air of time. Nothing.
Save the children
hallucinating feather pillows into bone,
the urgent thrust dismal music
soft footsteps in the reeds at water's edge.
Two shapes flickering toward twilight
  on synthetic seeds.

> *Our beasts marched for generations*
> *across the desert, unaware of pin-*
> *wheels turning in the sky above them.*
> *They felt no tiredness. No exhilar-*
> *ation. The metal burning in their*
> *sides their incentive to keep moving;*
> *the metal in their mouths their direction.*

Oh, mr. moreson,
      your wings...
the blank memory of a love-starved medusa.

                    so long...
so long the sheep have popped up
            in their beds
the grim wood fence
            blue sky
        the piggies munching on mast
so long this kinetic trap
            this holistic center

was circling down in growing circles,
the blue fabric of young girl dreams spreading
out enveloping as the dark and secret flesh grew close
    into the ground
and the hair spinning out expanding from above
laughter ashes ashes we all
bent in our seats to see the city swirling up beneath us,
one vast bowl of western exploration in the dark
    beneath the stars
but you could not see the stars when you were looking
                                down.

All of us remembering the last descent we took
and looking. The stewardesses settled in their chairs,
the drink trays glittering in their cabinets and you and I.
They came in a plumage from the plane spilling dreams
composed of textile mills they came
crumbling tumbling down the stairs
until they lie sprawled
        a cacophony of flowers
  and the majestic bird enters into them
taking care not to disturb the creases of
    their huddled bodies

            mr. moreson, Whaddaya do?
            mr. moreson, Whoddaya sue?

The sleet slaps into your pockets
           winter day
smoke rising from your neighbor's farmhouse
your footsteps coming to collect you
           the breaking of ice...

and it still rises anyway,
fanning out until the upper air collects it
equally with the mountain's mists heralding
   a change of temperature
standing far across the field
         an hourglass
of spent and unspent particles
rising up and descending despite the cold
         around you

> *When we came unto the Great City*
> *we knew not what it was. We dis-*
> *mounted and in our awe looked out*
> *over its high towers which reached*
> *even to the smoldering heavens.*
> *"What place is this!" we asked, "And*
> *why came we to this location?" And*
> *the towers answered not.*

Time disappeared beneath their fingernails.

     radon silver atoms
   impossible to see
the glaring burning terrible of their eyes
         Lost
the steely wolfsnap teeth
         hunger hunger
lost in that climb that will be
Will be some fragrant sweatsheened couple

   playing cards before the fire…
       winner loses nothing
        loser loses nothing…
Not written into history books/Never…
   But the songs sung!
   The notes embedded like Mozart dreamt
circling upward tightly until they burst

      H I R O S H I M A
     fleshwinged terror / /
            Ramayana

    turning the cards slowly
      eyes lowered
         the dealer takes three…
   the last silver bracelet dropped

And the murderer steps in.
If you were a doctor   this
      shining scalpel
 is what you would cut out
If you were a book learner, word wormer
           concrete layer
           window glazer
Silver-tongued orator of poor songs…
Alas, poor Yorick, your bottomless eyes,
your dusty folding into yourself
And Siegried even you slayer of dragons,
  that the leaves of fall fall to touch your flesh
  on the immortal spring…
If you were a lawyer
    a counter of commas
    a planner
       an OLOGISTforgodssakes…

Oh, Mr. Moreson,
stargazer,
what have you got, you tenement-ridden rat?
What star on a dark night drives you?
If you could have been a prophet
even then

> *When I go upon the hills with myself*
> *and a whiskey bottle, and the bottle*
> *full and the distance full, there*
> *are times I see whole clouds of*
> *luminescence*

Oh, Mr. Moreson…

In Arizona there is a city burned from earth's sand
   below the Superstition Mountains.
It is a nothing town of sunbelt tempera
        waiting
a city small by calibrations
mechanized sun-bled palatial walls adobe
   homes
a short distance from Los Alamos as the metal birds fly
a short perimeter from the machine gun towers surrounding history
a nothing town of supermarket cans
   of wire-tapped folk heroes whispering obscenities into phones
   of bead-draped music in winter nights
of importance   forsomeorotherlostlylost
circled by the hungry gnawing of train desert night
whistling in the darkness between space
and heading away on the heady dreams of California or NY.

Masked venegeance,

                oh, stargazer

my blood trickles through air as deep as your eyes
singing moonbeams where it hits the cool cool water;
my weakness the heavy thunder of three billion horses
careening across an endless plain...

Ah, but they could have killed you,
   mr. moreson.
They could have fetched your arms behind you
and sung the simple song of death.
The hollow caverns winding on themselves,
the rib-tickling music of despair,
the violent twisting on a sandy, rusted spit.
They could have sung. They did...
if you pluck a man of his heavy human marrow
   and only then, he soars—
his bloody hands the nail-driven holes
sucking into himself dark mountain air until
the neon signs of his assigned position are lost
as a flame beneath expanding oceans of stars.

The murderer looks up from the flesh
   of his victim,
through the red stained ribcage, looks up
   and his eyes burn:
"I am blind now maybe but have seen
the gravediggers set out in their trucks
piling their chrome fingers across the ash of a continent;
have seen them sift the molars of their ancestors
brushing time from their stone jaws;
have seen them plop their contemporaries in
               regardless
of the bottomless canyon they walk upon;
have stuffed their ears with the lutes of history books.
And in this I have been sane...have made my choice

And the Great Swan turned above him.

Where do you go?
Where do you go, dark wing,
night burner, where do you go when the ocean darkens
erasing your feathered lines into the swell of night?
Do you remember Mr. Moreson and his family
by the barbecue? The pale sheen of his daughter's face
in the white frame houses of suburbia?
Do you pant and tear your eyes out
at the silver screen or his neighbors' wives
turning inevitably unviolated into their graves?

They fed you books.
You should have gone into their burning pyres
to rise upon the updraft
instead of this.

>   They sit on a ledge surrounding your city,
>   steel arrows poised to hurl you down their feathered
>   shafts
>   leaving the rubber balloon of your body for the garbage
>   pickers, trade seekers, illusion syndicators/

>   They fed you books and you should have known
>   how to fly their omnibus souls
>   from the time you were a child, you tired design.

each man building
   a smithy of his conscience stricken time,
one rage-torn anguish of seething fire
   in the desert night;
each factory/plant/sexual
lantern crammed with the mindless
corpses of feathery white moths

tearing their souls to touch the fire
   of their attraction,
each corpse burning the fire of generation
the size of the conflagration
the measure of a man's affairs with himself,
small beneath the Great Swan
and the distances between its wings immense.

Form is a response
        to pressure;
forged arches bent before construction
   to meet gravity...
a mathematical response on paper
         determined
         necessary

you can't tell the trees boulders rivers
they will not be as now but
   as they are
you cannot tell the lovers
   the hungry the crazed sleepless
   the broken limbed
cannot listen for the restless shrug of flesh
the concrete-sore woman lost in her shopping bag
cannot stop to decipher ciphers

a man must eat.

A response to pressure...
        A light came down over our city from the
        stars. We called for the media men, but
        when they came it was gone.

A response to pressure.
And there there is none...

where television moonlit rivers
   are the blood,
where ore lies unmined
   barren cliffs untouched
scrub/sage/pine on postcards...

form is a response to pressure
is a response
is pressure

Mr. Moreson,
you could have been

NO!

                No...
                      I'm not as crazy as I used to be.
We sing the songs of dead men
   There is wisdom
         in the songs of the dead
Men rising on the chilly updrafts of our adolescence
               turning
                 and gray from height
                                   lost
repeating forever in our minds in death
some few notes of the billion spoken
      Where's the coffee, Marge
      Goddamn car won't start
      Left me and I'm drinking too much
      Hello, Bob, this is...
But a couple notes taken out of ether
rising from a hand-hewn cabin clearing
so far back in time it should have fallen
   if it were meant to fall.

My god if you could get those notes all together
            GLORIOUS BABEL
the clay-trapped lips and tongues
   not even
           memory
Structure is a response to pressure

               And

        the calculator walks in.

Set this scene:
he stands at the fore and upbraids you. You!:
Do you know that more people are living now than ever lived
That people are being born faster than you can point a finger
   at a clock
That in twenty years we will be eating hydroponic plants
   entirely that have never touched soil of earth
That even now you cannot understand the tongue of one
   tenth of those people
That they are dying by the millions in every country you have
   never seen.
Do you know? Do you know what that means!

And you: There are millions dying every day
       in the skyscrapers of Manhattan.
          And they have no peace. Calculator,
       you could have been...

So he leans forward and pounds his finger on the table,
   upsetting his wine glass and says:
What does it mean
          (*thump*)
And what does it mean
          (*thump*)

And what does it mean
               (*thump*)
And what does it mean
               (*thump*)
And what does it mean
               (*thump*)
                             until
You bang him sharply on the head.

                             And
               the murderer comes home.

From the cliffs looking down
   they can see it all:
The hammer poised in rugged sweat-stained arm
The downward sweep The metal against metal
The spark against stone The Flame The conflagration
The child becoming murderer in the burning down
The wild struggle The dark horses spitting bloody coins
       "a system beyond control"
ownership becoming capitalism becoming monetarism
The payment of the nothing wild laughter
       But the fire!

The smoke rising deep into starlight:
Can ya feel it, Man!
That in that death there rising somewhere, swirling
something stirs to hunch down over its creators;
to open its jaws and suck them in
         To where!
It's a pressure cauldron, Man...
this springing death from death, an incredibleincrediblyfast
   chain of life
like lichen eating lichen it goes by so fast.
And it maybe doesn't have a fucking thing to do with you

unless you're the biggest one,
$$\text{Man,}$$
   You better build that fire the best!
You better be that dark hulking beast or a part of it
or you'll be the lichen
unless you can be the whole damned beautiful thing
And whatifyou'rewrong.

Wrong...
but I see the lights are islands in darkness..

Lights?
The bones of your dead.
The millennia of death ignited in decay
flashing whatever entity is left them for you
lights/
and the flame too quickly smothered
by breathing darkness.
What do you think it takes/how many lives
choked in oil for the instant you spend before a television
set? Advertisements.
Form follows pressure.

> *It is said they were a violent people, covering their fear through the destruction of what surrounded them, including their own. Even toward the end of their history it is reported how one man in jeopardy of his livelihood killed his wife of fifteen years in ritual. Having rendered her asleep, he stripped her body naked and propped her standing against a wall of his house. Taking a nine inch spike, he drove it through her breast bone and left her body pinned there while he went out to share a beer at the corner with his friends. It is not as it seems.*

They saw how year by year the cities
molten splotches on night
engulfed the sands;
volcanic steams bubbling from earth surface.
They talked excited noises wind born by mountains
and the hulking shape above them grew:
planet earth a light
unfed by fuel
by life
and everything living at once by light,
the clocks radioactive eyes on dresser tops
unbreathing stretch of steel and cement

impossibly strong ungiving
supporting steel.
They were steel and forged by fire.
The monuments:
      The Freedom Arch
      The massive mobile of rush-hour usa
      The Washington Monument, a needle in the eye of night,
forged by fire and pain of their dead,
they will rise half dead haunting memory
through the eye of their bones.

Keeping the Outlaw Alive

KEEPING THE OUTLAW ALIVE

JARED SMITH

Published by The Erie Street Press

1988

Acknowledgments

Some of the poems and essays in this section of the *Collected Works* first appeared in the following literary magazines:

Bitterroot Magazine published "Autumn Is a Red Deer" and "If...but No"

The New York Quarterly published "From the Rigging," "Nobody Writes about Children," "One," and "Face of the Phoenix"

NewsArt published "The Incident"

The Smith and *PULPSMITH* published "An Evening in the Heartland," "Entering," "It Takes A Man," and "Keeping the Outlaw Alive"

Star-Web Paper published "Fast-Food Lunch: NY"

From the Rigging

What discontent is it
that drove our early fathers
across the breadth of this continent
this wide wide continent in one hundred forty years?
Our early fathers who had our fathers' fathers as children
so soon who had the finest homes of their times
or who at least had like neighbors by their side,
so like the homes and white painted boards we come from
and women whom they strove to marry and who married
and who went with them in their discontent.
What is it made them carry the hammer,
the nails of sobriety west?
What discontent found our distant continent
and nailed sails upon it from the rigging of windblown ships?

Keeping the Outlaw Alive

Next time you're out in Tombstone
checking out the wood crosses on Boot Hill,
having a cigarette while looking over the museum houses,
smelling the stale Milwaukee beer of tourist traps,
noticing the dry green bushes that smell like
    Noxzema skin cream
                    or
Are sitting on a green grass hill in Glenwood Springs
having a shot of red-eye,
feeling your lungs ache because the air's too thin
and you're plumping up your chest
thinking you're a long way from home,
    Have another drink.
Have two bottles.
And try to keep it straight,
because the civic tic-tac never did;
and a lot of people drowned in their blood
              maybe
for loving or hating the man buried at your feet.

In fact,
lie down. You have
been driving, John.
You're always driving.
You're on a holiday, recovering your breathing.
Watch the land.
   Watch the clouds spinning their mist above you.
     Lie back, why don't you
       stop driving stop
         and lie.

    What
    do you say?

In rain I hear distance...
the clap of dead horses in mud
stirring drunken carcasses with the power of my name.
  That flattened glint of metal
so carefully removed
antiseptically
the soul that drives a man
removed
in apathetic hatred on these white sheets
  a shell
of burned powder
      You/Me yes
laid out by caresses pulses ladies in white
needing to protect the rainbow fantasy
  It's all colors all colors their white gown
our eyes caught in tight vibration.

    Yes,
      but

Any response is stronger
than sitting in a room in cotton baffles
trying to cage yourself from the mad
  Shooting them
Ripping the throat of someone weaker
    than them
instills fear
    in them
and the sorrow/the tearing in your throat
    better

than disavowal
you are here to feel

rain and the sensual flesh are here
outside newsprint carpets of plush venom,
remember the tin badge, Wyatt was filled with blood of others
            even brothers
and the ballads brought to children on their way to school...

            A red wall
follows my wall follows
along red the narrow gauge canyon
    Progress
        is built into mountain granite
the gold dust air follows my lungs
blood on the country.
From the South this cell-cushioning roar,
this rotten stump fleeing brawls
its stained way to glacial lakes
  from swamp to desert to alpine stone
the shivered chairs, eroding bones of houses...

Talk. I am not thinking fast enough.
If a tooth of the law offend thee, rip it out,
as I have done. My license is to draw out the rot
the pain flashed smooth with blood my hands
crabbed with the suction bag of life...
I am John Henry Holliday.

John Henry Holliday, DDS,
born in Valdosta, Georgia, in 1852
in the like lifetime of Ike Clanton, Wyatt Earp.
William Bonney/Billy the Kid who killed one man

for each year he lived
to Civil War Georgia and Sherman's violent poverty
born nonetheless to books and dark suits
to studies in dentistry and
in 1872
to be told his diploma to practice was his epitaph,
that he would die within the year,
that his lungs breathed death into his patients' mouths...

I lie still unthinking/feeling metal bellows
a rusting steam engine wheezing mountains into its craw,
my back rigid the nervous fingers tapping cards into wood.
Moving my eyes in blood empty of oxygen burning my muscles,
If you look at the mirror the wrong way, friend,
it's easier for me to be the iron
sucking out that silver capsule that is you
than to ask your name.
They call me Doc and I drink two pints a day
        every day
and it doesn't itch as much as your wild thoughts
carry nothing beneath my belt...

    Yes,
      but

Watch him for a moment.
The bent man like a beardless Lincoln
riding his silver pocket watch into your city
full of cloth leaves dancing autumn color,
opening an ever hungry business on the vaginas he carries
unopened in his saddle bags whole rivers the moon knows and you
have never walked,

closes them and disappears leaving only a blood
tainting the nostrils of giant rabbits grazing by the city hall.
Watch them for a moment
until they turn the mad hill darkness of their eyes upon your dreams...

Have you noticed how they gather
so tight into each other while you sleep
their fur is indistinguishable their ears a torn fury
rolling their sex sign across whatever shred of yourself escapes
the snapping of incisor jaws so large granite slabs across the hills
until you rise screaming there being nothing else
throw your arms around them yelling Here...

> Doc, you're tired and
> I can't follow you.
> Remember

Remember. I remember a darkness opening between mountains
where The Snake River cuts obsidian from its banks
from darkness myself coming forth carrying a fishing pole,
laughing and coming toward me young
higher than any mountain
burning
and raising that pole
until it became a rifle, its barrel
twisted with stars off inlaid metal and looming
down before me/
remember freezing until that anger shook me...

When I grew sand dust kicking
    (The green shrubs.)
        Soldier boots bright in their sword sing sun

      rivers of cotton moonlight,
my father who sang the southern locust
practiced spinets in the parlor with
        my mother's fingers,
           an empty row of wooden boxes
             moving toward order
the European music of frontier gentility
smiling its faces in stories by the fire,
patchwork neighbors' children in the school of home...

And I had schooling,
oh, yes, Homer/math/reading a one
    room school
lucky beat it into me with a wooden board
until they burned Atlanta down
   rusting the silver wings
drove out my father's hearth/my mother's life
became Confederates in the Union camp
rode rails to politics
        to Mayordom from invested poverty asking why
        to Holliday Street all glitter in booming dust
        to Baltimore
   my blood congealing in my lungs
consuming the people in warehouses offices of trade,
oh, I had school
I spit it back in nobility's mouths...

Mattie...
    I could not have you
  beyond that summer by the river.
But I went home from Baltimore a doctor to Valdosta.
     And it wasn't there.
And I went home.

      They said I had six months to live
        if I went west:
I cheated them; I played the cards,
the doctor of golden fillings for our solitude…

      But why are you telling this?
      This isn't what we'll
        write.

The only woman I lived with afterward,
I laid bare her skull with a .44
and took her till she couldn't walk
after she buried a bullet in the mattress
  by my head.
I took her square for four days
before she turned me to the sheriff in Tombstone
when he was looking up her dress.
And when I was acquitted
I paid her off and turned her out of town…

Gold Watch Holliday,
my gray suit the back wall of every saloon
from Dallas to Dodge to Santa Fe to Leadville,
the miners' gold my hands
swift and cold among the cowmen.
The order of the cards
the always search for Law…

It was never winter in the dance halls
      train stars
         the trail
    the gas lamp housewife Bible-readers
  this   this is what I wanted

baking me biscuits.
        The cowboys different
killers of these as sand shifts hills.
But it was never cold
  in the dance halls,
their glitter heat in the smoke of distance,
    a turning of limbs on ice river mist...

       But what of the people
       and your time of law?

Virgil,
you remember
a blue star burned through his heart
which killed with the distance of the Union
which made nothing of night mountains
which implanted solidity
              No
No man ever saw me take my vest off
sand into wind
No man ever saw me mark the cards/
                            were terrified
each because there was nothing they could see
  of sun
dark tangles trails I never
killed a man
I the coldest temper a steel bough
feared by every cowboy
never killed for you Mattie was in my own mission
  all these years,
like your habit flung across the prairie
too had that hollow maw that must be crammed
whole forests/rangers/whispers choked

        into order
establishing the dead Valdosta...

      You're going, Doctor
      Holliday.

I always sat with my back to the wall,
my suit a cavern into flesh
or surrounded/melted
into Wyatt Virgil Morgan Ernest so that
no man ever knew where the scalpel flashed; I was not trained to cut the flesh,
but the bony framework of a man's desire: I, Doctor Holliday, Dr. Mardi Gras,
vision of a nightmare you cannot kill,
never killed a man without breathing
          deep into his lungs
and then   slowly   for his mistakes
there was no turning back from me/
those California bounty hunters backing me
for the swifter cutting away,
the steal of life too fast,
dying in pool halls or on the trail
or growing old out on the coast.
Not me, the molder of metallic light.

      But what do we cut on your stone,
      Dr. Holliday?

Cut that I have known
both sides of every jail,
have taken the blows
from both sides of the jury box,

have lived in Baltimore and Denver,
have drunk two pints of whiskey every day,
and stood,
have planted bullets in every saloon
from Dallas to Leadville,
have squared off at twenty feet with guns blazing,
and stood,
and never killed a man with any gun I held.
and never took a bullet.
And stood…

Cut
that I knew Ike Clanton
and Johnny Ringo, who sang like death,
and stagecoach gunner Johnny Slaughter
and William F. Bonney, Billy The Kid;
that some of them were friends and some were not;
that all of them were afraid of me; that I am only 25
and they are dead…

Cut
that I searched for order at cards
and made more money drunk than any sober man,
that I have cheated death through five years of death,
that I am the best dressed gunman of them all,
that I would not buy the law of books.
Tell them I killed a hundred men,
that I owned countless custom guns in velvet cases,
that I changed the history of law in Tombstone
in exactly thirty seconds,
and they will listen…

Cut
that my woman, who lives
praying in an east coast nunnery,
is the only person I ever understood
and that only her life has kept me here
drawn into mountain cold liquor...

Cut
there is nothing more
important
than
keeping the outlaw alive...

> "JOHN HENRY HOLLIDAY, DDS
> BORN VALDOSTA, GEORGIA, IN 1852
> GRADUATE OF BALTIMORE DENTAL
> SCHOOL IN 1872. AT THE AGE OF 20
> ONE OF THE GREAT GAMBLERS & THE SPEEDIEST
> MAN WITH A SIX GUN IN THE WEST.
> HE LOST HIS BIGGEST BET WHEN HE DIED
> NOV. 8, 1877, IN A GLENWOOD SPRINGS, COLORADO
> SANITORIUM WITH TUBERCULOSIS, INSTEAD OF
> BEING CUT DOWN BY A BULLET"

A Man Screaming

> *We carry knives and pistols*
> *and rifles*
> *Silver bullets too.*
> *We're the boys from Camillus.*
> *Who the fuck are you?*

You go through the house and down to the basement.
Inside there's another house—five rooms & a
bath hidden in the underground railway,
though you might expect two rooms from
outside. And you sit in the lower living room
looking out over the stereo with Muddy Waters
and old blues on it Taj Mahal, the room
strewn with antique furniture/bric-a-brac/
scattered piles of curling photographs dating
back twelve years and waiting to be
repressed having traveled to NY to Hawaii
and home some of them and others just
arrived from the black box and scattered
here remarkable photos in black and
white/in tints/in color of Jack Burger's
pate, of locks on the Bowery, of trees
and waterfalls, volcanoes and bodies.
And you're looking out the window
over the stereo through a latticework
of still-dripping eight-foot icicles
into a blizzard of flakes the size of
dusty millers settling on a summer. And
you're looking down a short and gentle
embankment of clean snow to an iced-over
canal filled with tree limbs and
beyond that a thirty-foot wide rise and
then a trout stream clean with two

foot browns and rainbows. A wall-and-
maze of fifty-foot saplings growing
along the banks and among them a
rusted corn-picker and busted silo
saying this was once growing land.
Beyond the stream a rapid rise
of white riddled
with naked trees. No fences. This
the first house almost built and in
the family for seventy years and
more. A wildness looking out into
the wild and laughing. What went

Fast-Food Lunch: NY

I start by the docks where they take the Day Line out, The Circle Line, scows of refuse painted fast on a blue river backed by hilly white houses clear as pine of the far side. Tar-painted timbers waiting for one-day vacationers, shaped into open rectangles around the memories of European trade, revolution's boots and the icy hunt for dead behemoths from the past. A steady stream of cars along The West Side Drive, but 42nd Street is naked at this end, only three quiet GM dreams passing me in the first long block. A cement school, I suppose it's a school—would someone bring their children to this desert on the edge of blue? No, probably a terminal surrounded by a chain link fence. Crates of boarded storefronts and bricked-over windows on small buildings. A marine supply store and a blue—I kid you not—police station complete with two cruisers straight out of a child's construction set. This could be the memory of a watercolor dream.

On my right The Port Authority Terminal, blank glass doors opening to descending stairs. Two young women are exiting, filled with the novelty of being lost. Flesh excited. The cavernous emptiness within those doors really is filled with the violence of open space you read about: the Minnesota girls hunting for fathers; the stolen handbag hustles; the bright fishbowls pushed out each night into the darkness of America.

The U.N. Countries beat ploughshares into swords here with diplomatic immunity.

And the Grand Central. How can you have a departure or arrival terminal in the center of a city? It is a black hole, a drainpipe septic system sucking the city's flotsam into the ground each night and spewing them out still dazed each day.

The furs, the glamour halls, Paris dresses from France and Taiwan here closed in one-time seamstress sweatshops, manacled between the gaudy sex shop signs, fast-food stands Americanized from every corner of the world—does McDonald's really use 1/3 of America's potato crop—and street swingers hunting for a place to be. The walkers here move faster, dancing around each other for the post position as they wait for lights. They are tall thin men, dark of many races and sleek sheathed younger women who do not understand where the limousines depart for Bermuda.

The Wall

Hey, Kim,
I tried to get by to see you today
eighteen years after you died.
After all these years remembering
how alike we were 24 years ago.
But it was raining and all I had was a suit
so I thought of how I might get over on a tour bus
anyway
and go with this girl who works for me
out to Arlington and maybe I'd find the black wall by chance
and maybe I'd find your name on it even though I knew the wall
wasn't there
and think it means something
beyond anything I know
to find your name among so many white marks.
But you see, we got to the tomb
of the unknown solider
when I realized I had left papers
that cost my company $32,000
unguarded at the Washington Hilton,
so wondering what it is to be dead, I
hopped a cab,
yelled at the driver
and returned…
        The papers gone
           disposed of by a bellboy.
I'm sorry, Kim,
I don't even know yet how to find the wall.
I should have said, Take me to Vietnam
  to the driver.
I've got a wife and two young children
and have just sold my house
and I don't know where they'll live.
What is it like, Kim?

Sitting Dark in Life

I'm sitting dark in Chicago,
blinds drawn white
my apartment...
no
this wording is not right
because...
well, everywhere you go
despite the wording in advertisements
you or I take our own
everywhere we go
but Chicago is not New York
and the ladies dream
Chicago is a stevedore
shipping bulls to market,
ribbons, heavy trains in the wind...
outside my window.

So Far Descending

The soft things are not soft.
Perspective gives us this:
at 30,000 feet, descending, I laughed
and the lights, warm animals, warmed your thighs
so far down there where life is.

This Town Is Young

It is the grass growing.
It is the universe of light years distant
   burned out
settling its dust on your car,
its oceans and love-wet women
dusting down from infinity
  on your car
    on your windows,

And as dark rises
she drops her skirt and sits
looking through plate glass
her dark hair up above her blouse,
leg-naked on fabriced seat looks out
then leaves in pirouette to the night
goes out to spread hot limbs on grass
spread-eagled sticking her ass
in the face of city
receptacle

Come,
this town is sweet.

An Essay on Illuminations

The other day I spent an exhausting lunch hour looking at illuminated manuscripts in a museum that won't be named. (I don't like to name museums because despite being "non-profit," they and everyone in them earn far more than the artists of whatever genre who created the work that makes them fat.) In any case, as I was looking at the manuscripts, I wondered the blasphemous thought of why these works are considered as exceptional and rare as they are. Certainly, their creators for the most part lived the rarified poverty of monkdom and never could or would have wanted to dream that the visions they went blind over would end up worshipped under glass. And then, too, these works, though beautiful and intricate, were all markedly similar to one another over the centuries their art was practiced.

Perhaps these gray meditations I was having were merely the product of a long telephone-choked day with a liberal dose of Tums thrown in. But I think not: the illuminations are very similar; and while some are technically more illuminated than others, they are none of them so beautiful in themselves that anyone attempts to duplicate the art today.

No, I think the worshipping of these manuscripts represents something far greater. I think the worshipping is for the man who devoted years of his life only to the intricate creation of those objects. It is a worshipping of there being something believed in which supersedes all other human drives. A worshipping of the quest as evidenced in attention to detail

It's almost too bad that kind of worshipping is only evidenced through the distance of death and the study of ashes. That may be because no one will believe a man will die for something greater than himself until he has. In this, as in poverty, artists of any media and saints are one.

Of course, if artists and saints were worshipped too much, it would destroy their humility such as it is, their perspective and their work. How about if we just wonder or ask why they cannot be *liked* or respected for their attempts, even as Marvelous Marv Thornberry was for the early N.Y. Mets?

We die too soon and with too little beauty to entrust all our future generations to the word and data processors whom corporate America pays handsomely to push buttons. We value those processors too much; we know that because they are paid well. And payment, as every employee in a corporate system knows, is for perpetuating the power of the one who *assimilates* the data—not processes it.

So who assimilates now: surely not Katharine Gibbs with a megabyte memory; a silicon doctor who someone pays to put his life on wafers? No, because these activities use all the time for assimilation. The artist, writer, builder on the bones and dreams of the living and dead? Who pays the rent with what for what?

Impossibly a Businessman

I too am now impossibly strong in a non-exist world,
a purveyor of white frame house
dark windows solid in bone
and trees.
I the businessman/educator
walking in flowers blown forgotten
somehow where I cry a starved wolf
keening its teeth on a stone of tongue,
trees beating their limbs against the moon
steel rayed tracks of purveyance out across the heartland.
I have come here drawn by fear
that the ocean always pawing
might come
that the earth shifting its shoulders
might reach out
greedily cupping my hands before I have heard
before my children have been born to hear
crickets rolling in the wells of joy.
I who now know only man
or only I (or only eye) know
there might be some thing to stop this sting,
some suddenness the swan in all her
    beauteous stupidity
does not question though even she believes in love
to the extent of holding to life for life.
I, the man, impossibly strong,
controlled control—oh, business of the gods—
go out here in the land of grain.

Give Our People

Give our people bread and onions to eat.
The onions should be large and pale as human flesh.
They should be dark as old blood.
The bread should be coarse
and sweet with the grinding of mortars.
It will dissolve their tongues.
Their tears will fill burning rivers;
their hands carve homes from the mountains.
We will live forever
as long as there are mountains.

The Mind

A JANGLED NEST OF WIRE.
WHAT THINGS COME HOME TO THIS???

If…but No

If I can draw myself into light
somewhere around sundown
in the midwest
a long way into clouds above
and into
fields of varying greens
I will be buried with the crops
to the music of crickets under moon.
If I can draw myself…
but that buzzing membrane scaffolding our wings,
we have too many eyes to feed!

This, Really, Is This

This is not poetry I can sing.
This is the pressure of my blood being
crushed into tin cans by media.
A poet, I am not
strong enough to sail against my culture
   forever.
I am but a boy. I have
children.
The sunset is beautiful.

When October Comes and the Wind Blows

38, with 3 children riding high school bicycles already,
they bought their first house
dreaming dying the American dream they
got a smallish house of white with a garage
knowing having fought nothing
comes easy to them though their sons sneer—
worked so hard seeding the lawn and
keeping the sprinklers going every day
and night smiling to look young
like they had time to catch, they
trimmed everything to make it grow.

Anything that grew they trimmed
until it fit,
like words—even if they didn't know
what it was it fit
because it was shaped like every other tree or bush.
And mostly it did. Except the
tumbleweed
growing by nature by the driveway in spring
the year they moved in,
its leathery green thongs
   a lost bit of something golden
they wanted to protect. It grew so well
so fast
so strongly wild
they trimmed it as a centerpiece/a
specimen
surprising them an upright young tree
perhaps
the only vertical in an otherwise horizontal green,

so they trimmed it
to look like a small pine tree
reaching toward some holy night outside their son's garage.

*

The mountains are, they know, cold animals
darting in at evening   in circles
about the town,
given invisibility by rain clouds or
morning mist or
smokestack high smoke technology.

Those mountains, it's a myth.
No one walks those mountains. No lights.
There are foxes breeding shadows from their eyes.

When my brother flew his iron bird,
pried open its fiery belly with plastic fingers,
the sun dragon suddenly rebelled,
tearing his arms until he pin-wheeled down into the rocks.

I wish in telling you
I could erase him.

What Makes the Man Different

There are deer moving in the night of our blood,
sailing across hidden clearings,
eyes spread on the tongue of owls—whispering.

This is our clearing in the city,
where after five we can cross the streets no one knows
and breathe deeply until our flesh falls from its bone.

This is the field we believed others knew
because overgrown drives led that way—
not knowing their hard steel eyes waited only for us to turn,
to light from the stream filling these branches.

This is what makes us
an opening into the stars
and as distant as a stranger's hands.

The Wind in Winter

Cold wind rises,
      wanders in a circle,
touching on the nose of wolverine,
passing over his eyes,
patting his ruff for something wild and free.
It moves south through the splayed legs of caribou.
When it leaves the north
it is vibrating with the surprise of life.

As Evening Draws

The time is new—
        always now—
and I walk a meadow folded by evening
and by the untrimmed border of man.
        It is snowing
a distant coldness on my hand
my fingers spread palm upward
        crickets into their warmth.

The Company We Keep

On days when I can take a rest,
allowed by the company and, more particularly, by me
and the rest of the country is busy
trying to see if it can survive
itself
without me as we both know it must sometime,
I will climb hills surrounding home
and turning paths once laid down by richer men
or even abandoning them to lose myself myself
see
from the translucent frieze of vine
and tree growth I stumbled on by accident one time
how in looking down on concrete dreams of steel
they are mosaic star maps, memories, pieces.
That they are islands quite as small
and isolated as the lost estates I walk,
though they are filled with men
and I with thought.

Evening in the Heartland

The couplings in life, the connecting forces, are uncertain and unsuspected as they pass. They are like a coal car rattling up a Colorado mountain pass on a dark night, where the desert mountains bounce back an unseen confusion of metal rammed against itself. One never knows in the dark, which shapeless lump among the myriad is the critical piece which will tip the balance of life or its direction as a distant engine grinds itself into manmade echoes.

Yet, all those lumps, or accretions of life do rustle and shift that way, constantly churning against themselves so that, even recognizing they are separate pieces or instances, they seem inseparable. The brightest instant is lost in the tumble almost before recognized, or worse, lies just beyond our grasp as our feet stumble toward it, only close enough to watch it covered over as the ground shifts again. Or, perhaps, we lift the desired moment once in a great while, and even then too often find that a new bend of direction has been brought about in our goals, so that this treasured moment is no longer relevant.

Our chances seem so remarkably small by now of finding anything. Yet, we carry on. What a remarkable genius man is in his survival, in his ability to look with amazement at even the darker rocks that will crush him when he falls, and to find mystery and hope in them.

Just to know, though! Just to know. Which instant of life even as you come upon it, is the one that will spin you on your way and swirl the other moments around itself in a giant maelstrom? Like the Socratic philosopher, we can only judge if we did the right thing by looking back on the shadows we created at the end of life. Like the Aristotelian, we hunt for patterns that are too large and make them simple so they will fit our understanding. Like you or me, we are, all of us, alive until the shifting stops and the pattern becomes terribly or beautifully clear to anyone who watches. Do not judge a man until he dies.

Whatever. Guessing in the dark is a crap shoot. Most of us lose and win at the same time because we don't see clearly enough to know, and because we're amiable enough to be adaptable and snuggle down like little puppies against whatever warm body comes along and calls itself god in our understanding. And then, of course, there are those of us who poise themselves by chance to spring from or to the right choice instant of life by chance, and spiral to jubilation. But even then on the blatantly stupid assumption that their choices alone were the key and they were astute enough to see forever down the rails ahead.

There are very few of us who remain at ease with our situation throughout life. Discounting idiots, there are even fewer. Those who remain even materially comfortable are generally born to the highest—and in this country, hidden—aristocracy. What can we do but be aware of these things? Perhaps this awareness can save our sanity, because something must if we are to remain alive and grow to understand why we carry these swollen bulbs of narcissism at the tops of our spinal columns.

Again, there are very few of us. Neglect the media. Forget about the Yuppies and the overnight successes. They are born of someone else's need to tell a story around a campfire to make a living; nameless ghosts or numbers like the players on a baseball team that always numbers nine but has a great many more players in reserve to play the positions that must be played.

Autumn Is a Red Deer

Autumn is a red deer
bolting summer's trees behind it.
Autumn is the day of the year
she remembers him home.
Home from the sky and the black rivers.
Home from the static drop of water falling off eaves.
Just turning there as he was in sun,
laughing easy one hand out to his son
then only three and growing
quickly between shadows.

Nobody Writes about Children

Nobody writes about children
   as if they were eyes rattling in pockets
following you and taking the world:
perhaps it is only because then
   you would have to admit it is given
in tiredness; in the day carried old,
gray on evening's feathers.

Nobody writes about children like
   they had children;
like the mystery between their legs
was colder than starlight
and followed them home then
thinking dresses flesh summer breasts
winnowing their teeth on night.

It Takes a Man

Noon noon
the corpses rose
rushed out dance tangle
    42nd Street
  the middle town
joined hands clapped smiled
parted on into the gray
washed away each night
a coat a scent of death, when
a dog smells of that breath
  he dies within a day
the soap scent the soap the
proudest of our time in plastic tubes;
it takes a man to be a mockery of time.

It takes a man
to plant a flower on his land;
a seed to know the wind;
you too
your eyes the hollow moon
their distance
    is not this...
too soft the capsule of the shell,
your love
    your hate
too great to hold the smell of self. It takes
three letters to spell impossible.

Finding Love

Strawberries on the beach
at Rye.
My son is two.
He picks a stone from the sand
says Daddy rock water,
turning takes my hand
carefully each foot slow toward
   the water
watching the large red berry ocean stone
  sand gulls sky wind wild noises
at once holding my hand.
Stops two thirds of the way
Says selectively More berry.
Waits until I too turn back,
then carefully over the sand again
and we sit upon the shore
eating the heavy red fruit of life.
Wind knocking tombstones across the sky.

A Day in August

A day like this I imagine
rolling through the nets of trees
crisping dew-spattered grass
enfolds everywhere.
Your hurried lipstick tangled
in the trim nylons of communication
as out of place as the next block
the next city.

A day like this I walk the fields
bordering every bedroom in America
touched by the warm scent of idle flesh,
running your ashen limbs through my song
and choking on the small gray stones of memory.

The cellophane windows of locust shells
dissembling wind in packets
on the ground.

The Incident

In Washington when they shot the President

This town is tired of you.
Maybe you are only riding in a taxicab
when the news hits.
They have shot the President.
They have shot the press.
They have shot the police.
They have shot the government.
The green lights are useless at George Washington.

This town pulls your entrails
into the black pit of 1963
where they first told you your color was wrong
so really wrong you could not listen
but merely tear your eyes out and
place them coast to coast of superhighway
marking the thin edge of concrete death.

This town is tired
of your hungry crying.
It wants you to build fences and schoolyards
to shovel the blank sheet of winter off your memory,
to forget another precedent has died.
Whether you liked the thought or not
that it was there
and you were a part of it
with your pearl-handled rhetoric
and your easy ideas of god and television news.

This town is tired of you
because you raged at the cameramen

zooming in on each spot of blood in dying color
and the urgency of canceling out
the sponsors' migraine aspirin commercials.

You'd best go.
Leave this town
before the plastic undertaker finds
you locked behind the walls of someone else's paycheck.
You'd better leave.
You'd better take your song and bury it.

Visions of a Pencil

The man who makes the pencils
   that write the world
knows nothing but the dark blood running your veins.
Thoreau so tuned in a pencil
   packing plant picked six
     by hand
       each time
         for boxing
           for sale
the universal eye picking arrow
   heads from Massachusetts earth
     not stop to look
       but there
        and known
for the city man media man
             vacation impressed
but didn't make them
   fill the gray American grain
     to the crushed limbs of trees
         America
the gray blank metal growing
         blank
the messages of madmen
the messages of numbers/proof
        of what
the semen-stained night aria of art
          somewhere
in a paper-cluttered factory
in moonlit aluminum dimestore windows
is waiting deafly for the breath
  of Man
blind as night on glass

Driving the Ashokan River
  in late summer
the peeled logs
      are frozen
in themselves the chute
    the spume
abandoned mine sites in Colorado
        sage

What makes the draughtsman fly
        is lead.

Morning Owls

Mist rises from beneath fields,
from between the heavy legs of corporations
grazing across our finest,
chewing them up,
spitting them out
and moving on in search of life.
Call them a computer
or cells of the Oversoul
or grime-encased machines...
they are the indifference
of blind owls staring into morning.

Exultance

As the plane flattens in its western rush,
I bend against its plastic windows curved,
my bones against its metal looking down,
to the red earth squares the checkerboard greens,
and I come inside the white paint homes,
the one in particular there beside the two-lane road
laid back about a quarter mile where a woman I can touch
fleetingly sits still thinking in painted walls
and feeling outward beyond beginning of memory.
And it is night.

There is no way
   through the starlight
  no way as the television clicks
  no way as her bedroom light
a shadow of her combing her hair
   against meadow-lit curtain
she could know,
   or know either that I pass as well.

A blanket of rain soft cloud
is the floor,
and I above it.
So far above there is no touching
   wisp of wheels,
nothing but a genetic bone-sent memory:
the holes between the burning blank eyes above me close.

In the plane's turning on its wing
   I am sick exultant.
I too am lost beneath the stars.

A Response to a Conversation with William Packard Where We Tried to Define Poetic Craft as Practiced by All Schools of Poets

Words so tight
they outline the vulvas and cocks of your mind
like Calvin Klein® cut-offs.

We are the Poets. We Live

We write about noise in the underground,
the dark slither of moonlight across gardens
leaving our saltless way among the bitter leaves of marigolds,
our trails staggered over seemingly harmless clods of earth
dipping drunken rolling among leaves or twigs unnoticed in day.

What magic mystery from our soft sides and bellies
left in the bedrooms of our visits to small towns!
We who feed on all things, for they look alike,
who curl in silence and bleed when touched by unknown hands,
yet move as slowly as the earth beneath oceans, as vast.
We who write about noise iin the underground silently,
yet who scream and writhe at the salt of human tears.

Hibernation

The bear sharpens its claws
   on old tree roots,
sniffs spring coming in from Montana,
making an oily rag of its nose
slaps toward the potted palms
and moves through just
that suddenly
standing on a cream-colored rug
hunched into your office silhouetted
by an urban landscape of glass.

Its eyes rheumy
play tricks on the pink-lipped teeth.
It has come to say something
or for some reason deep in its gorge
tries to roll earth over your bones.
It feels beautiful in its heavy hair,
and I sit in the synthetic light.

Beach at Oceanside

    you can tell   waveflock
  age is not   sand
something you are born   turning
with something the light spring   spreadeagled
  ing limbs   the curled
LOOK   shells
  the heavy flesh   wings of scythes
beneath bikini legs   into deepening sky
iron tanks beneath sun   a pin on the retina
oh, oh, the gravity   hanging where there is no
        age   age
But the untalking moment of her sunset
sweeping her knees the groundless churning
            white of aqua
                vita!

The Interview

I tell the newswoman how
what she thinks to ask gets hooked
into a screen mesh on its way out,
but without mentioning the moths and katydids
reaching for us with sorrowful eyes on silk
waving their human legs.
She says to be specific.

Lady, I
don't think this has anything
to do with cunts or money.
I can feel in your bones
you are also
something scared and watchful
where it is raining,
Lady, I am trying to be specific
in ways your words are deaf to.

One

One evening, her tree pulled up roots
and hit the road for California, gathering squirrels
out there in the darkness where the highway branches.
She learned that trees too leave.

Her car was like this also
in that its sides were the color of autumn.
A child in the back seat waited for heart operations...
Sometimes he gave, but more often he received.
It was not better that he did.

She danced naked in the moonlight,
spinning on one foot in the middle of Highway One.
The snow caught in her hair
breasts rubbed in neon.

Face of the Phoenix

We are all shadows
and have been shadows
from before the first tree defining itself.

Shadows talk?
Does air passing before flame thicken?
Does the air heat creating wind
and does the flame itself thicken,
then feeding itself on the infinity of its distance,
for light in its travels in infinite.

We are all shadows
and have been shadows
from before the first skirl of water
laughing in the swirl of itself.

We take the word
and it is a thickening of shadow,
it is a passing in the shades of our lives;
we take the word and we are shadows
and the word becomes our shadows
and the word becomes art
because it is our pattern.

That is why we meet ourselves
in the word we call our history
and in the eye of famous men we live in the shadow of
the young girls twirling down the streets
our songs
shadows
met and growing thicker in conflagration
as though feathers of ash
all of us shadows
are shadows on the face of the phoenix.

They've a Kind of Patronage

For success go abroad, my bard.
Go to England or France or Rome,
but once you've been to England, my bard,
you can never never come home.

It's in England the people pray for the poets
and in France they dance at your feet.
In Greece they'll love you, though they'll forget,
and in Erin ye've a gilded seat.

But you'll never come home the man you went,
a man among men who can't pay the rent.
You'll never fight like Americans do,
and you'll write lousy limericks too.

So, be a great poet, a writer well-read,
stay here where the pay won't go to your head;
remember what Hemingway might well have said,
with a hole in your mind you're just as well dead.

Model for a Romance

```
                        one man is s
                                    u
                                    r
She is a trapeze act                r
                                    o
                                    u
                        reh gnidn
        with love
            in that
```

trying to make her flesh
greater than it is
something to look toward
    always
    while
  one man
Another
    is also waiting
toward her a dark vacuum
and he will be the one
who removes her viscera for the grave.

The Eyes Too Walls

My skin, a loose cloth rolling
along glowing stone beneath sea, drinks
sober men exhausted to itself.
A locust rattles, blooms,
night a lightening flower crackling through its skull.
Skin covers all.
The eyes, too, left unstained,
empty now as hospital rooms,
beds changed and colorless walls repainted.

Evening Coming in the East

Nightwalker walks these valley nights
only alone when least known
after the barbecue/the day's work/the checks
   cashed/
comes jingling silences from silver belt,
long-striding comes loping red-eyed
antennae-fingered dream, disturbs the valley.

He reminds you of the undone job,
tears the curtains from dark women's sides.
Chants light through steely teeth.
He leaves you pitted with islands
like the night of understanding.

Invisible

I lie down among invisible animals
   fill my pockets with their soft eyes
and watch night unroll itself,
rising between my slackened jaws
and pouring down tree-stunted canyons,
billowing around the heavy rust of trains,
encircling men
a vision a dozen panoramas I return to
   seeping its moonlight into dust;
of the hat kicked crooked
the leather jacket dead again
       shining
while our footsteps shuffle homage
in sacrosanct circles of ourselves.
Of how at any moment
I will have one last explanation
and striking out
sudden will miss
everything.

Commuting

eyes ride their steel cushions along night
never into but wide wide
short hair framing soft flesh
and the glaze at summer's end

We are the people
We are the hope America
We are the children
still soiling ourselves in empty cribs
We the violence
The paternal order stern
    as rudderless ships.

In Memory of Strain

For a year after John Strain died
his family left his house unsold in weed,
and we got our courage up, going by
as we did each evening through the field,
our arms about each other's waists,
wondering what it would be like to wait
as ripening seeds behind the cutlery
for your lover to come home
tired and alone at the end of the day.
A child wants to grow
even if wanting to believe doesn't make it so.

And so it was one weekend we met there
whether from lust or on a dare
to climb through the kitchen window,
stumble to the parquet floor,
and hold each other by the hand in our uncertainty.
In truth, right then there wasn't much to see...
we went from room to room afraid
to climb the stairs, to open closets, but we did,
and talk as loudly as if this house were made...
well, for ghosts and nothing else but us.
So that when we had sex quickly, and we did,
it would seem that we were alone more than enough,
and in leaving we would grow
in believing what we feared did not make it so.

Except in raising that dust across those floors,
in having laid our bodies sweat upon those boards
in first hunger, we were unsure
that the man who died there might not still live
in the patterns of leaves shivering their lives

upon the walls or a light quick dancing,
perhaps the sun off a distant car's chrome passing
on a dusty road. How not knowing then we knew
that around us an unbearable brightness flew
that in its separation from our bones
had no basis, no majesty of being but mechanical self alone.

There in that twining light
built only of light and shadows and air
we felt an iron scaffolding of fear
and the promise of broken time
welded into the bones of night,
as if to be ourselves was in fact to hear
more than either of us could bear,
through lives neither planned nor felt
except in the mad moments of belief
that what we carried in our finest moments of grief
was in fact the pelt of some great animal
blanketing the universe with its pungent smell
and in its largeness being what we saw as small.

Perhaps that is why as we left
we moved so much more slowly than we went in, caught
winding our way to the foundations laid
by Strain for his garage, now fading where the dirt crept in;
and I buried my hands in the shattered masonry, not
in memory or any cheap respect for what was paid
nor in guilt for any missing moments,
but in sharing of that distant civilization
that leaves a man with only what he makes,
and locks him in
spinning beyond our words into his walls.

You Cannot Write a Poem

You cannot write a poem
that says I don't know.
You cannot write a poem
that says I'm not perceptive enough
to know what I am doing in your world
unless it can say my world is not yours
and I am doing in it what you cannot do
and doing it like wind on the face of a leaf
and you will have to take my word for it
unless you throw your family away
and your camels through needles' eyes:
That's a safe bet...we all
have our heavy camels sweating their burdens
through the miles.

You cannot write a poem
that talks of music
and cries.
You cannot write a poem
that breathes, and loves, that is cold,
that moans in its bed with nightmares
remembering what was said to it twenty years ago;
or that will sacrifice its life
to see your children through school:
you would not want it to
Would you
unless it could lead that stale breathing
from your own mind as easily
Would you?

You cannot write a poem
that answers anything
when nothing talks

and no one listens
you cannot write a poem
like a kid with an unstirred can of paint
dipping in his wooden stick to raise clouds of color
and shunning the opaque,
knowing you cannot write a poem,
being a part of the wordless clumps
clinging to your arm
and tearing themselves into liquidity
and being poetry
gone before you speak.

The Penitent Voyeur

As she looked then
walking between rows of tiger lily
her dress was blue her eyes green
as she looked across the chill
and still despite our words
echoing there it was not her.

Perhaps that is why I've always liked
the distant shots;
anonymous white of underthings bulging
to come forth anonymous of face
except the memory.

This eternal thing that haunts the young
that flutters from their husks with age
how often has looked out from foreign eyes
has pertly twitched some girl's hips
or driven a crushing fist before letting it lie.

Something I think wanders these streets
it forms as shelves for holding tubes of flesh
and sticks its tongue inside bringing us alive
so that if finding ourselves in time
the dream even then is good.

From Your Flesh

You walk into my room
highway-dark car at your back
sunlight caught in a bird's throat
your scent caught in my throat
we touch something between us
gives
elastic moment
in your entering I cannot
remove the hands of textile workers
from your flesh.

For a Woman Dead in Grand Central

I watch her rise in the morning
tired from the warm sheets not wanting to rise
but warm with the need to provide for child and husband
to hunt for the lover she left folded in paperback books,
drawing half asleep from her blouse a pale blue from a darkened closet
drawing it about her shoulders unaware
buttoning it in the mirror while she sleeps,
and not knowing
it not knowing because it is only cloth
but should since it is so much a part of her
it is the last blouse she will ever draw from the dark,
was to be even when wound onto a loom by a machine in some
   automated warehouse
far in time from mountains of Burlington, Vermont.

The Paycheck

THE NUMBERS   GHOSTS
SWIRLING FROM BEDROOM WALLS,
HUNGRY CLOSETS
  NAMING CAVE NAMES

For My Daughter in Moonlight

You are small
   huddled over a star
     in a dark room
        warm with the scent of sleep.

I would like to roll myself
into the infinite vision of your hope,
to be the green fire
   encased beneath moonlit snow
     heavy as air on your limbs.

Greenwich

This is Greenwich, Connecticut:
This is the end of civilization;
this richest per capita of America
where sleep pays to lie down by death.

This is the scene:
the houses some of them whole cities, stretching
down to trees holding somehow
the concrete road safe, or
squeezing it against Long Island Sound
twisting it so the car jumps
but only at what squeezes out between the trees
or at what eats away at them
from the other side.

This is the condominium
of the blonde daughters of computer czars
of the seltzer-swigging sons of landscape gardeners.
This is where they dock the Honey Fitz,
President John F. Kennedy's yacht,
next to the Showboat Restaurant,
tying the sterling silver taste of lobster
to the tainted smell of something not quite sea
rolling through the leaves of dark.

This is the scene:
on the Showboat Restaurant road—
and, yes, it is really there and
you are driving through it in the night
between tree-laden electric halos,
are talking to the silence sitting by you,
funneled between the partiers and trees—
you are suddenly at the opening of nothing;

at that precise place and instant where the road stops
and drops unwarning down into a night of stagnant ocean—
yes, here, just ten blocks from where I-95
plunged three cars through a bridge to death—
but this suddenness, this openness in the road was planned
or forgotten
or the struggle lost the way a defeated wolf
will offer its throat to attacking teeth.

This is the scene:
where you get out and take two steps
from your car to the jagged tarmac edge
where you feel the power of stone behind you
and the power of water before you and under you
and your blood dances on two thousand years of western music
where you stare only into what you are,
where your skin opens only to the light of stars
where your skin goes cold to the sounds surrounding you
of night sucking its teeth along your shore
and the gurgle of fear through dry grass.

This is the place
civilization ends,
where the only roads are followed by ships on invisible beams
where flesh goes down quickly
but floats on moonbeams up again
beyond the tearing of time.
This is the end of civilization,
and that gap in the road is really there,
and in turning back from it,
in staggering back to your metal case,
in hurling yourself against the brittle glass of nobility
in falling through into the Showboat Bar

you wonder why it takes money to live this way;
   in style,
to picket-fence eternity for daytime dreams.
And how much would we know
if all men were allowed to live this way
or Greenwich crept outside its trees at night
   and said
This is the end of civilization:

this broken, concrete street and the waves affront it.

On the Official 40ᵗʰ Anniversary of the Dignitaries at the U.N.

I wonder if it has ever done anything to save lives
of anyone except for making money for chessmen to buy chessmen.
The making of money is in a sense the saving
of lives
there is now little to see because of the glass waterfalls
where the river is the river looking at the river vertically,
except for the Dag Hammarskjöld stair and flagpole
and the Nelson Rockefeller plaque—I think plague when I write this—
on this plot of rosebud anonymity of power.

I look out over the East River
beneath armed rooftops,
watching for some time a page of the *Wall Street Journal*
slosh
a dying body fighting its last against the tides;
counting the unmarked fishing boats carrying rocket launchers this week.
Helicopters duck in and out among the buildings of Roosevelt
carrying dark tubes hunting shadows moving out of place against the sun.

I lean here in the open where generations of cattle died
twirling another helicopter in an arc above me above the people.
There are so many of us here with radios
binocularshifisetsnewpapersbookshotdogs with our friends
waiting for some news to come down the line.

Modern Man, Artificial Intelligence, and Humanity

Each day it is harder for man to achieve a personal control over his environment as technology passes from speed of function superficiality. Where does the ego come down, if it is to remain in evidence at all? Is modern man becoming obsolete?

No, his computer is a weapon of materialism; placed together the factors on an immutable mutable world, discerning immediately the weakest points in the walls of inertia surrounding him. In other words, if you were not you but a component, it would find what block in the architectural structure confronting you would be the keystone, providing the greatest change if removed—perhaps causing the entire structure to collapse without intent. And your ego, needing recognition in itself in this world of buttons, demands that recognition. The button is pushed—by the component you: and the better your computer, the more complete the devastation of existing structure. The greater or more infamous your "instant name"—a distinction built only on change.

Because the computer does not know one vital set of elements you need as a human being to direct your destiny, to be a human being. It does not know you or your interior relationships with the universe…and so it does not know your capacity for change, whether when you breach the fortress of societal mediocrity it will be to slaughter the infidels within the fortress or to live among them in greater health.

There is no replacement for the mind, if only because it knows the body it is within and is responsible for. There is no substitute for disciplined training of that mind. There is the mind, and then a large chasm before the Lucite blocks of clarity composing artificial intelligence.

JARED SMITH

Walking the Perimeters of the Plate Glass Window Factory

Published by Birch Brook Press

2001

Acknowledgments

Some of the poems in this collection first appeared in *Context South, A Fine Madness, Galley Sail Review, Rhino,* the anthology *Going 60 in Chicago: 60 Years of Poetry from The Poets Club of Chicago,* and awards ceremonies from Poets & Patrons in Chicago. Others were first presented through the Arlington Poetry Project and The Poets' Club of Chicago.

We were something slow happening in the mind of a cow.

—Robert Penn Warren

Lines Written in a Waiting Room

A slug walks into this doctor's office, you see,
and says I want to know if the doc's got something to handle the salt
that comes down from my eyes every time I cry and melts my skin.
And the receptionist puts down her bagel with cream cheese,
turns to her file clerk friend and talk talk talks,
turns sourly at last to look at the poor melting slug and then
peppers him with insurance questions.
And he cries deep within his soft soft sides.

Remembering the Union Dead at My Door

The blood of my ancestors is as hot in my veins as their thought in my mind
winding the spiral roads from Arlington toward the capital.
To have brought out the dead and buried them by my kitchen door is something strong.
It is bitter, but a growing part of us.
It is Whitman's leaves of grass and Barlow's columbiad mixed with Steinbeck's wrath.
It is the drummer boy on my father's side who fought in the American Revolution,
leading the troops that made a difference with his music that beat upon their bones;
it is the general who rode so well on my mother's side in the American Revolution.
It is the surveyor who laid out the early tracts of land and oversaw the early years,
who lived in this house where the Union dead were buried to build the living;
the gentry who served the middle states like the Brahmin served New England.
It is my father's father who worked in a factory all his life and built the unions;
my mother's ancestor Joseph Brant who led the Deerfield Massacre and went to Oxford,
and her father who was a minister and was well-loved and forgotten.
My parents and compatriots, the sargasso sea we call educators, philosophers, workmen.

Where the tall sea grass grows on the leeward side of islands, you will find no order
but the order of the winds churning across the landscape we have built in so few years.
You will find the sons of fishermen and hunters and architects of dreams
enriching the soil our Chincoteague ponies grow fat upon, building the roads and rails
that brought Rockefeller's oil to Carnegie's England, destroying the land and giving land.
You will find the outlaws like Holliday who played the spinet and studied Homer
and rode west when he could not breathe to find his future in Tombstone and Colorado;
the doctor of celebration who looked out where we later would teach spies languages
      in the war to end all wars,
and where we have an Air Force Academy playing football with the best that ever were.
These were outlaws to what we had, and allies to what we are, outside the formal,
still growing beneath the grain that feeds our souls.

The first soldier fallen in our Civil War
was buried by Lincoln, the pioneer father of our nation's heartland,
out by yonder oak tree, across the dirt yard of late summer, beneath the rope swing

where a generation of our government learned to climb and listened
to crickets in spring or fished the Potomac planning explorations that would not end.
We built a country out of this and the isolation of our forests and the continental divides
raising their cragged madness from seabeds gone millennia ago,
from the molten core of earth that traded around the world as silver, then as gold,
from the crickets' eastern chirp to the coyotes' western wail across arid plains,
the boot soles measured out their timeless tread to Arlington Cemetery…
from across all countries of the world to this back yard outside this kitchen door
were built the monuments to ideas that would be their time and pass,
reflections of all the classrooms, all the farms, all the factories, all the quilts sewn
in all the rooms we ever built for all the slaves we ever bred for our confederacy.

I pass between the graves this morning, flag a cab
and go on my way across the bridge to Washington.
A great blue heron is wheeling down the river toward its home among the trees;
A fish jumping belly white into the sunrise just beyond the shallows.
All these dreams and memories, and I descended from Lee and Joseph Brant,
mean nothing for this; but for the cars rushing to the heartland,
for the traditions that have built this civil war that never ends.
For these I play a part and carry the seeds of the revolution that started here forward.
No man nor government shall ever claim our soul while the wind blows,
and we can lie awake at night to hear it pound the waves against our shores
or rattle the leaves that fall upon our lawns each time the seasons change,
for we will rise above the slavery we have wished upon ourselves in our quest.
Whether black or indian or pakistani, I know now among these stones
we alone are human, our flesh softer and stronger than these monuments,
and our confederacy is to be one without our savagery,
unlawful and in the end, just.

Walking the Perimeters

Low buildings gleam in sundown
igniting the green grass strip along cement walkways,
centering Job's presence as he walks the perimeters;
and he curses to himself
until in the metronome of his footsteps he begins to breathe.
A dry leaf blows down before his face. It swirls.
A pigeon banks left and then right above the quadrangle.
Between these two he finds perspective...space to turn
and watches from more afar the suits drawn by.

The perimeters stand.
The night within has windows
and each window ignites laboratory tubes,
faces before computer windows,
bottles of chemicals,
time sheets and arias from forgotten tongues,
labyrinthine sculptures charting the stars
measuring the rhyme of ancient mariners
beneath a cold winter that hides
beneath the laughter of windup dolls
tottering to someone's beat.

Like a field in Nebraska
seen from thirty thousand feet
green golden with corn watered from far below the earth
from far down where the darkness wells up to meet sun,
and the gray beyond the Ogallala Aquifer impounds that field,
like that the perimeters spin away before Job's eyes
leaving petite parks and benches and
red summer skirts too small and light to see...
leaving the squat bone columns alone
staring back at that great outside
just glimpsed at in *The Nibelungenlied*

played only now and then on Wagnerian phonographs.
And the fog comes in on the setting rays,
spinning him aloft on a dragon's wings.

Fort Arrogance stands.
Its towers are the soul of a man
below his leather wings and burning breath
as he wheels first left then right away over
the walls to other buildings domiciles caught out
side the perimeters and dumped where they would fall by nature
in a cacophony of muted symbols
for mile and mile and wilder vaster outward from the walls,
the symbols crashing/taking solid shape
scurrying down into the rubble of their birth
and emerging in human eyes and hands
and naked bodies gyrating in vernal celebration
even here amid the bricked up yards of sensibility,
and then still farther out beyond the charted stars
uncharted and unnamed except as silent needles in the night of time/
between the spaces between those lights
and down upon the fog until he lost the muttered lisp of words
until he lost himself before the walls
with nothing to say his name in the midst of life.

The perimeters stand

and are a wall
surrounding all these miles...
covering such a sweep that from inside is everything,
but from outside is the moonlight
sweeping down across white stone roofs
and it is the moonlight before it strikes the roofs
or the crystal grains caught within the stone

and it traps everything
except the wind wrapping itself about a man…
and the moon becomes a cave
within which the very large is lost.
It fills itself, and
the moon becomes a cave.

He Who Says the Name of God Will Perish

Today we have finished the human genome project.
From the twisted spiral of our days we have labeled life itself,
untwined it to banish and recreate our fears.
We have tied it all into a paycheck that sends our children to college,
or have ignored it all and turned our eyes to entertainment,
so that our lives are filled with canned laughter and starvation
or are filled with tightly wound springs we cannot even see
that propel us to levels where we can leave the city at least once a year
and walk among the mountains or sail on starlit seas sometimes for a week.

It is raining in southern Illinois,
and fishermen slouch the muddy banks of swollen streams,
not because this is the place to come for trophy fish or for vacations that will be
        remembered,
but because so much of the country, so much of where the grass still grows high
is filled now with tar-papered shacks and hanging walls,
with doors that open darkly into nothing that can be seen,
through which these men come in need of food, in the waters,
and in the evening when the big fish dimple the stars of night,
come from their despair which is so far, so far
from the double helix we speak of in our universities.

What matters it then
if we know the name of the face of god itself,
but cannot recognize its face in the cold cliffs of our minds?
I have known the names of constellations our city dwellers have never seen
and been terrified spinning beneath them on the desert floor
while *I Love Lucy* filled the minds of our best paid and our most lost;
and it means nothing now. I have forgotten the helix
and the name of the man who found it and was written in our books,
even as it splits apart and searches for itself in the city lights where stars cannot be seen.

What is life
when we cannot reach out and feel our skin against the cold stone of night
and find the warmth we do not find within ourselves?
What is it that fills these sagging shacks in southern Illinois or Arkansas or Colorado,
rising up into the clear cold skies that stand above our laboratories and naming games
that has nothing to do with haste or quick response, but echoes
with the soft flow of waters running inevitably to sea?
What is it makes us turn our deepest discoveries to laughter caught on tape,
thank god I have forgotten the name; only this,
I have forgotten the name.

In the Plate Glass Window Factory

In the plate glass window factory they watch reflections of sky
and melt down silicon mountains before coffee break.
The sun rises and sets in iron vats.
It is contained.
In the plate glass window factory they build liquid frames
for pictures of farmhouses where the farmer rises early in the morning
or for train cars that ensnare the mountains of a continent
and for young women baking bread in little towns of red brick homes.
In the plate glass window factory as the day goes on the breathing hardens
and they pour their crystal lakes into featureless trays
which can be filled with anything,
sweeping time from the floorboards and cutting it out to hang on walls.
And in the plate glass window factory, the workers never go home,

not even when they fish dark rivers beneath the stars.

Not the Lone Ranger's Horse

I am the dark horse
you ride the fields of evening with,
but my eyes cannot see beyond the wood frame of this stall.
You have walked away
after pressing grains of the field to my mouth
and having pressed the scent of your flesh into my memory.
You have walked into the shadows beyond my harness
and left me to carry the night on my shoulders,
left me to support your world on my too-thin legs,
standing here wide-eyed at distant sounds while you sleep.

Master, I am alone
bearing myself with dignity
on cold days when you do not come.
The dark earth calls to me of roots and of seeds
growing from last year's graves and bearing fruit,
and you parcel that out to me touched with your flesh…
For that I carry you over the evening fields,
but I would have carried you far away, so far from where you want to be
had you not closed me deep into this stall.

Then Gone

Warm winds came in last night
stripping death from our fields, and the old man
with my name in his hip pocket walked down to the pond,
scattered his billfold among last year's cattails
called to the bass hidden in their weeds.

Something long, silver as water in moonlight,
ghosts by our windows
coming home.

Wondering What It Takes

Before there were people
I could talk with the clarity of mountain streams;
and even after people, before they were gathered together,
I could speak as one animal unto itself—
directly flesh to flesh and earth to earth,
in simple images without meaning, like clouds.

But wherever two or more are gathered together
in my name there are many names now,
and the words capturing those names are rippled against each other.
And though they all mean the same thing in the end
when it comes down to the end, and it will come down,
in the end they will all sound exactly as flesh to flesh.
In simple images, you cannot hear them

when people talk not only one to one
but one generation out into the next, one death
out into the next life, they are hitting against each pebble,
capturing each fern draped over the surface, each fawn pausing for a drink,
and emerging with the knowledge of all I would say
before there were people gathered together in my name,

and with names for every part of that which is all I would name
directly flesh to flesh and earth to earth....
But a universe cannot be kept within one people's brain
if those people speak in words that must be kept as names.
And on it goes....You cannot contain all the names in all the brains
that must be contained within the clouds.

Some Primal Memory

It's hard to remember what they built these buildings for,
these warehouses down by the river,
perhaps some primal memory rises,
but it's hard to remember why they built these factories
when what you see is the packaging, the ribbon cutting, the boxes
   brightly coming in,
the dresses turning like wrapping in dance halls.
It's hard to remember what they built these buildings for
or why the men are waiting all day in lines, are traveling miles,
to come here for or what they hope to see
or what the architect hoped to build from paper as he slept,
or why the windows and what the entrances and exits are
when everyone is rushing off to sell a needed need to someone else…

Sure, they say among themselves they know,
that they built these stones to form a store,
to be an arena, to keep inside something you might call merchandise.
But over years you can see the change,
you can see it creep into their eyes as the buildings age…
the knowledge that you cannot build a stone, you cannot fence the air,
that something else, more hidden, was meant to be kept hidden deep within there.
That at last it is likely to come out
when the paint has peeled from the ceiling beams
and the walls are slick with sweat-stained tears, when men have died within
and have been forgotten by all the men who laughed with them,
when quietness settles on the river and the heron is frozen into time among
the reeds the last thing that comes out from all those carefully fitted boards
is a darkness soothing about our shoulders like a cotton sweater warming us
until we disappear.

Believing That You Understand

I wanted to tell you how everything changes and doesn't change,
how currents in the river near where you were born often twist back upon themselves,
without our even being aware of it watching from above; just smooth glass
reflecting back sun above mountains reflecting back nothing but morning haze.
But how or where do you find the words to tell what you cannot tell?
At such times I would put my hand on your shoulder, and time would pass.
You would point to a flower or say I love you, and I would be amazed,

knowing that the spark of life that flew between us at your birth still flew,
and that you were gentle with it, had known long before I took you out into the fields...
knew that you were also walking with your son and telling him these things
some year a long way from where we stood, watching the leaves that fell and blew,
saying almost nothing with your words because they mean so little until one feels
the wet tautness of a spider's spiraled web in morning grass or hears a wood thrush sing
the last song it will sing before autumn, knowing it will not be back.

I have given all my life to words
as a sculptor gives his blunt hammer to the purity of stone,
and have perhaps hacked out less of the essence I would pass on.
My craft too is of the gods, but perhaps not enough of trust to keep the blade as true.
Odd to think that we have been before and like in stone the images are there
beneath the brute grunting we engage in for our food, our love,
beneath the ritual matings we are met in for our wanderings,
and that these words so painfully chosen are but reminders of the art we know.
Socrates would claim it so,
he who was so careful with his words and definitions,
and who also wanted nothing more than to pass on to someone else what he knew
to be true...but I have never felt that words were solid enough for that,
though I have tried to make it so...and they are harder stone than anything I know.

Look instead to the snow settling in an alpine valley
and finding permanence until the spring rains pull it back into the ground.
Take your child's hand and hold it while you watch.

Pebbles in a Stream

These words are pebbles in a stream
where sometimes there is water flowing and ferns trail their fronds;
or sometimes they are locked in ice crystals
so you cannot see where the stone ends and the ice begins
and everything is white wherever you look
except the dark wood pillars that hang above it all;
or sometimes the water has not come yet,
and nothing grows nor has ever grown;
or sometimes the stream becomes a river or an ocean
and these hard shapes that formed it are hidden far beneath its surface,
back in a time and space that set things in motion but cannot be named.
These words and all they hold and all that they reflect
are the pebbles of all that we will ever be.

On Mr. Peabody's Estate

You can't stop life.
I've sat beside this willow for ten years of evenings
casting my lures into the water beyond its shadow
while its green curtains hung down hiding the termite rot eating its heart,
and have watched the other fishermen come and go,
suits or more often long hair and loose knit shirts and jeans,
neither kind of dress doing better and neither kind of dress right for the world
they enter, this tree spreading shade that drew the large bass in evening
that drew the fishermen.
But it was struck down by strong winds six months ago
and rolled out, the grubs at its heart exposed to sun and dying,
the termites too moving on to other challenges.
It was winter when I found it, and was sad to see it go
bare skeleton into the lake, its lower branches still holding it above the waterline,
but dead. And now
in summer, Oh, it is easy to be wrong,
because it grows, its leaves leaning up now not down but toward the sun.
You cannot stop life, not even when you strike its heart,
not even when you eat its heart,
but what is it based on, what hope fills the green green leaves
as its dead heart sinks into the shoreline...
what moments/and what generations of insects.
and what fisherman will still steal those shadows now that I have gone old.

There are fences now rising up along the lake;
Eleven years is a long time in the life of an aquatic animal,
but they still keep one shore open, where the willow lies and its leaves are green in passing
and I visit it at times to sit and look upon the waters that
  the men on the other side can stock with bass
because they do not fence it all; they can't fence it all.
And tonight I watch a young boy of maybe ten
sweating and casting his line into the shadows.
I would smile and offer him advice/instead I smile and walk on down the path.

My own son chooses not to fish, but has other things.
He will not read these words, though he loves to read and reads well,
and I will send him to college next year wherever he should want to go.
My wife has polished her wedding ring and reset the stone. She will not fish with me.
I walk on down the path, turn a corner for discretion and piss into the bushes,
marking my own willow tree, which means nothing in the end.
You cannot stop life,
nor see the termites eating away within the heart of Mr. Peabody's estate.

My wife does not think of sex as I do, nor roll in the grass, nor ever has.
My wife does not make money as I do;
I am a money machine with a rusting cog.
My son does not like to fish and will not walk with his old man;
he has the Internet.
My daughter rides horses and plays viola.
She chases younger men.
I walk and watch the sunsets and see the fish dimple their universe in evening.
My wife believes in having fun, and I don't remember how
on Mr. Peabody's estate where they have begun to raise the fences up.

The Reservoir in Drought

The water is three feet down from normal
where I walk, skirting the banks of the reservoir.
Not that it has not rained; drums beat down hard on our lodge last night
and for days of moons the skies were clouded/the wind cool and brisk
as if autumn had filled the days of summer forever.
Every third day for a month the thunder came, and the rains.
The streets of our city filled with water/the gutters overflowed.
But it did not come here;
it did not fill the fields that border on our drinking supplies;
it did not soothe the dry red gills of the dark fish surrounding our cities,
those that come from deep in the earth beneath our feet to feed upon the stars.
And now the rains leave these fields as wasted and sere as this beach where water plants
    once thrived.
They leave it to the animals that walk along the land, losing contact with the mountains,
losing contact with the dark spaces beneath our feet,
those spaces that we dance over in uncertain times.
No longer even muddy or touched by life the cracked earth I walk along,
the wide burrows that are the caves of nocturnal animals I pass leading back beneath
    the old water line
where no one knew them when it counted and they were walked each night
back into the paths that lie beneath our city,
smoothed and patted down and shaped to glass by mysteriously passing feet
and eyes that saw not the water nor the land but both and then the dark
the dark that even today holds out the sun
where I walk
and the waters run so low this year…
and where do they go when they leave the sky where do they go?

In the Year of the Comets

Our thoughts have passed so many miles
that years are laid out behind us like empty cigarette cartons…
our days smoky remnants filled with the importance of the universe.
Somewhere in this swirling cloud of dust
the animals we hunted now turn their attention inward,
circling back to us with inquisitive cold eyes.
They wrinkle their noses, burying them in the damp earth
as if to follow our ghosts on silent feet where the stars bloom.

Ode to a Goose

You goose…
I was walking that way, it's true,
and too quickly almost my fishing rod in hand
but something caused me to look up in time and see your nest
just steps ahead of me along the deer path in the woods,
and you on the far side stepping back from me
head turned over your shoulder so I could watch your eyes
and your open mouth hissing despair at my speed…
You goose…
can't know the horror I felt in my heart
whether at my almost going too far or at the pain in your eyes
as we both looked at your eggs huddled there, each knowing
as they lay in the neat earth circle you had made them
the circle you had built with the clay of your wings
and had sewn with the wind of your feathers
and had sat upon and sat upon after life had taken you cruelly,
as we both looked at them and thought each in our way
how they would be destroyed in their helplessness by some man
or by some other animal while they sought your warmth,
you can't know
why my turning away so quickly was not from fear
was not because you hissed so ferociously, but because
I know better than you that it was the universe lying there,
that your spirit is as deep as the sun and as fragile as
  an eggshell…

You don't understand me,
goose…
There are things in any man
he cannot admit even to himself, or understand.
I am the wind behind the sunset
as evening drops down upon your lake,

and move across your feathers so swiftly that we are gone
almost before we have seen each other...

And what I have left inside of you
is of the earth and of the night.
It is reflected back upon me in your eyes...
And what you have left in me is the distance between us
and the desolation of the moon on your waters,
the white round sun waiting beyond the shoulders of our earth.

You do not understand,
you goose, that your reprimand
is the same distancing my wife uses
when I try to bring my latest battles into my own home,
when I try to tell my children they also will find stones
scattered on hidden beaches even as I have
and will not be able to lift those stones because of caring
any more than I have
or will lift those stones from the water
   only to see their colors pass into memory as they dry
   in their hands like stones
and my wife will only smile sadly and move away drawing them
   with her,
for she sees these stones as nurturing
and sees that I am the wind
and that something in me pulls northward as the days grow short,
that something howls loudly above the clouds when they are tinted silver
and shakes the leaves of the trees towering above us...
something that is cold and distant and cannot be seen.

But she does not know
that it would hurt no one if it had the chance.

Walking the Shore

The freeze line softens
and we move through it, slowly at first,
our senses stumbling:
how can we move through this time line…
how can life or motion take place where light does not
reach…Yet all winter it has been so…
curious fish have nosed among the dried weeds of our garden,
snails have scoured our sidewalks,
trucks preserved with salt have caromed through the night streets
while we have slept, waiting
all of this has gone on, but today
the stairway is leading down, the walls eroding into water
and leading us down beneath the roots where lilies grow,
down past the eyes that have stayed bright all winter
that have moved with ease through the ice that has bound us.
The freeze line softens
and cherry blossoms climb into the night,
bright with reflections that carry the color of dreams.

Putting the Passengers Off in Small Boats

It is evening, and I have heard the gray heron's last call
fading into these salt marshes that surround our home, have seen
the wind die away in the oily swells that pass beneath us,
have seen the sea and the land and the sky become one,
and have dropped my hand loosely into the water.

Again, I stir my fingers, and again green light halos outward,
phosphorescent plankton whispering into being.
I stare deep into the quiet where nothing moves,
raise my hand into darkness, and light drops down
becoming green globes of flame within an unseen sea.

Reaching into my tackle box,
I drop small pieces of grass collected from other trips
and they sparkle before me, flickering, and gone.
I drop a small split shot I bought for fishing with,
leaving a spiraling tunnel of light
downward so far I push my face beneath the water to watch.
My hair too, and my eyes, burn:
I am capable of seeing beneath the night for the first time in my life,
and the light comes from me and from what is outside of me.

Though we have lived for all our lives by this sea,
I have never seen these lights before. I know that I will bring you
and tomorrow we will sit at this same spot against the coast
and will drop our small boats upon the waves as I do tonight,
but that these lights will not be here again and this time
is all I thought and all that I will see.

You too no doubt
have visions you would share with me,
but the night is quick and you are far away.

Where Wind Shakes Our Bones

I sit at a rail crossing
with evening rising around my car,
spreading until it fills the high clouds,
and still the heavy wooden boxes pass
filled with dreams of lives that were
put together in summer homes, fitted in distant factories,
and nailed together to cross the fields before me.

Small red lights block the roadway, flashing,
the hollow Christmas lights of home.
I see children sitting cross-legged in them
      singing reindeer bells,
chattering about what will come in tomorrow's packages.

I am coming, Mother Earth,
having left my office, having raised metal grains
to feed my children and paint their homes.
I am coming to wash in the soft light that ends our days,
to step from the hard road we have circled our cities with,
to live where wind shakes our bones.

Putting Your Money In

What happens if you select the wrong one
when you're standing at the vending machine,
and having dropped your quarters in, you think a long while,
and push the button for Zippy-O's
leaving a full rack of Smackos corn chips sitting there
when packet crimper O'Reilly is having a bad depressing day
and is about to be laid off because no one buys Smackos anymore
and his six children will be put on welfare just before John the Baptist runs for president,
and that means he won't spend seven bucks to go to a movie to see James Bond
and won't tell his buddies who won't go and Pierce Brosnan will take a fall
so far in the ratings that Steven Spielberg won't write Revenge of the Goldfingers
until long after O'Reilly dies of consumption
or something strange he coughed into Smackos corn chips just before hearing the news
and sealed up in that one bag sent to your workplace vending machine.

And the Beat in His Chest Goes On

The lucky man in the corner office
gets paid to see it all from his window at the top...
gets paid to see his childhood wash from misty days,
sluicing down across his pane onto the roofs below,
the little people (truly little at this height) running and
throwing something white to each other far below...

But the lucky man cannot take it long
before squaring his shoulders and putting on his hard lucky eyes,
striding like a lost elephant down his gray corridors,
knowing the light is above him but will shine off his executive hair,
peering into the unlucky cubicles built by Queen Ant & Uncle Sam,
noticing how their soft walls quiver when he passes,
hearing the buzzing drone of gastrointestinal machinery,
glimpsing the drones suddenly falling into silence,
wondering which one will bring in the food.

The lucky man in the corner office sees this death
every day as it seeps into the stone walls that surround him,
bounces back from the all-reflecting glass and beats inside his chest,
while we who work in the darker storage bins along his halls
see nothing, dear god, nothing but the images of moments
frozen briefly in a camera, pinned by us to whatever is in front of us,
the crayon of a child
we work for not seeing there is rain outside
or forgetting...
forgetting the liquid flowing from our water cooler is not
the stuff of man-forged pipes pushed through building walls,
but an ocean of long-forgotten possibilities.

The Board Meets in November

Two rows of coat racks have been pulled across the front foyer...
empty when I came in, they are now filled
with the heavy wool of shorn animals that have never been inside an office before,
with the glistening dew that collects on autumn evening grass
with the dead fibers of the cotton plants
with thirty-six closets swollen with the memory of families growing older
and buses taken cross-town, and aircraft hangars...
certainly with the hotels from countries I have only read of...
with heat and struggle and with the alumina silicate that keeps these coats
free from the sweat these businessmen have come to dole out on paper votes.

What woman or what child made these coats
who would reach these select and indifferent men and women;
who was not allowed to hand over the coat after its hours of preparation,
the hours of sun and the warmth of animals huddled for comfort in the night,
one rack onto another in a dark factory to a dark warehouse to a dark closet
to this room; these men like their coats are the same as you and me
in that they too will go home to pressure and nitro tablets and scotch
if not beer, in all ways the same except that they have hung their coats
in this foyer for one brief moment when all of us could not,
and cast their paper votes; the *chance at least* to
choose wisely from the proper cup before it rolls away across the floor

Something Natural Happening in an Office

In the very center of a scrubbed white room
on the linoleum
is a stone...
you can find it sometimes linked in silence with another.
Gray afternoon light fills its pores, giving depth.

It is raining outside
and blinds across the windows hold it in.
A square box defines what is inside itself.

Between the sounds of falling water
a phone rings
and rings.
The stone responds as you would imagine.

Between Meetings

Your voice comes out of a tunnel twenty years old.
I reach into its darkness
wishing I had the nerve to run back down its length
or the time to get there,
to see if your hands are still as perfect
for tossing pebbles into streams
and sending out ripples that will keep on going
long after the sun moves behind these hills.

A Memo Torn Along the Dotted Line

A row of birds is a dotted line along the phone wires overhead.
One might cut out a line across the clouds beginning there,
might pass into a warmer, more exciting place, I think,
if one were to gently push the birds aside, pulling apart the fabric of clouds.
The circulating pulses of our words warm their toes, excite their feet,
until as one they rise and sweep in one tight circle before settling again,
natural and contained as a swirl of wind over prairie.

The light changes, traffic parts, and our car sweeps forward,
but the image remains uneasy in our silence as the miles unwind.
Perhaps it was not a phone wire at all, I think, but a power line,
whose high frequency thrumming made their eyes bright lights in dark places…
maybe not our words at all that made them shift so fast or made them realign.
But you smile as if thinking the same and say
No, no power lines no matter how taut could light the soles
of the feet of God's creatures enough to carry them so lightly up.

Another Saturday Night with Cassandra

I can't turn the light on,
Cassandra,
come in and feel yourself at home.
Who are we going to drink to now
when all the bottles were put up
by dreamers owned by glass blowers,
put up there on bar shelves on full moon nights
by werewolves wearing white aprons?

I know you are going home,
but who is going to pay the bill
for this frontier on wheels
and the angry men it carries in its belly,
given that you will drop from sight?
Don't tell me what you see
until we pay the rent.

Tales of Silent Men

There are partings in the whiteness filling this space between willows
when I first come upon it this morning through the still wet grass, the gray trees.
No crickets sing. No bird yet challenges my presence or stakes its ground:
this is the middle time, or a little bit before,
and silence is an upwelling that begins just beyond my sodden feet.
It is an upwelling that parts the whiteness with its sheer force,
scattering into columns that grow denser and hunch over upon themselves;
columns that rise upward from their evening nest,
parting from each other like dancers releasing hands to pirouette across a stage.
Sunlight comes between them, releasing them, hurrying them,
as they part to scattered shrubs and trees distanced along suddenly visible water.
Still solid, swirling gray, they pass behind foliage on the far shore
furtively sliding away into suburban greenbelt, passing without imprint over grass
and outward toward the buildings hugging our near horizon.

From behind one tangle of brush where I watched one slide away,
not really farther than where you are sitting from me, remembering it was still early,
the shape swirls back, counter to the others that move on along their missions.
My whole body tenses as that swirling gray from beyond the brush becomes a man
walking back toward me, still hunched over somewhat, face hidden by his hat pulled low,
walking as tiredly as I had been just moments before myself, plaid shirt hanging limp,
toward me around the bend in the shore through the tall prairie grass and purple thistle.
Good morning, I say, remembering that this is what one says to an unknown neighbor.
And then the day rises and the mists are gone; the prairie grass unbent.

We all have miles to go and things to see.
Kitchen lights come on across the field beyond the green belt,
suddenly defining houses that were not there a moment ago, and I think,
yes, I think I can see a person standing far at that white house there, before a stove,
reaching down to raise a cup of coffee to start the day.
But no, what I really see, I tell myself is only a quick flittering of shadow across light.
The distance between where we are and where we are is just that long,
and we make nothing out beyond what we tell ourselves.
The day is merely time to move along.

The Eyes on the Coin

                    You look out the window
just before the phone rings.
Maybe someone from across the street is calling.
You do not answer this time,
suspicious they will sell you empty curtain rods
like they once sold you a used carcass of keys
before nailing their doors shut and dropping from sight.

Winding its way across the face of your watch
are your hands, and their fingers are pointing
to every sensation that will come into your life
every sudden pain that will fill your chest
every secret hiding place in your darkness
        rattling
     until you listen
     and listen
wondering how many bells ring for what
that you can buy with a quarter in a metal box.

You find only a disk that circles back upon itself
calling to you with the face of every relative
of every girl who tried to fill her heart with you.
Looking out the window
you briefly see yourself duck behind something
gray and heavy partway down the block,
as if afraid that you would be found there
        pointing at yourself
           before it rings.

At Evening

something man is afraid of comes into our cities
along their arteries;
something slinking on its belly
dodging from bush to bush to pile of trash,
nosing through scattered bricks and rubble
until it flattens itself out of sight
as the trains rush by.

It is in every city…
sometimes where the iron rails reach out
allowing entries where exits are meant…
sometimes where effluvium washes out in drainage ditches…
but always where only the homeless ever walk
and wind calls unknown names just out of reach.

Some thing it is that is never quite seen
but brings the breathing of decay toward our buildings,
that means home for strange rodents and scraping behind
 walls.
Some thing that leaves a path wider than a city block
that has no beginning either way you turn.

The Sun Finding Your Hands...

The doors of a city open slowly.
When you look in a mirror there are no trees behind you.
Trains come calling when the moon is high,
whispering your name again and again into the earth.

First to give out will be your eyes,
because such soft light cannot contain stone—not long.
Men on their way to war will go down to the sea in your
  ribs,
leaving them beached in the great white way
far from what you see.

A tangle of magnetic tape is a nest
the wind blows into down along Lake Shore Drive.
Perhaps it is the place a candy wrapper will choose to raise
  its young.
Perhaps it is only the tendon which will snag a page going nowhere.

You open a door in leaving for work;
the sun finding your hands poised like paper sparrows.
You see this and it fills you,
and the stones are so thin that they are light
falling so deeply into your thoughts they do not land.

It Has Started

It started with the squirrels eating their way
down from our attic,
their eyes finding the liquid gleam of electric wire.
They dropped from trees above our house all night
as your eyelids quivered on your pillow.
I know. And the birds too, finding their way
down the tunnels of our chimney. I would
listen to their picking at the mortar,
then in morning lift the damper so the dead
  would drop out.

Sound of Late Moonlight

Memory causes the man to fear.
Moon ripples across his eyes.
They are midnight.
A mink crosses between shadows.
When he touches a woman
strong fingers massage his shoulders.
He breathes Arctic winters
where wolves steal his scent
burying him in the tundra.
When he was young
he took his family here
on a boat built by strangers.
Now he comes alone
and they are waiting for him.
If he turns his head just right
quickly
he can still catch the sounds of car horns
rushing upward to rescue what remains.
He spreads his fingers
feeling snow float down between them,
melting down into his bone.

I Wish That You Were Here in Spring

Your letter comes in sunset,
outlining every reed along the shore.
I walk along the dock beyond our cabin,
spreading my arms to become the light and shadow filtering these aging boards

A merganser flashes down from the low hanging clouds,
sears between evening and autumn's red haze,
lands in a bright spume of light and dives beneath the waves.
He will come up somewhere,
his red head now dark against his dark plumage,
his throat filled with straining fish going into night.

I wish we had come to this,
because even in this distant time
the scent of your body still enfolds me.
but the wind is blowing into evening,
and in evening mists rise from this lake,
erasing first the distant shores, then the trees,
the fox that comes down to drink, eyes bright, ghostly;
finally the single man who steps out into the white, swirling darkness.

Returning Home

This evening after returning home
I rise upon the warm breezes of the heartland,
my wings heavy and musty like a pioneer's shawl
knitting together the cornfields and factories…the hills
        and rivers…
sensing again after so many years the tense excitement.

Far below a church bell echoes.
I tilt into a spire so that the moon fills my eyes
and trace the hidden paths of back alleys
the deer trail down to the highway's edge
the coyote carrying something warm and bloody to his brood.
My talons are the night.

They say a man does not ever get to know this freedom,
to leave the control over wires he has in his office
until he goes out in death,
but I think in giving up these things I have forgotten
and in giving up control of them there is control,
and the sad crying that fills my voice is victory
and the wish that you would join me.

The Last Trip We Took Together

    Grass is flashed with reds and yellows
winding its way down to water
        winding its way through grass rivers....
           Summer is leaving this mountain valley.
             Water begins to slow, anticipating ice along its edges,
and all the rivers deepen in my heart. I turn my eyes upward,
        imprinting the landscape to memory
            where it will be typed out on paper as a road map;
a road map of colors and the winding spirit that is life
              hiding beneath autumn's dusk.

    We were there together,
           walking down from our car, feet catching in the long grass
and dragging us back as if it could from cold blue sky that was our horizon.
            We did not walk together, but apart from each other,
    each one seeing what we would see, each one
        stooping here or there to pick a weed or lift a small stone to take home
            to warm ourselves in winter;

        and both to write our own maps
      to keep in our empty rooms at either end of the highway running between us
      so that with these few short notes we could remember
          the meadow we have each been a part of.

Our Last Walk

The colors assail me.
They are the colors of spice cabinets
left open in autumn's wind.
Seed casings swirl before me
withered with seasons yet to come,
gray with the sun that will warm your lips
  next year.

This is a changing of time,
a removing of masks.
The colors, again, catch at my feet.
Not what they seem,
they have abandoned the dark wood
holding up our sky, and flown.

They would hold me, I think,
but then are gone
quick as the last dry insects
flitting between strands of prairie grass.

An Apology

I am not easy. The demon is in me tonight, he who speaks
from deep in the throat with gutturals
imaging me as a bear heavy from hibernation.
It is not that I want him here
or that he can be conjured from a bottle or a weed....
Worse, it is that he feeds upon himself
even as the dry papers of our days blow across his eyes,
and in that self consumption he grows cold/
colder than iron on ice...

That is why I go out this evening
having taken my fishing rod from the rack...
to try to draw him out,
to place the right lures into the dark water,
to draw the bright flesh from darkness before the sun sets,
to settle light as an insect on the skin of the universe
before the stars drive their holes through my polished smile...
because I know that he doesn't care.
That he is in me and doesn't speak our language,
That he comes from the very soul of the universe,
whereas you and I are small and passing
and are far from beautiful when he is here,

Nothing comes back in the fishing,
not when you come back into the electric lights at the end of it all though...
and if you do not come back he grows madder,
still madder, swirling his gloved hands in widening gyres
meaning nothing absolutely nothing
     nothing
is what I feel for your smile or your laughter
until finally only he can destroy himself
and I pray for that when the demon is in me.

And I pray because he is tonight the only light,
believing still that fire can fill a man's veins
and that a man filled with this demon can dream so strongly
that he can heal his body of the money placed over the eyes of our dead,
rising above them…
so far above though that we cannot touch what we believe.
The demon is in me tonight
and all I can get past my lips is that he was with me
the night we met, and I think and hope
you must have seen him then as well.

Andrea

There must be quiet times even in the lives of outlaws,
        Andrea.
The moon is setting over our lake
and its silver is a music that passes through the dry reed
pressed between my lips deep into my bones.
I am filled with bright caverns that no one will see.

At Home

Not being well today, I watch you
from a distance as you sit and uncurl into afternoon.
Your eyes look out beyond our fence
beyond the flowers I have bought and you have raised.
Your hair blows across your face
and its whiteness is the white of your jeans
and your body is poised in the music of time
to reach out in those spaces I have almost forgotten.

Before the Fire

We sit before a fire...
autumn chasing leaves across our living room windows,
and it is growing darker across the corners.
I reach out and poke at the heart of the log,
flinching back as sparks leap toward my sweater.
You laugh sharply.
The log breaks apart,
its darkened skin rolling back,
a mouth opening into fire.

We think upon this in silence
as an enormous tower of wind sweeps around our house
moves the curtains, steals beneath our doorway and moves on.
That wind is filled with the dead husks of our days,
with the eyes of the very insects that ate from our garden
  last spring,
and cold though it is sees nothing of us now.
It is cold so cold upon our skin
that we draw each other close and our skin wrinkles
becoming the suits we wore to work or the slacks we
gardened in and nothing more that the wind cannot shake.

But you, you are the light
burning at the center of this...
beneath the shuffle of factory looms
beneath the flesh that gives away nothing,
you and I are the matter that burns,
are the energy that is all matter
and are reflected deeply as pirated moonlight on the waves of
  darkness...
and there down beneath where the moonlight lies
lies something else white in the dark
where we can almost make it out.

In the Parking Lot

Cars in the parking lot
are nestled husks…shells of animals
spotlighted by arc lamps on a concrete sea
we are in New York twenty years ago
in one of those cars
and have parked to walk a Hudson River pier,
smelling the ocean washing among typewriters at 2 a.m.

we have a beer and look out through moon on water
at the soft animals with furry dice hanging from their
 visors,
wondering how empty they are or if the flesh will return

I will not be with you
when we wake tomorrow, but
rising to turn down the alarm in a Chicago hotel,
and these husks will have people in them,
heavy with forgotten dreams.

Turtles

live on the edge, unlike you,
slowly
but on the edge between aqueous worlds
They lunch on dark spinach beneath the waves
over the three quarters of the earth you cannot go
and whatever miles deep caverns fill their thoughts
they are free to ghost among them
slowly
while you comb your blonde hair
watching into the mirror
stranded
they come lumbering up the beach
leaving deep trenches in the sand and moving
from one world and one time
across the edge into another
unlike you
stranded
half of them breed only once in fifty years,
while the others never come ashore.

Information Superhighway of Death

This land is not the same growing field you were born into,
but twisted into dark, broken cities...destroyed
by the schemers who say they have much to give...
and who have nothing at all to give but death to the spirit
who have said behind their polished office desks they would drive us onto an
      information highway
have said they would create super markets spanning every hemisphere of our earth
would put our generation to work building other lands into brotherhoods
would keep our sons and daughters well educated and well fed
selling the needs of life itself to the Pacific Rim
would not buy the drug cartels of Mexico or corporate deity
    of the Orient
having finally driven every vestige of the peoples' empire
    from Russia and Cuba and Korea and Vietnam and half
    the world
because the peoples' empire was not of the people but of the schemers themselves
having broken the workers' unions and bound their shackles to the poor metal of
    materialism
having bought the men who grow the drug of hate and importing it every day to
    every city in our land,
and have heard them repeat the lie they believed as machines took over the too-
    human tasks of reproducing the inane
how when they created information highway production in the great white service
    economy of the world
we would all work far shorter hours and have more leisure time
and would read great books and write symphonies of desire...
Instead writing sympathies
as first one and then another of our comrades was forced from work
and had to move downward through the septic drain of society
so people in Argentina might buy more tv sets
so people here in our home town might buy more tv sets
so we could make rich the boys who told tv sitcoms of the rich
every night in our living rooms...
selling us Polaroids of where we were sending the founders of our prosperity.

It is enough.
It is time to stop
laying off the men and women who might be our sons and daughters
or giving them the job of merely slinging hamburgers
or playing their guitars to no one in hungry subways
staring out into the space of human history…
if we have been doing so only for the schemers
because every time one of us goes down for the benefit of another's paycheck integrity
and that paycheck goes down too to the MBA's promotion
and the MBA takes one more dollar home to feed his wife on our loss,
one more human song fades into the lights of neon used car lots…
every Lotto millionaire wannabe who has less chance than dying by lightning
but trusts his desperation to johnny jingo writers and finds his salvation in a bottle
> turned-up beneath a late-night street lamp,

who learns only in that way what he bought when he bought his tv dream
what he gave away his bright future for
what he bought his wife—how little he bought her—
goes into that fat man's wallet,
and it is time to slam it shut
to cut the credit cards in half and make him pay
make him put the song back into America by building
> *something*

Restore the arts Restore the songs you sing in dreaming
Restore the image that you learned when young was America,
because it is the image the dream the song that makes the
culture worth dying for
and America as it is isn't that at all anymore
on the super information age highway to oblivion…
the one world one mecca one flat idea world culture of the
elite is what it is going to…and we're all everyone of us left out.

Published by The Puddin'head Press

2005

Acknowledgments

"Finding Oneself in an American Fairytale" appeared in *Juice*

"Eyes," and "When It's Time to Go" appeared in *Spoon River Poetry Review*

"Lake Michigan" first appeared in *After Hours*, and was adapted to stage under the title *Jared Smith's "Lake Michigan"* for a 2004 opening in Chicago

"Things to Remember," and "Of Moons" appeared in *The Greenfield Review*

"Returning Home" appeared in *CrossCountry*

"Passage from Home" and "Mood in Grays" appeared in *Dacotah Territory*

"An Erosion" appeared in *U.T. Review*

"Erie" appeared in *Illinois Review*

"Talking to My Son" appeared in *The New York Quarterly*

"Controlled by Ghosts" has appeared in *Trail & Timberline* and at *ChicagoPoets.com*

"Seven Minutes Before the Bombs Drop" has appeared in *After Hours* and at *poetrypoetry.com*, linked to *Poets Against the War*

"Coming of Age" appeared in *DuPage Literary Arts Journal*

"Getting Ready to Move On," "Tossing Jobs Around Like Manhole Covers," and "When All Is Said" appeared first at *ChicagoPoets.com*

God is that than which nothing greater can be conceived.

—St. Anselm

What have we seen beyond our sunset fires
That lights again the way by which we came?

—Edwin Arlington Robinson

Getting Ready to Move On

The last flowers blaze their dry color
like Easter baskets left outside all year into the first freeze of autumn,
their reds and oranges flaming from dry frostbit stalks.
This is the last day after sixteen years we will tend them.
In the spring rains, a new enormous house of fieldstone
will fill this garden with its family of four and three-car garage.
This is the garden that glowed the golden color of my wife's hair,
gone cold now with memory and the need to be elsewhere.

We will not be here,
having followed the leaves in their last ecstasy,
The empty rooms of our children will have been torn down:
our children will be lying with their own in other beds.
They will come and go with the turning of books in far-away towns.

I think, if we are lucky, the photographs from inside our house
will be carried on a coyote's wail into the night of western mountains.
There will be parties by candlelight on desert slopes with desert friends.
There will be winter streams that lay a black ice over these years
so that we can skate over them dancing above our aging friends.
If we are lucky, there will be no pain in letting go.

Passage from Home

Far down   where the road went out to dust
flickers rose in thickets from our tires.
And that was where the girls went for their first affairs
   with rock
   with the waters
where their dry casings afterward rattled the earth
   as locust wings;
but also where they learned to grow eyes for seeing in the night.
There.   Here.
where the office buildings now stand
row upon circling row
forming natural arenas for the strips of meadow grass.
There is something sad about this town—
in the ease with which it perches in expectation
   of the coming boom
even when no children return at night to drink their milk before the fire.

A little town
formed of the webs of young thought
and abandoned in the granite of time;
a flat stretch beneath the volcanic columns of cumulus clouds
which hold the light for many hours
after the evening news is first turned on.

Mood in Grays

Snow fell last night
burrowing through the minds of white moths
whose crackled legs spring the shortness of life spans.

The sighs of the unfed
who turn down the liquid throat of dreams
having never been conceived
half-haunt the recorder taking notes
of blackbird shadows among the first reeds of day.

The turbulence of the father's oak
planted thirty years before earth took shape
prime-moves the cattle going home…
flicking ambitions in a dead man's skull
paving the way of forgotten trails.

Lake Michigan

Understanding Lake Michigan
    is like shoving a small straw into the nozzle of a fire hose
& sucking while someone turns the pressure up...
Twenty-two thousand square miles of surface pressure/
forty-five thousand four hundred and ten roughly if you include the Huron lobe
    narrowing down to between three and five miles in the Mackinac Straits
        —not that narrow even then
to be going through a straw and out through the back of your head;
        very few
that's like understanding Lake Michigan through a strand of neurons.
It's like broadband when you've got a phone modem stuck in your head.

        Heavy, rusting lake-to-lake freighters
        carrying dark-grained earth metals from the north country
        and light-grained earth grains from the east country
        down to the southern lake steel mills
        swirling among each other and some of them catching out
        into the chain of water narrowing to the St. Lawrence
        where they exchange cargo with the ocean freighters
        going off to Europe or north or down along the southern coast...
        deep rusting corridors of time containing life.

Try telling *that* Lake Michigan to the young stud selling *Streetwise* on the corner.
Try telling *that* to the businessman you meet from out of town;
it's not something you can put into everyday conversation.
I mean, it's big...
this thing that caused all the eastward bound limestone and iron ore
to back up against it and rise up into piles of office buildings.

        Where the wind blows it is cold and dangerous,
        and your hands bleed as they grab wet metal, cold, feeling nothing.
        You are a wraith of oil skin plastic held by knotted hemp in the constant gale
        and the buildings so close on shore and the eyes from the offices on shore

                    cannot reach you as the waters roil about your feet
                                 off Milwaukee Chicago Gary
                                                it is night
              and the dark is pierced with stars and corporate windows.

It ought to come through eventually though,
   maybe intimate talk like late at night,
us being sixty-eight percent water,
it sure as heck ought to come through for us in Chicago
                     awash in this
drawing our drinking water from the Lake,
that what comes into us is what thinks about what comes in…
is the Muskegon, Grand, Kalamazoo, Fox, and Menominee Rivers
   along with all their fish and plant life
               and human sweat
in the form of sulfur, coal dust, mercury & heavy metals,
   pesticides, fertilizers
and, well, fertilizers among other things we hold close.

                                  Curse and sing in the wind
                      as you batten the hatches, you lords of Lake Michigan.
                          Your flesh will be battered as the rocky basin itself
              and your lungs filled with icy cold 'til they can take no more…
                              then only you will fly as angels.

                      A great blue heron fishes the calumet.
                      It wades among a vertical landscape of greens.
                      Its sleek gray plumage towers over its domain,
                      and it picks from among the schools of fish
                            drawn to its shadow for shelter
                      so quickly that nothing is disturbed.

What comes into us in Chicago
comes down from the cold north woods as well,

from ground springs drawn from aquifers with hundred-year retentions,
                        sea of experience
from among the deep roots of hidden pines on unsold acreage,
swirling down along the whole western flank, stopping by Milwaukee and Green Bay,
fingering and then bulling its way through the impediments we've built up
        working at undercutting and filling in our built-in swamps
    and swirling itself out into arid dunes if it misses the city
and gets past the Calumet and other manmade harbors to the south
it hooks back up for another pass or it goes down inside itself.

                                Eyes bloody, faces creased with time and sun
             invisible in the nighttime until you have led the way and lit the lights,
                                      your clothing hanging in shrouds
                          your face looking upward from unclear distance
                                       and your lips silent and gone.

                Sitting around the table, thirty men from UC
                are compiling data sheets on their PCs.
                "You can get ten cars per interval node
                through this sector across this stretch of road
                block by block across the country." And NOAA,
                and EPA doing the same trick by cubic feet of lake
                compile the same to see what they can make
                when data are combined and you have a map.
                PCs to PCs data tap data tap data tap.

                I think I can see what we have here, says one.
                What can we sell it for?
                Hey, it's a life.

This thing is so big that when it breathes
                        are accorded
we reshape the city.

When it goes down in drought every heavy freighter on the lake
unloads 350 tons of cargo for every inch the water goes down to remain afloat;
now when you're talking ten-year drought that's a heap of jobs per inch
trickling out everywhere from the western quarries and mines
    to those rip-rap towers of glass along LaSalle
        to industrial centers in Germany and England or France
maybe nine or ten thousand tons per trip per ship lost when the rain don't fall,
and when you're talking heavy rains and heavy winter snow cycles
    then you're talking about giving land away because we build too close.

                              Saying something startling new
              about the young laughter in barrooms and casual getting to know
                    that goes on beneath bitter nights torn with rage.
                                  And you will succeed
                    you will in this city that comes from the earth
                        as much as the stars are from the earth
                       and as distant as thought reflecting off water

Either way, it's high-cost maintenance
    and it's in Chicago's bones…
this thing that came out of the last ice age
                the opportunity
left by something massive slouching down from the Arctic,
something like nothing else in all the world to fill the arteries of Chicago brawlers.
It takes a pig-headed fool, a hog butcher with a penchant for getting into fights
and a delight in coming out even but with new adrenaline in the blood;
It takes that Captain-of-the-Plains mentality to belly up to the bar here,
to recreate the grandeur of the glaciers and walk among them,
to reflect back the jagged ice floes of winter stacked up along the outer drive,
to grapple with this thing in all its seasons and take life deep.

        sometimes lightly as a sandpiper darting along the shore
        scrutinizing patterns in the way sand is piled on pebbles and
        grasping life from what is tossed upward by the elements

        From the Hancock observation deck
        cars disappear into your shadow.
        They do not have anything to do with you.
        You yourself are as tall as anything on the lake,
        and you are blind in the early morning sunlight.
        Nothing is disturbed.

It's a fang-toothed, snarling monster of an idea too,
this idea of ever making partnership with such an ancient relic.
Hard to think about while clinking your ice cubes together in The Prairie Restaurant,
        to reflect
but this lake has pulled the life from more men and women in Chicago
than any other natural force; and we keep on coming back like we need a fight
whether relishing the crafty hidden power of lights along the lake
    on a midnight cruise celebrating prom night
        or a sales meeting success night
           or a dinner with the out-of-towners
knowing that this is not something that will last unless we take it in/
or whether meeting the gales of trade straight on where cargoes shift and ships go down.
Seventy thousand tons of cargo shifting is a lot to think about,
and it's something makes a man learn to do his job carefully in the heartland.

        Sometimes a shear dress clinging to young hips
        pressed across a taut belly bearing an impossibly young birth
        with the sun setting just right along the shore…
        and she with her lips parted and moving silently
        so that you could almost hear them if you bedded her

I mean, this thing is big.
It brought the steel mills to the heartland.
You could see the train cars pulled up by the steel mills
    waiting for the men inside to finish pounding out long
    ribbons of steel into bands
    that wound back and forth across the factory floor curled
    around supporting posts with the heat roaring off it and the ribbon just
    flowing along except when it got
caught on something and then
go snapping off the supporting posts and I swear those workers would
        jump
    straight up high as their knees without pausing to think about it because
    if you didn't, you lost your legs cut clean off
    and everyone knew this
    and it was part of life
until the whistle blew and then everyone would take his lunch pail
and head for home but lining out squeezed against the factory wall outside
        on the experience
because that white-hot steel gave off so much heat still when it was piled
onto the trains. Talk about *Rust Belt?* To Hell with MBAs; it built America!!

    But either way or in whatever image before culmination it gets
        pulled away beneath your feet
    and you are standing as if on air, the cold
    thrill filling you and your framework your understanding
        filling with the cold waters of time. This
    is how you learn to work quickly and surely, Chicago man.

    Honey, what are *you* looking at?
    This is the third place I've been in tonight.
    Last week I was looking at the museums.
    I've been to the cafes. I'm always looking.
    I've tried a few on too, let me tell you,

> but I know what I'm looking for…
> cool, hard as thunder…gray as night,
> *I* know what I'm looking for.

You can still find those steel bars in every industrial nation in the world;
You can find American-specified steel piping under every American city built
   beyond the best specs. Washington or New York ever asked for,
bringing oil, and water, and natural gas and industry to every city.
And you can find those steel bars at the bottom of Lake Michigan as well.
It's not your garden-variety pond.

It is a deep body of water, and that means it rolls over every year;
as the seasons change, the cold ice water from the surface swirls down
and the dead debris from the bottom rises on an anaerobic cloud
while the bright, living water drives downward nine hundred twenty-three feet,
   scouring around the bottom
      swirling nutrients into the mix
         washing along the ragged boards of ships sunk long ago.
It's not so far, not too deep to go, to travel back two hundred years in time
to probe among the wreckage of commerce long forgotten…
                    they are participating in
to rise back and drop down again along a clear-lit tunnel of time
where the living and the dead pass constantly in this tunnel in the Midwest,
dancing past each other repeatedly as the seasons change.
The Lake itself can chill its surface 15 degrees Centigrade within 3 hours,
bringing with it whatever has lain upon the bottom until its time has come.
These are where the storm-beaten boats went down, where it is deep.
In shoals, where glaciers left their jagged boulders
are other ships with cargoes of death, reaching out to snare pleasure craft;
sometimes a fisherman's line hung with Christmas trees for salmon will catch,
and a dead man's fingers will hang on for a moment saying *come back*
Come back; all things are as they ever were and there is peace within the lake.
Things have not changed so much from when Marquette and Joliet were where you are.

A drop of water that enters the lake remains within it for 99 years before passing on.
All things are fluid here, no harsh banging upon the wind and rocks you know above;
just these cold dark caverns and their chandeliers of weed.
We will rise on silver wings in the spring, you and I.

                                                                                                  Yeah,
                              this rocking and turning platform
                     with its impending life and street corner
                                    leading nowhere
                                        is pretty special
                                            is the focus
                                              you've got
                                              is a window
                                     looking through time.

    The natives used to scare deer into the open by setting fire to the prairie.
    One whole side of the lake seemed to be in flame that ran
    high as the head of my horse, according to one pioneer's journal.
    It would blow in the wind and it was as if it were the wind.
    I have never been so scared or so drawn to anything in all my miles.

The numbers begin to mean less than nothing;
the tonnage of water and facts to be more than unconnected.
It is a big lake,
but not too big to rise from within itself
and be drawn down into the cribs that line its shore,
to be pulled inward through rock tunnels to the Chicago underground.
This lake is a masterful arena for pitting man and woman against the elements,
                                    before they are
for burying those that fail and forgetting those that win.
It is a lake without natural outlets,
a lake like the urn Grecian gods drank from that never emptied;
but every man and every woman in Chicago drinks from it.

Every man and every woman in Chicago carries the lake within them,
and every plant and blade of grass that draws its water from the lake
is likewise of the lake,
with a memory that has no memory
that can be seen.

The lake thinks with what is within you
and what is within you in greatest part, Chicago, is the lake.
It is pretty big.
It reaches up to swirl the jet streams that whip above our continent,
deflecting them north or south around its borders:
look at those loops you see on the weather map each night!
It is at the end of *Tornado Alley*,
a wall that breaks the elements,
                             a part of
and it is in us all more than we have ever known.
It is a hungry, ragged beast
that glimmers blue on the horizon of the ordinary,
tying every man who lives along its borders
                             it.
to every other man by everything we carry deep inside.

                             Somewhere over 787 rectangular boxes
                     filled with glassy eyes that have gone water into water
                        and have taken bone into water into time
                            are located just offshore looking up
                               where the strongest swimmers swim
                                    in the heartland
                                    at the bottom.

Controlled by Ghosts

The snows came in early over Monarch this year;
cold right behind them, whittling away at the firewood.
I stacked it extra high this year, seeing how thick the fur grew on the fox,
for all the good that did because it's already smaller now than usual.
I dragged dead aspens down the hill and chopped them up, piled them up
as long as my heart could take it this year; just until one day when I said
that's enough; that'll do it now;
and I went blank deep down in my bones and went inside and lit a fire.

The snows came in early this year, though, even so,
and the cold; it was so cold. And the snow was so deep you couldn't get out,
you couldn't climb the hills after awhile even when the sun was out.
You couldn't climb the hills to pull down any more wood, even if you had the heart.
The woodpile just kept getting smaller one day's heat at a time.
And the wind, it just kept coming in through the chinks in the wall,
so I'd sit there at night burning as little wood as I could and huddled
until my mind started wandering and I'd think about you.
I'd think about you and Pete going down to the store last winter,
his arm bringing you in under the wind when you turned the corner,
not that I could see that much up behind the aspens where I worked.

My whole life has been controlled by ghosts;
that's mostly what I think about as I take the last cord of wood, piece by piece,
take it in and pile it by the cast iron stove your Momma bought.
It was a Christmas present the year we built this house, black and hard,
sitting here in the middle of our home waiting for winter.
Well, it came, of course. It came early that year as well
but of course there was a thaw come February like there usually is.
Not this year, though, with the woodpile all but gone.
I saw Pete, I think, yesterday way down the road,
saw him walking almost lightly over the snow as if it wasn't deep at all,
standing near the corner where the two of you used to pause,
looking like he wasn't sure where he was meant to be going now.

Then gone, of course. I suppose I should have got more wood,
but I thought I'd got enough; always did before.
There's a first time always, I guess, the cold comes down
and stays around until it finds what it's looking for.

Seven Minutes Before the Bombs Drop

...everyone still has names.
Sand is gritting against my eyes when the wind blows,
scraping counterpoint to the dry coughs of my son beyond the wall.
There is no medicine that will help this, I think,
but music is playing on a radio down the street.
Everyone I know will be gathering there:
we will barter for what we need; trade scraggly chickens or dates for shoes;
trade shoes for drinking water before the sun gets high.
I will seek medicine among my friends.

Seven minutes before the bombs drop
we are sitting in the dim lights of a church reading poetry
talking with words meant for little animals we might keep tethered
or lock into our kitchens so they will not soil the rugs while we sleep.
Between the words, though, we are talking of other things,
are bartering whether we will wear chains about our necks
or will make it into old age in one piece ourselves;
and we are reflecting on the words of other solitary thinkers
who talked of war while drinking cognac in bomb shelters in the blitz.

Seven minutes before the bombs drop
we are crying, running, our bladders filled,
our muscles quickening as never before in Kansas,
and we thump our open hands down on throbbing metal fuselage.
We throw ourselves into cylinders that have only one direction to go.
The painted gray of the runway trembles, breaks loose, and falls away;
becomes the endlessly wide sere blankness of the sea...and then light
will begin beneath our wings. Sand into sand and dust into dust.
Testosterone may be a great thing, but it does not last without love.

I am going to go home when this evening ends
and sit with my wife and children around the dinner table;
we will light candles as a centerpiece, and we will drink wine.

I will turn the CD player on low and listen to the ancient songs;
the songs that are no longer written, and will cry.
Yes, I'm going to go there down the highway in my '96 Lumina;
faster than I should, outside the law, but in my Lumina.
That's okay; you can come too. You come too; there is no guilt
in holding onto each other in our despair through the miles;
there is no guilt unless we ever reelect the darkness that envelopes us.
We are the light, if only by the choice of fate and mystery of words.

Finding Oneself in an American Fairy Tale

An artist arch-backed to the room,
   flexing the flesh at the base of her spine, she twists subtly.
Gaunt street lamps glint through the gauze of her hair
and her lips part to speak of holy babies crawling in the alleys.
She croons to them, offers herself each evening,
for evenings are the times of native american fairy tales
as much as days are built of eurasian fantasies.

She is the girl who danced naked for boys even before reaching puberty,
whose eyes led them farther even than her gentle fingers could,
beckoning to wind-tossed prairies moist with april's yield;
yet she is supple only in the night,
for the day has caught her clutching at her pocketbook,
looking over her shoulder, doubting herself and her reservations.

She dreams and lights a candle,
and the candle is a coyote whose calls surround the city.
The ululations are stories of the earth mother and sky father,
of the happy turtle carrying the universe on its worn shell;
but they are tricks
she finds, waking to the crash of paul bunyon striding onto fifth avenue,
and the blue sky is the blue eyes of his babe dumb-faced over an empty land.

She would stop johnny appleseed in his tracks even now,
but she is an artist and impales herself upon him
taking him deeply so that the urgency of her body transforms his seeds
and their steel skeletons twist and groan in the wind as they grow.

A Quantum Species

                Life is that brief
          multiple point in the cosmos
where entropy and energy reverse themselves
                  in contemplation,
        a blemish on a gray monotony.

           All that matters
                agglomerates.
    A woman in red blouse/black slacks
passes suddenly between a light and her wall
                 is reflected
through the web I detect motion within all my molecules.
Her message is on the night as it passes into electrodes.
        .

              I am a spider
        tending its net between the stars,
    a quantum species seeking for security.

In Our Attraction to Electronic Media

We are dark in the heart of stone,
but one flint of light is enough to give you air.
You draw the air from that light and put it out.
You are alone.
The moon is rising above you
over a deserted field of dried grass
and the air is dark and cold.
You light a match
and the dry grass catches hold.
You are a fire lifting the dry life around you,
and are drawn yourself to the fire.

When I call you on the telephone, I am reaching out and stroking your flesh with my mind. But I see the telephone I call from, perched on its white plastic end table, rather than the muted candles you are surrounded by or the man who places his hands upon you so that you murmur uh-huh uh-huh as I try to tell you that I am with you in this place.

You are on fire and are the fire, lady,
at the same time that you rise twirling into the sky.
You are a campfire we built of driftwood on the beach,
and the ocean is moving in upon you without thought.
You are that fire, and yet, as evening draws deeper
you sit in front of your television set or computer net-
work is the alluring of us all, and is the heat that sends us up.

It is so hard to know
as each ember rises into the night,
whether it transfigures from the logs that give it birth
or from the gnats that with evening rise toward destiny.
The music of the waves are the same whichever way it goes.
We are a slow turtle dragging our bellies across the sand
to lay eggs in an environment so harsh we cannot long survive.

The embers rise on warmth or catch the currents where wind blows.
A lightning bug flickers green in the grass, an invitation to eternity.

Picking Up the Empty Packages

I have seen summer flicker in the flash of your legs running across evening lawns,
and have sought comfort in cold beers and hot charcoal grills,
in bluefish pulled from the cold Atlantic darkness charring with garlic sauce;
in laughter on aging wooden porches left behind by other families,
gazing beyond you and beyond the fences toward where crickets sing.

I am heavy as the night as I pile empty boxes and Styrofoam popcorn into plastic
    bags.
I wish that I could know that these are indeed only the empty husks,
the precious packaging that held meaning in…
but regardless it goes out now into mustiness and trucks and then the earth…
the Christmases and birthdays we have shared and put away.

I will keep the cards, hand-drawn or store-bought,
with their simple words and line-drawings
that go on forever into my brain.

Driving Small Town America

what is it to play michelangelo's adam
            and reach out a Sistine finger
                        to   BOMB
with a fingertip
            when nothing comes back at you?

Look to the video arcades of the service economy:
America is only days away from waging war in Iraq;
I paint with blood, and it is not recognized as blood, though
your work, America, has folded up with the streets of back hill towns
and your police force and your teachers and your firemen have boarded planes
that scrape the edge of night from your pallet and lay it deep

nobody counts the fish killed
by a rock falling out of another universe

in Mendota, La Moille, Princeton, Galesburg, Macomb, and Lewistown, Illinois,
in every little town and cluster of slatty shacks collapsed in between,
the streets are empty of strollers, shoppers, lovers;
the cafes are closing down
the town renovation and revitalization programs running down,
the nightlife nonexistent even the cruising of small town malls is gone.

If you make atoms behave like they behave in the beginning
when it is not the beginning
they will make a beginning that is like the birth of the universe

This is how Historic Americana along the 1950s gateways to tomorrow is playing out
                                                STILL/SILENT
around barren courthouse squares in the spring of two thousand and three
there are no newspapers that tell readers what is going on in Washington or the world
            or that have for christ's sake more than a few pages on the local issues
                        and who is doing what or marrying whom

there are no news stations on the radio or television that provide perspective
        if there can be any perspective
between the peeling rust of infrastructure we drive along inevitably
and the markers by the courthouses listing those who died in World Wars I and II:
64 names listed in granite in towns with no more than 200 families now—
as if some gigantic force had sucked all the vitality out of our past
and we have not yet caught up.

In the beginning is the word
        and it is   BOMB

Evening Along the Outer Banks

Because we are endless in our separation
        because in our separation we are infinitely far from each other
                because the shadows on the cave wall are insubstantial and have no depth
                      because we are by necessity one in our infinite separation
and the illusion is as permeable as limestone carved by rain
        and the limestone is formed from infinite forms become one
                and is washed away
                      and the shadows play upon its wall,
we wander these streets without direction
        and the broken street lamps are shaped in metals factories ignited deep
beneath the earth to burn dark upon our commerce and molded
        all to be the same,
facing up different streets and destinies laid out upon a grid.

Because we are tossing within our bodies,
        carrying within our minds,
                are tossing within our minds are our bodies
swept as through kelp beds off familiar shores
        our skin smooth against each other in creating or destroying
                and steeped in our sweat
we swim caught in this fabric we spin
                because
to reach out is to reach within ourselves and to breathe
is to take in what is outside and make ourselves anew,
we are spinning our skins from dry reeds on forgotten riverbanks
and are spinning our skins from the infertile roots of cotton plants on dying land
and are spinning our skins from polyester strands of fossil ferns
                in our reaching out
are the meshes we cannot reach through but through our weaving
from the abstract to the physical to the abstract
        there are the kelp and marsh grasses growing
                —the universes between them!—

and the cottons and the polyester polystyrenes we whisper into
become the disks and the clothes and the words we wear
swimming outward through the mesh we weave
   in seeking words we reach into the ether
      finding shadows on the limestone
disks we carry from computer to computer in our pockets,
rocketing into the dark each night from our interweb homes
   each day from our interwebbed offices leaving tracks
      traceable each to each along the hollow streets
we seek what is within us each.

Because our portals are our eyes
   because our portals are our mouths
      because our portals are our lungs that bring the world within us
and our lungs drive our thoughts and drive our fingers
      because, some say, our thumbs are opposed,
we build cell-like structure to match the meshes we create
because to create, we must take a moment to ourselves within the night together
because we enter the world through each others portals
and our beginnings are our endings.

An Erosion

Dark rivers which are not there
separate the grains of earth and roll
out among the particles which form our eastern glacial plains;
waters channeled from rains which do not come from here
quietly collected while no one looks
packaging themselves in cement and metal pipeways
circumventing/going under everything we are;
the great fishes which slide with the speed and stillness of thought
filling their dimensions.
Under highways and the flat pavement of apartment office buildings
they are descending devoid of thinking things,
carriers of dying specimens of vegetation,
they roll out in greater speed and volume
until they pass in one black leap upon the oceans.

And there where it comes to the surface...
He's sitting there turning your white belly in his mind
as it tumbles end over hairless end
somewhere where the artesian well brings it all
   to the surface
tumbling it through his workworn fingers...

...He stands there thumbs
knitted through his belt
or he squats there leering into the space before him,
but whatever/whoever/however he stands,
it is through the lean tiredness
he extends from beneath his brows
and reaching out caresses the earth with

so when he laughs
as he does now
when first thinking he is seeing

   your limbs flash
like distant fish…
and then again when he knows that they are not…
but he stands there
and he stands there.
The lights come on in factories along the shore
and in restaurants and he
watches the one wave disappearing into the next
and waits the wait of the fisherman…

leaning back, he flips a silver
             med
    al
       li
          on
     high
into the air above him where
it turns glittering inscription over inscription
in tight descending circles beneath the clouds.
He smiles as it traces through the trees.

Offshore a white bird rises from the waves
and dips into evening.

Erie

The far side of Erie
moves against our continent behind strong winds,
eating its way into shallow inlets,
cascading between countries.
On the far side, metal buckets capture what is lost from trees,
boiling it down to be sold to Americans.
Summer houses huddle in box-green door frames,
hanging from their shutters along dirt roads.

Louisiana jazz man carries his battered horn
into the swampland where the moss hanging from trees
is an envelope for secret communions.
Sometimes I am sure it is the river uncovering our song.
Sometimes an owl's wings in silhouette have the shape of his lips.
Always it is raining, and when you get beyond high-rise cities
paint is removed from buildings as quickly as put on.
We are far beneath the level of waves, where music plays
and undead animals occupy the shells of others' lives.

Between these
gray stones lie in a field
outside my hometown.
I see them but cannot find my way.
I have dreamt of them each June evening
while walking from here to there and back
listening for your name in the wind.
Water is as deep as it goes.

Talking to My Son

I want you to remember this:
how city stone in evening softens,
how, like limestone, the heaviness settles,
how what was meant gathers in caverns
sweating with the coolness of patience;
I want you to remember how translucent the stone
was in its reaching out, how
you were not sure where its boundaries ended.

I want you to remember
evening people are not the same as day;
that because they are fewer they are important
as the gray space settling between lamps;
that their force fields are cut sharp
as the crystal you drink from,
and their power to produce change uncertain,
since little happens in the city night
that has not happened before,
but when it does it is beyond control;
that there is no direct association
between a woman's words
and your love.

Eyes,

What have you done with the lakeshores
I have fished along each spring among the tall grasses
speckled with goldenrod and fiery purple loosestrife,
tinged with sunset swallowtail butterflies
        hastening each to each?

Wherever you have stored this
it is inside a hollow skull. Your hollow centers tell me this,
your round portals of hope leading into despair.
Yet the halos of tiger's-eye that border you
reflect the fringes of meadows that are always with you.

Why have I carried these vacant spaces with me
to fill them and carry them on mile beyond year if only to leave them here,
having no bottom and containing nothing or everything?
Why have you swept the horizons and stared into star-filled nights
and sought the inky darkness of words on pages written by the dead
if you are going to filter them into a bony bowl to be left behind?

Having Passed the Solstice

At the end of June, the country is dying,
shriveling its skin. People are going on through nothing,
televisionadscarsbythebumpercroploadbursting out of new car lots,
seeingweaponsofmassdestructiontoo in malls,
we reflect like a polished kitchen table by candlelight used to do.

The drought is severe this year.
Grasslands in the Great Plains suburbs are in flame,
and a culture that has no belongings to cast a shadow cannot stand.
The sea comes in to claim its own at last inch by inch and year by year,
as millennia ago, but as then it is a sea of salt where little holds.

A man tends what a man can tend and disregards the rest.
I have buried the parent generation of my family on both sides
before and after the Trade Towers fell and before Al-Qaeda was a base or a deception.
The trees around our little plot of land have been cut back from our lot in life
without knowing in their slow-growing hearts and heavy trunks the world has changed,
but the drought is severe this year and a man must do what a man can do and leave the rest.

There's a symptomatic breaking down, I think,
that has nothing to do with guns or renegades but with the seed of man
and what happens when it shrivels like a weed from too much feeding in bad ground.
There's not much pretty about weeds breaking through the bricks on dust-locked lots
with their thread-hair roots pushed above ground trying to steal water from the sun—
shallow roots open to an earth bright by day and a universe black beyond black beyond.
All that weed can do is put out acid from those roots and break more down to find the
   earth it came from.

Sometimes there comes a rain. Sometimes the roots take hold,
dig their way down into a softer soil formed from the things that lived before.
But they never believe even in a wordless way that "That's enough. That will hold."
They will always grow beyond the resources they have formed,
great leafy vegetation that knocks down houses and institutions when the year is good.

Imagination and the Man

A falcon landed in the apple tree outside my window yesterday:
a bird of the sky and high telephone poles, that would not act like this.
Yet he sat there, focusing the small twigs and leaves around him,
drawing the whole vast structure of the tree into his intensity.
Until in the end there was nothing but his eye that I was looking at;
all else moved around it as fog moves across a meadow.
I sat on the sofa facing him, not six feet and one pane of glass away.

It would be foolish to say I think that we were matched
or that we were bound together, but it is true that time binds and we were there.
Had either of us moved, the surface would have broken, mirrors shattered.
It was a touch of magic in my home, empty of people and filled with life.
And then it spread its wings, tangled briefly in the tightly wound limbs,
and was gone. I will not sleep tonight, nor for many more.

It Is Time

       It is time.
     Your hand reaches out and punches the button.

       It is time.
    Each morning the slab of your hand clamps down.

       It is time.
  To get up and drop your suit on your back and eat toast.

  Every morning
  It is the same time

And every morning we go out
  to the same meadows where you hunted yesterday
  and it is the same time
  and you stalk the same kind of game.

It takes time we do not know for a field to regenerate itself.
It takes time outside of a watch for a stream to flow clean with the swift gills of fish.
But every morning when the hunt goes out, we go out to the same field
picked so barren by now that the only game to eat is ourselves.
This heart that we keep clutched to our chests, eating hunched over at the end of day,
is stocked there by common taxes, and is bitter, and is our own.

      It is time
by another meaning in the dark soil above tundra line,
every morning when your hand clamps down on what is important,
there are very *unimportant* flowers close as our mountains,
paper thin whites and blues and yellows smaller than postage stamps,
brief as six weeks of winter in the sunshine days of August,
farther than a roadmap of our cities,

with petals rising one maybe two inches above the frozen soil
and roots reaching down five feet *pushing five feet* into the ice
each morning when your hand says it is time...
they are frozen into winter and into the rock soil beneath them,
but with their roots flexible even through the ice to twist aside from the rocks that surge
    beneath them.
From rocks that break loose from bedrock it is so cold,
heaving and rising through the soil like leviathans the size of school buses,
because of the buckling, creaking soil down where summer's heat does not go,

they smash their way up, even like your hand coming down on time.
And the unimportant flowers, still unthinking, shift their roots to escape severing.
There are the lichens also unlike you who live their lives on the bare rock of their
    necessity
so slowly but inevitably each lichen itself can live two thousand years.

        It is time
        but each morning your hand comes down
        and your body gets up for the feeding ground
at the same time even these rocks themselves rise from the ground
and silver thin root fingers swirl paste them into the darkness of earth-time.

Reflecting on the Visions

If I were Pablo Van Gogh
and were to go to a window, and looking out, say
I see a multifaceted tower of lights that moves when I move
and the sun gets in my eyes so that I squint and see bright swathes of color,
would I know if the far side of the window were backed with silver
and the gyrations of the tower were gusts of wind slamming against that thin sheet, or
would I know that slumping red and brown Monet beasts hunched down in fields,
and would I hurry to take their sketches as I imagined them;
or would I look at that flat misshapen beast slouching toward me
and say this is me because I recognize the ravages of war?

Would I hear John Cage playing in the music from a farther room?
And in such confusion, what would I tell you then, or where would I lean,
when I do not know the color of my eyes or shape of my limbs?
The photographs I have seen are of an old fat man with flappy hands,
not the lone wolf who streaks through silent streets at night.

I shall be Hamlet listening for rats behind the curtains,
and their toenails ticking on the castle floors will be the minute hands of clocks;
I will put them in a shining metal case and wear it on a chain beneath my vest
for important evening parties, for the white-haired Albert Einstein scribbling on a board.
If I were to go to the window again and again and again, I would take you all
and write that my name is Henry David Thorough and I will simplify,
and either I will miss it all or take it in.

The Lessons of Millennia

We learned that in the midst of ourselves we were most alone.
The best among us would sit in rooms filled with books of the dead.
The worst among us also, for that is where the words were written,
and the beginning was the word.
We learned that it was written in many languages and meant many things,
that it sent men into the spaces between stars or destroyed them,
that it was memory from one race of people to the next, from one
long-dead pioneer to the young descendent writings letters to her son
across a continent sitting in his room listening to rain fall outside his walls.
There was not much else, though we gave degrees for this,
and we changed the word; oh, we wrote whole technologies, whole analogies
and learned infinite separation of the inseparable in all detail.

What it came down to, though,
was I liked to have a drink in the evening…
drank of the grasses that grew golden on distant meadows
drawing into the hidden words of my own world,
having bought them on labeled bottles in the marketplace.
And the marketplace was the same for every one of us who bought,
whether Plato or Caesar or Mr. Jones,
whatever the choices was it really so different for any one of us then
when we drank the draught that brought us all together once again?

So Much Growing

Something to count the days by
        Red-hued husks from a dogwood
                Wind that issues seasons in

Our peach tree blooms in northern Illinois
having produced one swollen vulva in its life
which we sucked dry as the stone it grows from,
still specially sweet in its landscaped swirl of Bradford pears, flowering
   plum, magnolia cadence
working the soil for memories.

Ducks brooding in the flower bed on Easter
        beneath pines where magenta straw flowers grow
               so much growing at the edge of the great plains!

Doktor will see you now
something in your tummy yum yum
is eating its way out as despair or as tomorrow.
The last thing anyone will want to see of you
is the last thing they will ever see and will bury deep.
I do not want to think of ejaculations between bone
and yet in that blank socket lies
all the eyes you have seen and lips touched.

Within the Islands of Solitude

This season as the death chill grows upon us and our seeds are carefully stored,
wind shutters about us like a cat worries a raccoon. Tentative because
it might catch hold of what it's up against, but of course, wind isn't a thinking thing.
Wind is that which passes over all else, shudders dimly in the back of consciousness,
grabs hold of worm-worn wooden storage sheds filled with what we seek to hold
and hurls their boards apart to reveal the emptiness kept inside.

But the wind, the passing wave of change, is not itself what comes inside,
not when all the photographs and recipes and matchbooks have been stored
and been burst apart in immense conflagrations that the scope of time cannot hold.
These are dull thoughts in a dry land, but will not be eroded because
like granite beneath the fields, they lie beneath inhuman consciousness
tearing apart the bedrock that supports each green young thing,

A case in point: Achilles' armor washed in red, a battered thing
which life had emptied out of, leaving the empty space of a blind man's eyes inside
to describe those things beyond the scope of human consciousness,
to find words for the winds that carried ships of wisdom stored
and lost in seas that were crushed between jagged rocks, seas crushed because
even the water that fills our thoughts, that is our thoughts, cannot hold.

What then, if we could set our own sails anew might we seek to hold
beyond the goatskin saddlebags we carry and each rusted metal thing
we bring home to lay upon the necks of our children, who snicker because
we have got it wrong, they know; we have it wrong deep inside...
know somehow the grains we carefully selected, fermented, and stored,
are lost to our words, and with each draught distort our consciousness.

Blind men always are the greatest singers of inhuman consciousness
bringing forth the greatest dreams of men, dreams of the skull and what it can hold,
dreams of the ocean and continents beyond, of the sky and all that can't be stored
in cylindrical metered pipettes on lab benches, with each labeled thing a thing
that is unlike anything else there is when you get to the blankness deep inside.
Blind men are the heavy hitters in this, with their far-fetched imagery because

there is an emptiness that fills all water and the eyes of men, and because
water itself erodes all things and is filled itself with all things. Consciousness
among the other dragons, sculptures, *piano fortissimos* whirled about inside
wraps about itself in the vast oceans of space that lie about us and grabs hold

of the sun, the moon, a young girl's legs, of any image that can make this thing,
this goatskin bag we call ourselves worthy of being words, of thoughts that can be stored.

Because in the distance of time, wind isn't a thinking thing we seek to hold,
consciousness cannot be measured. In the traverse of our lives there is no thinking thing
inside the wind that distorts and shaves and spreads apart all things before they're stored.

Witnessing the Writer Who Tried to Raise a Family; Dark Matter at the Beginning of the 21st Century

We could have done so much
Had we not been waylaid by electronic screens,
thinking data was information;
thinking information was our job.

Thinking back, when I met you, I laughed
not because your cashmere sweater was one of Lot 345026
but because your timidly hopeful fingers had touched it,
so that when you put it over your young flesh you hoped
you would be something more refined or romantic than you are.
I knew then that that was impossible. I knew
something I have forgotten through the years,
and through the years we could have done so much

for you
and the tendrils of civilization
you plucked without knowing anything,
but believing that there was something worth it all in me…
and I, believing we knew everything,
stayed awake at night, not thinking about colleges or food or bills
but you

and out of that for all these years
as we have searched each other's needs across the country
turn forward the clock

take a man with a high level of education
who has learned to live among and serve those who have wealth
and has learned to generate capital in excess of expenditures
in a job that he has served for the primary benefit of those around him
        —the public good—
through the sun sere years when he thought he could *make a difference in the world,*

and through the years when the icon of innocent wife and children had a claim,
and let him be smart enough in his own skin that he does not put his life on credit,
and then and only then deprive him of his job through downsizing
when he is still young and in good health, and he will still
be bored
pursue sex
tear at the fabric of society
be dangerous to other men who are raising families, and if he is a poet
do something about it.
He may rape, riot, kill, or just do crossword puzzles as befits his nature.
He will be unhappy until someone wiser gives him destiny
or someone younger makes him young.
You cannot kill the onus of learning when you let it out of the jar;
you younger fellows take note, you bureaucrats and social engineers
take note lest ye be paid in ways you did not dream.

Gray suits gray
       landscapes clothes for the silent shark gliding
  his way around the coral landscapes. The shark draws no attention;
matches his environment silently;
manipulates the clown fish bright in their orange and white scarves
  bright colors that signal sexual attraction media coverage sales of gum-snapping jeans
   leaders of populist votes that get out the army and drive the guns across continents and
  oceans
without their even being aware as one then another twitches slightly to the right
looking exuberant come get me get me I'm the one;
he eats when he is hungry and is invisible when he is not;
he lives in wall street washington and the east coast corridors,
endangered gray, but muted
as the land is muted in all its colorations
forming patterns that merge into a star white light upon blackness,
one of many too many to be counted.

A society of arrogance and assurance,
but *la via del tren subterraneo es pelagrosa.*
Our gods are more of swan than of Aries,
though they do not act the part;
more of Aristophanes than of Euripides.
Proud Ilium, you have fallen so long ago you are in shards
described only in the words of a blind man
who saw the darkness of armor clattering around him
rather than the shadows of republic on the wall.

This is as things are after increasingly knowing everything for two thousand years.
We have eyes that we might perceive those things that give off light.
We have ears that we might perceive those things that give off sound.
We have writing that we might perceive those things that are dark matter
and make up all that we cannot see or hear, and that is by far the greater part:
it is a moot point. All things expand from the moot point by inverse ratio.

Somebody's got to pick up,
has to make the time to sort the days,
find out what happened between purchases from the store
       that are already stored on data discs for further purchasing indicators
              sweating the little things
someone has to judge the blank patterns because
that's what holds us together on the bank of Walden Pond
       not the purchases that are known
with our twenty-three rows of pea plants that someone somewhere stored away,
or to think about the things that were never written down about each blade of grass
              between them,
some bum who has no need to be told or sold the little things.

Does this have meaning,
that *in vino es veritas*, and we have come so far from our homes
to meet in a bottle before a candle in a dark-paneled room in a sophisticated mating dance

that we don't rut and sleep,
that I have stayed awake so many nights
thinking I wanted nothing but to lie in a field beneath the stars
      listening to crickets
            loved and loving in the eternal youth of animals
                 killed and killing without thought
except that there were children who wanted these things as well,
and since I hadn't gotten them maybe then they...
does this have meaning when you put on your sassy spring outfit
and go to town after so many days are gone.
Somebody has to take the time to think it through.

The Endless Chairs

School chairs lined up across a room
              empty in any room in any school in america
      are one-armed bandits waiting to take you in:
  Ya pays ya money, ya takes ya chances…
They are chairs sitting with one arm out flat, waiting for your notes,
waiting for you to try to pull them down.

Note that the chairs stand there after you have gone
       they stand there through the cold night
          they are so important that they are empty in the cold night.
They are egg boxes for various vicarious cargoes,
are refilled/re-emptied/receptacled long after you have gone,
are sitting there in a blank room, arms raised eternally.

You might paste the teachers and their textbooks, most of them,
on a long print scroll, wind it like a conveyor belt with mosaics
and press a button to keep the thing rolling around and turning out chairs;
a mosaic where only an occasional bitter bitten stranger—how rare—
  jumps down
to raise his own arms and lift them up against the stolid chairs, breaking them apart.

Note that the strangers who stand outside the chairs are the bearded ones, haggard ones,
the angry, bony witches that don't know *HOW GOODLY SIMPLE LIFE IS*
and expect someone lost within the chairs to Do something outside the class.
Note how quickly the administration packs them away, pastes them on the mural,
and how easy it is to give them empty marks in memory.

Tossing Jobs Around Like Manhole Covers

Between places that belong to other people
   there is no money.
        I think I will sell cars.
I will link data bases to windows.
I will look inside them and pick gaudy ornaments
that reflect the light of old movies.

Everyone is a clearing in the snow;
       a coming in;
             a vacuum.
Leaves that shaded us last spring
are brown bodies swirled across fields.
They are gathered in by our industry
         and it is silent.
We are waiting for someone to live.

A sound
      would make the air vibrate.
The cold would shatter, cascading to the floor.
     There would be
         a floor.

When All Is Said

Private First Class Williamson floats in a small rubber boat
on a wide and blank sea
feeling the swells of the ocean lifting him
      sliding sideways
           pushing against his flesh
  and circling
as though something powerful were holding him
to take him somewhere with a secret purpose.
The swells ripple at his fingertips and swirl his belly deep above
      some dark emptiness.
The sky is the horizon, and he is gray with evening.

He shoots his last flare high into an endless mist,
where magnesium roars into a statement of experience.
He is alone, cannot drink the water, cannot reach out any further,
is afraid that something powerful moves beneath him implacable.
He has circled the constellations, he finds, as darkness rises.

Again he fires his last flare in memory,
                  and it is a star;
    and the stars reach out with all their raging energy to answer him,
        and the arms of his lost companions far below reach
  upward
  as thirst fills his throat until his tongue blackens in his mouth.

He drinks from the waters, and the thirst fills his mind beneath the stars.
He is rocked with the blood of the lamb in his dreams.

To Remember US By

You drive me out of work
with your games
with your situation comedies
with your halftime announcers
with your video machines that are accountants
with your catlike attention to bugs in the corner
with your luxury cars with wheels that fall off
with your picture windows that come into my home online
with your financial pornographic striptease shows
with your short orders fast tippers businessman smiles
with your palm pilot fingers that rile my wallet
with your talking heads talking
with your fine shoes that cost more than I eat in a week
with your clothes sewn in sweatshops and sold in your stores
with your soles that feel nothing
with your games and your names and your thirsting for money
with your charges for medicines I wouldn't need without you.

I've sold off everything I have to you
given you my lungs and my lower intestine
my car my house my home
the books I spent my life writing
the flowers in my window boxes
my children and their future.
No apology. No hyperbole.

Wait

The child running toward you
        sun tumbling from her shoulders
                eyes bright as fish scales is a bomb
molded more from textbooks
        than the poverty of assembly lines.

When It's Time to Go

When you have done what you can do,
        when you have been thanked
and are standing with your back to an open stairway
and a stone courtyard of tradition surrounds you
        in all directions
                sometimes
                      you go inside
                              and listen
                                      to the walls.
They vibrate with madness
that is so dense it cannot scream.
It cannot flake off like the paint in your home.
It was quarried deep beneath the earth
        where it is dark
                and light comes only
                        with a chisel
                              or dynamite
                                      and is everlasting
except that some part of the stone retains darkness
and holds it deep within its heart
        while the boot soles of other hearts bounce off.
You wander there
        after the thanks
                and you go home.

Unhinged at Last

        I walk off the page of my calendar
  and
the h-suddenly
          -unters who tracked me 26 years are stunned. "He is
   outside the grid!"
               a bird
  I am aloft leaving only feathers against wind.

Your Room by Candlelight

There is no knowing most things.
Only the imagining.
Your words are clear drops of water
passing through sunlight. I see
the colors I have collected.

The Perfect Mirror

The lake is a mirror.
Mountains are bulked up against it in sunset, cradling.
Insects drop their life before spiraling from its surface.
The lake remembers briefly in spreading circles.

Mountains will wait a longer time before they move.

Trout Fishing Along the Allagash

A trout moves up into moonlight
and sucks life from the surface of his pool.
The life knows of nothing larger below it,
but is gone before it is aware of life.
Each day, year beyond year, the river dimples.
We are folded into our desks, ears clamped to a wire,
fingers tapping tabulations.

A Space Between Time

In the first three months, her new car
has measured out 1595 miles
of rain-swept black roads that I am unaware of. I can read
the numbers. I can see
the wheels, and feel their heavy erasers passing over us.

There is a space I do not know how to fill,
inhabited by fear-soaked suits waiting to be worn again.
These suits have flown about the country to speak in meeting halls
so many times they have nothing to fear from missing miles.
They carry the junk of hotel rooms in their pockets.
They carry the words of twenty five years lived alone.
I can enumerate
the deals. I can taste the cocktail glitter;
the meals. I can read what I have failed to do each day.

Things to Remember

(A Protagonist Poem in Nine Parts)

1.
The smoke detection device hanging by the kitchen
contains Radioactive Elements
    according to the label
and may someday save your life.
If it cracks or must be disposed of,
  you are ordered to send it to the factory.
Someone in your family must package it.

2.
All things are alive.
The gas storage tank ½ mile away is waiting
   for the perfect moment.

3.
You are not holding the wheel
as your wife or husband drives to work.
You are not even in the car.

4.
Sometimes you will think
you recognize a coat sleeve or a hat
passing out of reach in the corner of a crowd.
Sometimes it will follow you.

5.
The Christ child may even now
be leafing through a book of verse
   and reading Yeats.

6.
Oranges are sometimes green.

7.
If you walk to work
you will save yourself the cab fare.
Every taxi driver approaching the intersection
   is aware of that.
He wants to earn a living too.
There are six intersections to be crossed
   each morning.
He has twelve times to reach a decision each day.

8.
The can of mushroom soup
is three years old today
and is dented deeply on both sides.
It is the last can on the shelf.

9.
The sun is shining more days than not
somewhere within the world.

Of Moons

In the worlds of the pigeon
lying as wax below the air conditioner,
the air does not smell of birds;
there is no reason to walk through old feathers
   upon the ground.

I stretch the sun like a needle
      through the turrets of an old church in the Bowery
where glass bottle ships unhinge their sails;
this is tomorrow   in its only form
and seeds crackle like slingshots under feet.

Sweet Mother of the western plains,
   your son is forgotten where the crows eat out his liver
     in sweating bars   in the Great City,
the city of the plastic trees and artificial dust mops.
He does not speak your language any longer,
   building signal fires from aluminum canoes.
He cannot swim the mighty Hudson or Potomac or Mississippi
  in order to reach out to you;
     he would be lost upon the Colorado, although he pays paths to lose him more.
Your stone teeth are almost forgotten in the sudden quiet
of a farmer eating peaches in an Alaskan spring.

A pool of coins
sits under candlelight,
the object of attention
in a quiet room.
Men roll up their sleeves and curse
as sweat rolls down their hands.
The windows are vacant.

A pigeon tours beneath the clouds
in a vacuum
between stones and air,
and is hated from both sides—
a meal or a leaver of debris.
Its eyes are painted barns from Pennsylvania Dutch
and it walks among craters of the moon.
The year is early, and wings make hollow noises in the streets.

Coming of Age

The lantern lights on the screen make you unaware.
You focus on them and their dim halos,
but the white walls are your incubator and albumen.
They are Mother Hen, Mother Media, Mother Medea,
and your own wing flaps are scarce heard
tucked into your body and clipped off as they are.

It is written in the band about your ankle,
registered in the game warden's book for your collector.

When we made the Pullman cars, it was to pull men.
When we made the Pullman towns, it was to pool them.
When we made Carnegie mills and Model Ts, we built a caravansary.
When we built computers, we computed men. And then
when we built the Internet, we commuted them.
When we let the people in,
we let them pay the bill at the gates of moral bankruptcy,
and nailed them on Christmas messiah trees,
became cubicles watching walls across America
while America was watching us outsourcing prophecies.

Long life! Long productivity! Drink the drink.
Enhance life with the dance of lights
and we pull the mind of men apart again,
running ever faster to our smaller spaces
inside white painted rooms with airtight seals.
The warden waits to check us in.

The Last Snow Fell

I have stayed out in the snow a long time.
The wind blew it round beneath the street lamps
until they were turned to plaques of marble in the trees.
It is easier to understand everything when I am not by your side;
I stayed beneath the big tree in the meadow across from your home,
as you turned the house lights off and passed from room to room.
I stayed as the roads grew invisible and silent and wide.
I stayed, remembering what we planned to do and see

when we were still talking to each other and had plans
to share our memories only with each other; it was a long time.
The snow fell, laying blankets over me, turning the ground cold.
My bones were cold, my eyes dark, my flesh stretched parchment.
You will never know I did not mean to leave you to grow old;
nor to leave us apart forever that evening when I went.

Hollowman

Hollowman has no ears…
the bones in his head tremble.

Nothing yet registers
the bonework latticed beneath metal
or that Hollowman has gone,
has swept as smoke through the windows of his own skull;
his metal liquefies itself tirelessly
slowly filling Prism
eating at walls
until holes begin to curl their lips back
and the entire structure then
                       collapses
in acrid smoke of seething flesh.

Nothing then fills his veins
unformed perfect his mind
since nothing had come before
save shells singing their hollow oceans
    into time…

So, Here's, Then, to the People

So, here's then to the people who care:
who don't huddle in the dark cold corners of the city
but though screamed at by the wolves of money each day
can come back for one more round the next
or leave it alone if they want.

Here's to the children who believe
women and children are children and live forever
though childhood passes from them themselves
like the ball game with its perennial nine players
and go singing discovery forever into their hands.

Here's to the man who wears a gray suit
so that the twisted, scarred metal of his sides is hidden
so that his entrails can be contained to protect family:
to the man who wants his sons and daughters to know country air,
who wants them to sing the songs of sirens;
who in beating his brain out through the back of his skull
finds escape in the oceans beyond thought.

Here's to the woman who learns Business
thinking to match friendship with the boys she knew,
but finds mannequins in the aisles of fairy tales;
to the people who never had poetry written of them
because they have given their lives for something they don't understand,
and are poetry or would be if they spoke.

Here's to the people,
Remember the people!
What about the man who forged the gun, or the man who molded
the bullet that was employed by John Wilkes Booth…or by
  the man

who killed President Kennedy and Bobby Kennedy and Mary Jo
    Kopechne anyway
or the miner in the lead mine dragged down below light
to earn food in a radioactive afterglow.
Here's to the people.
Remember the people!
Molders of fortunes and nations,
as subtle as penicillin in a petri dish
or the cash register...
Here's to the people
writing ballads strummed in alleys...
to the saints!

Here's to men,
for being but men
is being God,
for it is that than which nothing greater can be conceived.

Brain Creature

Brain creature comes down from the hills
snuffling light through wrinkled nostrils,
pads its way among stone tombs,
studies the fire of figurines,
howling as it breaks shadow fingers.

*

Windmusk calls to itself

*

Consciousness fills itself with the abyss of
falling trees in silent films,
leaves becoming fingers
white with cold

*

Something begins to move inside the fragile bones of Hollowman.
Something that lies waiting in the nocturnal presence to
pull him into our time and north america filling his blood
    as a song that is history/
a song carrying other men and women in its bones…
a long drawn light exiting toward the horizon
a
bridge binding gelatin starlight to its length…
massive iron bones grinning out midnight's heat,
holding up the crush of commerce on floating pads of concrete
undulating over miles of silt washed down,
breathing life into its absence.

What fish pursue this river canyon now/
What scales tossed glittering where there is no sun?

There are no footsteps
marking their progress over stone
no wind
chilling a man's collar
no rattle to the timpani
welcoming his autumn eyes
as they open beginning the migratory sweeps of pale gray birds,
the dark crush of oceans toward equator
  and round again
a surging upward through earth gone soft.
His fingers will never come to the surface
nor will they cease pushing their way farther into the ocean
once they have left this bridge.
No one will speak his name
as they drive cars across this span.

They will earn their memories
will drive their wives to hospitals on the other side
hearing their blood pound with the wind against these girders
but they will miss this man who built their magic carpet.

Like moths
small white moths
settling their whirlwind courtship of fire
they will perish dust in dark.

              *

Birdman calls out into the gray mist surrounding him.
He sheds wings of molten candles
and cocks his head to
Infinity.
His heart fills with water

splashing its cool distance to the underground,
a memory of violence he carries within him.
                    *

Moonlaughter catches at your spine
fills the herringbone beneath your shirt.
You turn
your fingers kneading at the gray
pulling out your weight
in computer time...it goes
markachaggachagga markachaggachagga
boot soles on the intellect.

You have seen how your sun comes through
one spot in the cloud of autumn days
finding one tree burnished on your hill
isolating it in time
and memory.

You are a spindle of white
of milk drawn down by gravity
into a cupless lake of coffee
a Mississippi bayou heron tipped on eyeflesh
—a sleeter of motion beneath liquid—
drawing out concentric circles perhaps oolongs
where they brush against infringement
    then circling on again
concentricity rushing after its greater parts
but reaching down as well and warm,
folding like a Möbius monster in all directions forever...
unseeable as a blank white wall
you are embedded in

your brown eyes, fawns
leaping over logs before the gun goes off
first forged from autumn's leaves,
the color of your hair
or of my mouth hanging open in its sorrow
over sand and pebbles our feet move among,
moving among the cypress knees
we leave buried in our estuaries

the shattered crystalline reflection
    —these are real substances around you dissolving!!—
a ray of sunshine in clear water,

*

The people carry their desks outside.
They plug their typewriters into grassy plains
      their business fax machines into the trees
           their cell phone stock quotations into clouds
and listen to the slow call of soil,
signaling to each other how the trees respond.
Some of them take off their clothes.
Others open their collars and lie back.

This
is the peoples' choice.
It is their decision and for once
they have not forgotten the implications.
Pretty soon they get down from their swivel chairs
and smooth their hands along the ground.
Rising, they embrace.
They go off alone or in twos
listening with puzzled looks upon their faces.

                *
These are things that do not touch
        Hollowman.
He looks for a long time before disappearing into shadows.

He drops his wallet…
sleek black it wanders across fields,
gorging grass and flowers through multiple stomachs.

Motion seeps into his shell
but so slowly
that
without moving
from his case he is sailing
upright on his feet across a sky two hundred feet
above where people will turn in their fleshy machinery.

A telephone rings in his crystal,
and he of course
has no ear opening into the world
        his word is gold

It is someone
some part of our future
calling to say when
it is time you will know.
You will walk the moon
searching the inside shape of self.

                *

Because the earth in living could not speak
it was dead.

Because the furred animals were warm in night
and were not buildings with nametags with green water.
Because we could not imagine that stars in our own skulls
were worth the stars that our sons sought,
we could not speak,
but felt with the space between our ribs.

We go down to the rivers
filling crevices in earth
rolling where it rolls between stars
singing our sighs of molten metal
like a redwing blackbird on estuary's morning.

              *

Song comes down,
tears the marrow from our spines,
separates our groins with desireless fingers,
fills our feet with shoes for walking,
casts spiderwebs against nova suns in dew dawn.
Song is Song,
and its caviar rattles our memories
like the fence posts of hungry fields in autumn,
our words squat pumpkins rotting into loam.

Distance,
if you think of it,
is a star immense with molten helium
in its rushing upon you upon night;
a snowflake, a star,
small indefinitely small until it settles
upon your rivers and freezes them,
bringing night wolves soft as feathers into
shadow
singing the costume jewelry of untamed talons.

Where Images Become Imbued With Time

Published by The Puddin'head Press

2007

Acknowledgments

Various poems in this collection first appeared in print in the following literary journals:

"A Matter of Degrees," the first section of "Symmetries," and "The Intensity of Light" appeared in *The New York Quarterly*

"Along Back Roads from Illinois to Pennsylvania,""Wallpaper Memories," "Little Cowboy Geniuses," and "Not Time" appeared in *AfterHours*

"Father," and the first four sections of "Symmetries" printed as a set appeared in *Juice* and *The 2005 Juice Anthology*

"Nanotechnology Man" appeared in *Home Planet News*

"Observing the Constellations in Grand Central Station" appeared in *The Iconoclast*

"Storm King Mountain" appeared in *The Pedestal Magazine*

"Unforgiving" appeared in *The Bitter Oleander*

"A Mountain in a Suitcase," "Translucence," and "Why Put Up with This Anymore?" appeared in *Presa*

"Being Born of Bone," "The Hand-off," and "Helios" appeared in *The Seventh Quarry* (Wales)

This is the end of the whale-road and the whale...

—Robert Lowell

The planetary fragments broken lie;
Distance is dead and light can only die.

—Karl Shapiro

The Word That Had Many Voices

The word became a long drawn howling wind
stripping the flesh from men and babies and women.
It beat against the small bones of their inner ears,
and wailed into a crescendo of fear and hunger
that permeated every thought. The word
that was a simple follow-up to a smile between strangers
was gentle when it began and planted grains on dry land.
Bringing water it began to whisper and think on its own,
but it sounded gentle in the distance among the grasses
where the grasses took on life of their own and whispered back.
They whispered to the intestines of dairy cows, and milk flowed sweet
while the word formed another mouth to sound its need. The word
found its way around campfires on cold desert nights,
easing its way into the mind, burrowing into the earth,
melting down land where the grass would grow, setting up dichotomy,
it began to form lunch buckets and assembly lines which broke only
each day as evening swept new words across the prairies speaking
first by dream and then by horse and then by train and then by car and then
by jet and then by robot where the word became electronic data interchange,
where it sang the song of Circes lulling pigs to sleep while it built upon itself three
billion voices building the machinery of a word that could no longer be discerned.
There were so many ululations in the word that it beat a timpani within itself
and the timpani became another word, no longer a timid smile,
nor an engineering term, nor political solace, nor trade-off any longer, nor
the word in the beginning.

Storm King Mountain

Chewing on a stalk of jimson weed,
looking down from Storm King Mountain
where the river flowed its columns of autumn colors,
Pete and I would toss small bits of granite like paperweights
out over the trees and listen to see if we could hear them coming back.
Once in awhile we did hear a distant clink
like the meshings of a gear coming into place;
a squirrel's bright eye would leap from our fingers,
a barge of rusting iron would swirl about and pause on the river below.
It would be a dingy red square upon a blue ribbon
far removed from the sun igniting our valley.
Something dark is coming this way, he said.
I nodded, but what is a man to do.

There was a military academy below us.
There was Vietnam. There were heart attacks.
There were clocks with metal tongues counting our days.
There were gray-faced women with gay lit bows
wrought in foreign shops by lives long locked away.
And the sun was beating down upon us,
so that we shed our shirts and began to burn;
Would it be so bad, we thought,
if something dark were coming this way,
when we could see it all so very well.
We have the time to plan;
we have a vista spread about us.
We can feel the roots of the earth taking hold.

We looked to the sunsets and waves of grain to our west;
even there along the marsh-drawn margins of the river
where mallards and mergansers nest and long-legged egrets
stretch between two cosmologies to pull coins from the waters
while wild rice rises into evenings catching fire along its flaring tips.

Deer fill the dreams of our suburban alleyways,
always moving, shifting shadows at the edge of sight,
and wild maidens clasp them to their hearts, run bare-legged
into thickets of desire we cannot understand but will come to cope with.
Why would it be hard with all these flames of life
swaying with the waves of autumn and a rising sun:
If something dark were to come this way, it would be filled with light.

In time, a shirt turns into a thousand pounds of metal at 80 miles per hour.
It turns into thirty tons of metal at 100 miles per hour.
It turns into a factory of crushed stone where life sweats into the cellar seeps.
It turns into a lair built of fallen trees, wrought iron, and electric needles.
It becomes a game of rock-paper-scissors
where somehow the paper shears off mountainsides and cuts metal.
Shadows come crashing through our windowpanes
to take small pills at night from bedside tables;
and, yes, an older man needs to sleep sometimes while the world keeps up.
And, yes, I can sleep, and can still keep it up as well as any man:
Even when something dark is coming toward us I am eager to pump light into it.
There is nothing gentle in a big black box barreling down a concrete river,
though its heart and soul and every shadow within its bulk is filled
with grains of the earth that could feed an endless multitude.
Not with the sun's rays igniting all it touches at 100 miles per hour
contained within the dark.

Father,

your grandson is struck sterile
among choices you have left behind.
The compass that carried you through Eagle Scouts is gone;
the badges worn across your chest, dust like the degree from Harvard.
I am a cold point beneath the winter sky,
a dust mote upon a string played obbligato between galaxies,
and soon enough there will be no mountain meadows
for your descendants to walk among.

Darkness burns away on the wings of a moth
flaring itself into a place you have come to know.
The maples I climbed on have gone,
with no more power in their roots to shade your window.
The driveway I carried your suitcase along that last day
has been blacktopped three times that I know
and the weeping cherry you never knew was planted
by my son whom you never knew
and dwarfs a house on the other side of town.

You knew the lady slippers and mayapples,
showed me where tiger salamanders lay beneath logs,
called ground cover by all its varied names,
spoke 16 languages and read from the books of the dead,
strode with an urgency through urban forests
and took the train to work each day. Tickets, getting
tickets please. Sandwiches in paper bags.

The *aurora borealis* blows through the cells of my bone,
igniting them so that they are torn apart and scattered in the solar wind.
What was it that you wanted to achieve? Why
did we wear our tight shirt collars to expensive hotels
or spend long years sweating our fears into foreign sheets?
I am older now then you were on that day

when you lay down in a blueberry patch and died
on vacation beneath a Minnesota sky.

After the stroke, we had three days before you rose,
and the light in your eyes seemed to go on forever without finding words.
In listening ever since among the stars, I have been paralyzed
and have raised flawed children who are as wise as you
with no desire to pass it on.

The Alchemist's Stone

Joe Naper built a smithy at the edge of town
at a widening of the road, near the brook;
he wouldn't have far to go to carry water to cool the load.
Only cicadas matched his hammer against the steel long days.
Horses rode through night on wide blank eyes.
Grain came into town on metal feet and wagon wheels,
and Joe worked the smithy block year round, turning nails for homes,
turning yokes for oxen, heavy-handled blades for soil,
on this one-sided block of stone
that grew upon a field of tangled root and gain.
The corn doesn't grow here anymore
nor the grass grow eye high in the sunset wind.

As the sun rose, you could hear the hammer fall,
shaping the air and town around it as we walked to the fishing hole.
Lunch pails began to fill our hands as the sounds swelled out.
Whistles blew at noon and trains swept through
as wrenches, screws and scraps of steel congealed from air
and shattered among the debris of autumn leaves we
tripped among on our way to school, barefoot boys no more,
but soldiers carrying bayonets and lightning into night.
Cars came, malls opened, bands played from the metal he made,
and though Joe Naper is residing in the dust, he is forgotten;
his anvil which rings still concentric circles into permanence
is draped with spiderwebs in Mary Conlon's antique shop
where Mrs. Lilly hunts for gifts for home.
But the corn doesn't grow here anymore,
nor the grass grow eye high in the sunset wind.

Why Put Up with This Anymore?

Whether it is by spoken words or written ones,
men cannot bring a people together to extract wealth from what is natural,
men cannot pull iron or gold from the darkness that is earth,
men cannot shape steel to climb into the sky on cocktail wings,
men cannot herd men and girls into concrete towers
where nothing grows except their love for each other,
men cannot grow corn or wheat or marijuana or cocaine,
men cannot turn water or fossil fuel to the fiery entertainment of electricity,
men cannot carry their ill-gotten produce from one town into another,
men cannot plant seeds with any expectation of what they will become,
men cannot drive down a highway with no car and no hard surface,
men cannot remember where they are going or that they are alone or not,
men cannot lead invincible armies with evolving weapons,
men cannot even feed themselves or their wives or children
without your fluttering your lungs and your lips together
and without your fingers trembling on the edge of something great
and without growing up among others who likewise shape their lips around air,
telling stories that decide who will be the most inclusive mover of words,
whether journalists, engineers, generals, singers, politicians, or presidents,
there are ultimately no others who can come before you
whether it is by spoken words or written ones, Poet,
I cannot understand why you hang your head down
and skulk in alleys eating poverty with your words.

A Mountain in a Suitcase

A computer makes you think
that you do not grow.
A computer takes your words,
burnishing each in time
each
single
one
in the context of a splinter.
Ragged
pulled away from its roots
festering under the skin…

an angry thought
interlaced with desire to grow
stands out forever
with no context.
Twenty years from now
who will remember
the context of words are
grunts
you make trying to build a life…

the shavings that you leave behind
are not you, but things that do not grow.
They are leave-behinds that leave you better
in the context they leave behind
outside the computer,
but inside the computer they are twisted seeds
stored without water waiting to grow
without the context…

They are your calls in the night to your lover
and your subnotes to yourself to help you grow
striking an electrostatic charge that freezes them.
And they are carried in the hearts of your children.
And they are carried in the heart of your pink slip
in the digital photo of your leaving work
they are no more than pixels
in a box that remembers every cry of anguish

out
of
context

a mountain that fills the night
is packed into a suitcase
going from street lamp to street lamp
in the hardened hands of a muttering old man.

Symmetries

—after reading Symmetries of Culture
by Dorothy K. Washburn/Donald W. Crowe

I.

Weathered picket fences hold back
the cold; cradle the last dust dry husks of grain
blowing in across Montana plains white and fecund as a virgin bride.
On the one side, snow mounds drifted high, and the other much the same,
but as good an attempt as can be made to shift the blame
and shift the scales whatever bit can be wrought against the balances of universe.

A wind howls through these fingers as I hold them up,
slipping away between simple bone linkages, sweeping stars and planets
into slipstream assemblages that draw meaning out to lightlessness.
I could place these dim integers in a throttle grip of ghosts
and build structures that would enthrall us all. Yes,
I could model them and market them and sell them all
from where the wind whistles on these cold, hard plains
to where they hold back sand upon the east coast Outer Banks,
and still everything of value would trickle through
pausing long enough only to be seen and be forgotten before being lost.
Ten fingers, integers, post markers, fences retreating to forever
which lies as flat and pale as paper waiting for a message.
Though I step upon the empty grains of summer, or grains of silicate with which to
communicate, to build upon it a foundation, a field,
we dare not step between these ragged sentinels of insubstantial and uneven length.

What is between the spaces, the digital integers, the on-off lights,
escapes quickly when the sun goes down beyond the dunes.
The cry of a plover carried on autumn's tide before the surf is proof of this.
So much escapes into the dark when most of what we see is never seen.
The universe is dark matter thrown by dark energy held apart by integers,

and I suspect that one is one. I suspect I am the sea
and the cold barrenness, the hopeful foundation, of bone
that is as permeable as the plover's cry, and you and I are one.

II.

An ocean blows through your home.
Dark matter penetrates your flesh unsensed and is gone.
Nothing breathes. Nothing fills your lungs, for they are empty bags.
Your fingers are the current, yet they escape themselves
and meet themselves coming back.
They see as the moon pulls upward and the tide comes in,
or as the moon pulls outward and the tide comes in.
You have felt this in the Church or Synagogue or Mosque,
and would have written it but that your fingers see beyond themselves.
You would have spoken of it after walking mountain canyons
but that your lungs were meant more for breathing air.

What of the nautilus in time,
what of the gleaming pearl corridors that are the sand
building into a skeletal spiraled corridor of time that is a chamber
that erodes into sand and passes between our measurements beneath the waves?
What of the spiral as a thing itself that builds a continent
and erodes away.   What of the mineral core
of our planet distilled from infinite nova suns blown across night,
built into the spiral and eroded down mountain streams into the sea.
   How will it all regroup in time.   And where are we?

Think upon the many-chambered.
Think of Babylon with all its multilayered gardens
as a culture thinking in base 60. Think of spheres being measured all at once
in all their angles outward. Three hundred sixty points of arc
beyond and before the Great Bang the beginning prime mover in every direction.

Remember Babylonian stargazers eclipsing into runes of ruin, or earlier
remember the spaces between even those lines that are inscribed on cave walls
at the beginnings of symmetry...no boundaries...think of how you might think.

III.

I believe it was from the river end of Sutton Place in Manhattan I descended
a spiraled cement stairway and looked across the sunlit street where
that morning there were black helicopters buzzing heavy-headed overhead
          something going on
and I was surprised to note that right there where I had walked on lunch hour
beyond the waist high iron barred guardrail fence spiraling down
          —good fences make good neighbors, it might have said—
across the street swept totally clean of yesterday's dogs and pedestrians
lay the calm façade of the United Nations, so I paused,
looked behind me, read "They shall beat their swords into ploughshares"—Isaiah
and walked over the clean streets to pace unmolested the fenced-in playing fields.

A similar fence lay along the edge of the cement I walked
and beyond that the East River.
I was not far from Hellespont or Spuyten Duyvil,
nor from the Unicorn Tapestries the Rockefellers brought from Europe. Not far.

The same fence has followed me across the eastern seaboard in later years.
I have seen it lined up linear and intractable and reassuring
before the Indonesian Embassy in Washington and before the White House
and within the Old Executive Office Building and around the grounds of Virginia homes,
and even around old New England cemeteries...sometimes high and sometimes not,
but always keeping some things out and letting others in.
It's the sightless things you feel on the air that still come through,
the little things, invisible, that make you what you are;
and they're not linear.
They pass between the digits and digital equations.

I think it is only the residue of our lives
that can be mapped in electronic impulses…only the residue.
The vacuum of space itself is a compressible medium
yielding a B-Flat moan across infinite time.
Though we push ourselves outward across the linear planets
and dance down the rays of light beyond time in metal ships,
we are only passing through today,
barely touching the depthless surface of the word.

IV.

The fence
      standing upright through snow
            is the pattern.
The white is the salt of human sweat.

The pattern
      expressed in symmetries
            is one thing against the blankness of the infinite.
It is symbolic of our culture.
It is black and white in mathematical terms.

Beneath the salt of human sweat is color.
      Color gives dimension; it gives new symmetry,
           the symmetry of color
                making highways visible
making institutions.
      If you want to come in
           there should be no fence.
If you are in and are looking out
      it is white and there is a fence.

A shadow cast by the first ray of sun

      is a word
            becomes a break in monotony
that culture picks up.
The unshadowed
      is all that is unknown.

Break the pattern.
Speak loud.

A Matter of Degrees

Imagine a society of stargazers
who know only that the lights in the sky are round
and that year after year and generation after generation
those spheres pull the seasons into place behind them
while grain grows in rows that reach up toward them;
they would see these as spherical as opposed
to that which is linear and finite
and dies;
and the wise among them say
it is the edges of these spheres that are important
because it is the edges that always come back upon themselves
and the seasons change greatly in their progression
but the edges change little through age;
it is those little changes that change all things.
And the wise then study the edges of the spheres,
and they stand with their backs to each other
scanning the horizon in areas where there is no grain,
finding that each step gives them a different unit to view,
and pivoting slowly three hundred sixty steps
inch by inch circuitously to find degrees of perception.

These stargazers in their sheepskin coats
will grab at anything to remember. They will hammer rocks into pillars.
They will dig holes in the earth to melt down metal.
They will rip the skin of wild animals.
All to note down a system of 360 degrees that reaches out
toward those distant lights that control the warm spring rain.
Perhaps they will give degrees to each other.
They will study units until it is time to pass those units to another generation.
It too will go around in carefully measured steps.

Each unit will become a sphere
and each unit around that sphere will be another sphere.

The counting of 360s will be the counting of one.
Imagine that they build so many towers to reach out toward that one
that the earth becomes blanketed with metal walls and plate glass views of clouds.
Imagine then that they begin to hurl those towers themselves upward
forgetting that there is no upward in a sphere within a sphere
and that the stars are not indeed above them
but are in their very bones
back beyond time.

I've been there, have gone through it,
when the company wants its records back…

—Twenty Years of Empty Spaces in the Rolodex—

What they want when they come with boxes on Friday is all that was formatted;
They don't know that you can use what is there all about you…
the dried wood that can be painted on or notched,
the cave walls that become running bison,
the sand patterns, papyrus, stone tablets, electronic radio impulses…
these are the commandments handed down—use them all
within the dark container that sits behind the company desk.

Unforgiving

Streams of moonlight surged through your body:
I could not say how the moon had gotten there.
When I cut you open, and the cat people came out,
their eyes spilled embroidered diamonds.
Coyotes ghosted down suburban driveways
nosing among ashcans, scattering autumn before them.
I swore knee deep among our garden weeds last evening
with the fiber sinewed clutch of root memory about me.
Reaching down, I lifted a last winter squash from the earth
so that it nestled, an egg-white phallus in my hand.
On the one side of its shell was evening and a Midwest sunset;
On the other the dark earth that begat our last year together.
At its heart, the fiery orange flesh of thanks.
For months of darkness this strange flesh can lie silent,
its lives hidden inside thick wax shells.
It takes a hard knife to chock them open
and a firm hand that will not slip in blood.
Until a man can see himself
he will never see the 100,000 civilians dead in Iraq.
He will count the shells that he has skipped upon the sea.

At Christmas, Just Before Midnight

The women in the room stamp their feet
and crowd around each other in a great restlessness.
Like horses in the deep pockets of feedbags,
their eyes do not quite fit their circumstances.
There is a rawness that flares their nostrils.

In Age

whatever is light
has swept across your face:
the cumulus clouds of cottonwoods,
the grey feathered streak of sparrows homing into evening,
the green leaves of May maples melting into June.
Fifty-five years of even the softest kisses
wear down the flesh, erode the dreams.

But your eyes at eighty are the same
bright blue bordering the edges of the ordinary:
blue skied windows of passion frozen into experience,
treacherous black ice at your center
where so many men have slipped and fallen.
These orbs still are perfect and unweathered,
these equalizers that see all.

Snowball, Gregory Corso, and a Village Stoop

In November 2003 an albino gorilla named Snowball died in a zoo in Barcelona.
All things can go far/
No things have space or time.
The gorilla connects me with Gregory and with you.
It was born in New York's Bronx Zoo while I was in grad school
and Gregory was drinking Village nights and shooting them down/
that is to say,
he was writing poetry, and I was not so particular about what girls I knew
because I thought that I was writing poetry as well;
and it was poetry,
at least to the point when I came home one evening and he was outside on the stoop
we recognized each other and I sat down and listened and smoked.
He was bitter, locked out of the building by the girl upstairs,
and I would have let him in but thought he was better off away from her,
and she wasn't mine to own,
so shared a cheap night of cigarettes on a New York stoop.
And it wasn't long before he took on about how
a baby albino gorilla named Snowball had been born in the Bronx Zoo
not long ago
and how today its parents had fought over it and broken its arms.
Well, what can you expect, he said, if you treat animals like people
and you lock them up
and you crowd them out, of course they're going to go mad.
He waved his hands around and cried and cursed.
I recited his "Mad Yak" like I had the first time we encountered each other,
and we never heard about Snowball again until I did today,
but of course he who cared most never did
and I don't know about you.
The papers said albino gorillas are very rare
and this was the last known one in the world that died.

Translucence

for Chauncey

In the picture window, my dog sits
in this place which is his,
watching everything that happens
where he half dozes in the morning sun
as it warms his halo of carpeting.
He sees bright-eyed beetles go trumpeting mad uphill
and herds of small snow-suited children scrambling down
as warmth passes over him and into him.
He watches shadows lengthen dark darts across our yard
while I make numeric memos to myself, eyes closed.
And at the end of day, I'm not sure what he thinks
as the lights goes dark. I often find him still sitting there
staring into the darkness with eyes and ears alert, waiting
when I go passing quickly from room to room,
thinking or waiting for something to go by or come on in…
wondering maybe in some unsophisticated way
where the world goes when it goes away. Or, if like I
when the light comes on quickly like a symbol crashing to the floor
when it is dark outside and there is no world, he sees himself
shivering there in sudden inspiration before the glass wall.
Maybe it's just that we can't take too much light too long,
I say as I run my fingers through his long grown hair
just like we can't take too much night.
We need the change like all things need the change.
It has nothing to do with suns or moons or distant things
that we have not held close between our paws.

Dead People

I'm tired of dead people coming into the room
when we have sex. You never know
where they're going to stick their cold fingers.
Talk about mourning breath.

Being Born of Bone

Men become nightmares
behind the white paint boards of suburbia.
Pigmentation is drawn from minute skeletons
dredged from isolated farm ponds.
Dream catchers open their nets into night.

Fossil

Plants that have been dead so long they have withered beyond dust
turn turbines that reach through night to light our books.
These things that grew from the sun
and were buried in stone
are lamps
and we are the moths drawn to them.

Full Moon Above Main Street

I try to make myself aware of time, rather than clocks,
but am stifled by my shadows, standing shoulder to shoulder,
thickening the air on all sides. Perhaps
we have lived here too long even for the mountains.
If I do not have the strength to leave soon,
I will stay here until the earth grows cold.

Ka-ching!

It don't mean a thing
if it don't go *ka-ching!*

Scholars are nice and give good advice,
but they don't do a thing
since they're only coaching.

Computer storers like Gates
sometimes have what it takes,
but mostly they're stashing
far less than they're caching.

Something sounds right between the *ah* and the *ing*,
something simply metallic that makes our hearts sing.
Not the *ka* sound alone—who wants crows in their home?
But the catching and batching and otherwise snatching
of all that we want always answers *ka-ching*

Stroke!

A piece of fat in the artery
ends it.
The complexity of patterns
recognition of symmetries
echoing of histories;
understanding
a pot roast
becomes a blinding light.

Leaves and Spit

A wasp begins to work its suburban maple.
All day and into evening she eats
swirling her hands about her,
her saliva becoming arms and eyes,
passing leaves over her mouth,
chewing them up and spitting them out
cementing them into cells
that have meaning larger than anything she can understand.

She eats the sun where it gathers into leaves.
She pulls it from the sky, whose darkness is in her eyes,
and the darkness grows outward around her, until
into each pod of darkness she forms she spits light
and the light fills the darkness until it ruptures.

Briefly intensity whirs against the darkness
before dropping down into light
flying to be eaten.

Ramses Visits the Cradle of Democracy

Struggling to comprehend the Museum of Archeology and Anthropology
from a gray grained room down the street from The Wharton School,
Ramses' *bas*, despite the university and museums, does not speak economics.
It perceives a different kind of degrees, a muted room of Egyptian obelisks and sphinxes;
It is itself the sphinx with five engravings of the pharaoh's name along sand blasted sides;
its tail is strung around haunches, along its back warming its sphincter muscles.
The *bas* thinks upon Benjamin Franklin and James Madison who crafted the Declaration
       of Independence down the street.
In the thinking, it goes weird. Its head and shoulders that remained above the sand
through centuries of lifeless erosion are worn beyond the strength of its testicles;
his face no longer Ramses, but a grey elephant. His beard is the trunk, his headpiece the
       ears.

His eyes are the blank of egg-beaters, the formaldehyde of Dickey's *Sheep Child*
personified in sandstone. He is the centerpiece, looking out through the musculature of a
cat until the shadows fall; for then his life comes out and inhabits the living, after dark.
It draws energy from the city streets, the troubadours, the call girls,
penny ante stuff
that is all that he can see, for his *spiritus mundi* travels and partakes only at night:
Not sheepish in the least, it partakes of what he sees and believes is the best, poor tired
       king.

America, you are left behind upon mummified wings.
A half block away, the draft cover page of Darwin's *Origin of Species* is on display.
Linnaeus charts the sedimentary layers of history. The shops shut down at four.

Masks and Carved Animals

We live in semicircles of lust.
      A wind is blowing us away
           Autumn with its soiled ottomans
           Dust bunnies under rumpled beds
                  television sets and CD data impulse
                  striking invisible music into the air
        Spiraling between domed walls
Not reaching doors we entered by.

                  I would place a candle here
                  if there were a table to place it on.

Wallpaper Memories

On my desk is a desktop wallpaper backdrop
beneath excel-ent spreadsheets, realplayers, and instant messages.
It is of a broken, hollowed habitat of lava laid out before the 1780s
overlooking an arid, isolated ridge lying above the Pacific still.
I was there this year, walking the sands.

The men who laid it out are barren now, their bones long gone.
Trees and bushes grow where their women lay;
some green in the ocean wind and others whitened and fallen away;
still, four walls of blackened rock around a white sand floor
are now shifting in memory on a desk in Illinois…

Behind this wallpaper words are written,
temporary disturbances in electronic fields cached,
balances and assets recorded. Tectonic plates are shifting
in a very small way beneath our fingers.
I do not know that we can begin to measure the increments
with which we draw apart, or how we are reformed.

Where do these thoughts and images find you,
whom I last left standing in an empty railway station
as far before the beginning of computers as time itself?

Rivers in the Ocean

A vast green current divides upon itself in the north Atlantic
because of a decrease in solar activity or the passage of an ocean vessel—
it matters little when the tonnage of life presses down
and what is swept along is swept along and crushed by ambivalence
at depths of life where the sun has never been.
This coldness sweeps southward unseen, unsettling continents.

Your breath over the telephone wire
speaks tonight of a winter fire filling a white room
where a black piano sits unused. I know
your fingers would play the notes if I came to you.
But the time for playing has passed,
and whatever damage we might do the world
if we lived wrong ourselves has been done
and multiplied by our miscalculations.

What is set in spin is an empty eddy,
and will not be recognized no matter what its end effect.

An Arborist's Taxonomy

I like to think there were trees once
that met our every need, as the eucalyptus meets the need of the koala,
or dry grass rustling like ancient wings meets the need of locusts.
That we could not live apart from them in our symbiosis.

But these trees I find in my walks
are so filled with the aromas of peaches and apples and plums
that will unfold from delicate sun-filled blossoms,
I hardly know where to turn, each breath deeper than the one before.
So much to choose that must be harvested to make us whole!

Though I have raised these trees from boyhood,
made them part of me, and planned their balanced boughs, it is more for
     saying
how they are different one from another than how they are the same.
Coming down the road, you would say all their leaves are green
and, see, their stunted rows all bear fruit. They are an orchard.
You would have to wait until autumn had begun its harvesting of color
or step closer to see where we had gone wrong and the patchwork maze
was less and more than pattern seems.

The Hand-off

Heavy planes have flown over all night.
Somebody has issued orders.
I hear the newspaper flopped by my door.
The delivery boy is gone already before I hear.
There will be nothing in it but ads for real estate.
Mortgages are low. Everyone is buying houses they cannot afford:
Houses like mausoleums with Lexus hearses.
A child is lost in these rooms.
His eyes are windowpanes set off against mirrors.
Water drips somewhere down a corridor.
A chipped cup hangs by its handle in an empty cupboard.

The Intensity of Light

It comes in shells now,
a form of miniaturization of the barbaric bonfires
that lit distant shores and launched a thousand ships;
from something dark in the ground melted and misshapen
through a Menlo Park man's mind, a scene for motion pictures,
smaller and smaller until it could fit within collective comprehension;
grandma out on the back porch singing with crickets under her breath.
Reaching to light the tallow candles, blow away the smoke,
stopping mid-sweep to lean upon her broom, swoosh,
softer than a spider's scuttle
between floor boards.

Dust motes come down like paperweights on history...
        moth wings dusting the glass,
shadows fluttering in from all sides.

As I approach the house from different directions
        darting/sloping back like a barn swallow seeking morsels,
aspects of time and outlines shift,
neither being more nor less right, but lighted differently,
different flecks of flesh being swept from the air and obliterated on the tongue.

What is in these lights that sucks life from the world about us
        and fills our intellects?
How many insects have been enraptured, drawn in,
filled our ears with bloodthirsty whining or clumsy dust-mop wings
as we tried to catch the last glow of sun going beneath the plains?
Lamb chops from the skillet.
David Brinkley signing off.
Crickets.
Every effort has been expended in communicating.

When the first seventeen-year locusts swarmed across her hearth,
she was a young mother with twins: one blue-eyed, and the other dark.
It was the blue-eyed one that followed them six months later into the soil;
it was the dark one that would bring them back, she knew.
Latticework
is how she thinks of their wings;
latticework that is just wide enough for stars
        so far away we can only begin to measure the intensity of light.

Proud Ilium,

on the lawn at Ravinia.
Swan Lake
we on the expanse
cicadas in the trees of august heat
insects and the swallows
at five heights
the passenger jets
the fighters...contrails in sunset
A man came among us
jittering among us a violin
against transparent wings
Odysseus
Jesus
Laborer
I am but one of many Russian dolls.
The sun is darkening,
a train going into night.

Nationbuilding

Give someone a long enough childhood and he will endure almost anything in later years.
Give him a past that he can go back into with his children in later years…teach them well.
Give him bright plastic baubles to hang upon his boughs,
for these will hypnotize him, will find his center of peace;
we are drawn to brightness like moths to flame.
Train him like Pavlov's dogs to hear an angel's harp whenever food is laid before him,
for this is what it takes to make a country stronger than the men who make it.

The Gates Are Set to Close

Across the green green grass of home, iron-barred
gates are drawing down in the name of Liberty;
I take these items from the *Chicago Tribune* and the *New York Times*
in the week of May 15th, 2005 in the year of our days:
more than 80 highway gates are initially to be installed
to lock Chicago residents inside the city in an emergency;
automated they will clank down to the tintype tune of homeland security
  keeping inside what is bad and inside what is good in a suddenly frozen tableau;
and in Manhattan in turn tunnels and bridges will close
while police place little trinket locks on Washington Square Park at night
where the *Times* says "dissenters" tend to gather after dark,
and I used to sit long hours into the midnight music of folk guitar.

There are plans in place.
There are scenarios, and either way we go, you lose,
whether caged in bars or blown across the landscape.
I have no answer;
I do not know what cars come down our roads,
nor whose fingers turn what keys or send what impulse.
In this perfect storm we are covered with the ash of autumn
from four years and three thousand lives ago.
It is getting hard to breathe, America.

Little Cowboy Geniuses

A heaviness is settling on us,
a smog carrying the flaking cells of our industrial skin,
a cloud with hairy brown dust mites burrowing through it.
You cannot see them but they fill your pillows in evening;
they ride last roundups through the pages of your romances,
drop like cowboys from your scalp to coral dust bunnies.

It is a dust
wearing the old skin of minutes that have dried in a desert sun.

Fine Bone China

You were walking between the campus buildings
bright dreams and warm woolly jackets between the buildings
long hair brown in the sunlight blowing in the wind with books between
the buildings at Kent State
when sharp reports that would fill your years forever thudded into flesh
driving out the color of your eyes and the color of the children
you taught in your class
on American Literature: Philosophy of Romanticism
gunned down by the National Guard because they were carrying books
between classes on the campus of Kent State
instead of boxes of bullets in Vietnam.

You served me years later
bowls of homemade soup in your garden apartment in the Village;
and the soup was brewed from bones nestled in China,
from heavy American oxen from the Midwest
who lay down with a cleaver between their eyes
and filled the bowls you placed before us.

We couldn't fit our spoons down into the broth
between the bone and fine bone China.
They carried you away on Thorazine.

Not Time

A not understanding of time is a not understanding of symbols.
The wrist disc I wear leaks lithium, not time;
and it ticks, meant for men of my generation; it ticks without meaning
loud enough that I can hear it, not time, even above the engine as I drive.
We speak the social symbols: you have enough of me for this,
I care enough of you for that, not time or money for the other.
There is someone else for that.

I think of a shadow in a murky lake
rising into my awareness as if I were there.
I see it take the shape of a predator and then melt back.
By the time I arrive there will be nothing but moonlight.

The Little Things

It's the nearby things that bring us fear…the thrashing legs the feathered wings
      of cicadas scratching their eyes in parched summer leaves
      of commuters rushing to the too-late meeting
      of AIDS waiting behind every lover's eyes
      of unwatched packages ticking away in airport restrooms
      of Culex mosquitoes carrying West Nile along suburban streets
      of the dark-skinned man who runs the magazine stand on the corner
      of the middle-aged white man who walks his dog all day long
      of the dark earth which grows wheat and fruits and holds lakes
          irrigating into our dreams
      of anthrax-laden letters that come from long lost relatives
      of the lover going out the door and never looking back
      of the long long days and nights when nothing happens
nearby that is notable in any way that we can buy or sell or write of.

These are the little things that get beneath our skin and kill;
they are the terrorist bombs that will eliminate us but once,
and all the money that is spent to notify us and remind us of their presence,
the quickly glinting teeth, the televised giggle and guffaw, the barrage of ads,
are just to bring it all, the great nothing, back home within our bones,
to raise our anxiety to erase the melodies of largeness from our minds.

But it is the very large and massively immeasurable that leads to life, the pull and balance
      of a tide bringing nutrients to estuaries
      of the moon balanced in a groove about our earth
          drawing crickets and owls into our darkness of lightning bugs
      of the smallest tug from Pluto keeping us from spiraling into the sun like nine
          egg crates crafted of burned-out ash
      of the Fallopian tubes that carry Janus seeds from nonexistence to beyond
      of two sets of pupils dilating into each other's space where there is nothing
          because they are infinite bowls captured within bone
which look toward life and light as a rabbit trembling at dawn on a suburban lawn.

This is where life has come from, this giving out into others, is where it comes from, this taking into ourselves those things which are farthest from us and ease our sleep; from these we build whatever we have built that does not shatter walls
nor burn libraries.

With No Return Addresses

This is a white Christmas coming on, snow falling
after years that the plows have chained away.
Beethoven is playing on the radio downstairs.
I am writing addresses carefully on packages
on old boxes that carried other things to this house
and sending them off not, it occurs to me, to people,
but to addresses, numbers, in cities on a grid.

Each number disappearing beneath gilt ribbons
opens out far from where I can see it
to parties filling, neighbors coming in, laughter,
children coming down the stairs in night clothes
their eyes as bright as all they cannot understand,
factories letting out into the cold metal silence of winter
and the wind ticking glints of snow against silence.

I want you to open this box the way I see you,
and your soft hands to curl about my gifts
with that intimate knowledge that says you know I am not there.
I want small grey mice to snuggle back into their dens,
and warm cocoa to fill the corners of your mind.

I add other boxes to the stack as well,
carefully inking the numbers of palaces and asylums
where I have lived and send them out
      with no return addresses marked.

Helios

I take my understandings
from cows that feed all springtime in the meadows,
from trout preparing life voraciously beneath wintered streams,
from cabbages growing to fruition outside my kitchen window.
I gather these pieces of light
in my evening walks and bring them back to the table.

And so these diverse moments build my bones,
and Helios comes to me with the grace of life
sauntering in its own way along country paths
I have not yet known but been a part of.

What Light?

What light would be lost,
how much warmth from the ground beneath our feet,
if all the stars but our sun were to go out.
Each one insignificant…but all of them,
I think that we would freeze.

Nanotechnology Man

gets every atom in the right place,
does not measure his life in coffee spoons, but in nanos.
Now this now that, nah this nah that,
is very particular and very slippery
can repel water or turn coal to diamond at great cost
can walk upside down on the glass ceiling
is smaller than you and therefore larger
is a classified document in jpg
expanded far beyond the smallest pixel of identity
is above the lego block universe of mass consumerism

is a building block for something
that slides away in tight fitting white coats.

Roadhouse Restaurant & Grill

Two girls are sitting on the curb as I drive by,
one putting on her roller blades and the other restraining
a large black Labrador eager to move on,
wrapping its leash about the handle of a scooter.
This is an entertainment or a disaster about to happen:
two young brown-haired girls in autumn
depending on the training of the dog and likelihood of traffic.
Three souls push off, a screen of color-tinted leaves between us,
a plate of glass, and a long, long flight of stairs.

In the Roadhouse Restaurant & Grill
a pale shadow pushes a damp mop between chairs,
leans forward, thinks of college, leans back and moves on.
Think of Baudelaire, I say, drawing green sketches of men upon my tablecloth;
think of Modigliani and twisted shapes, I say, as I count out a tip
and chew the chef's tartar. I give her 40%
and the solemn promise never to look back.

Big things come from little towns,
from amorphous shapes that pass through institutions
learning languages that are not their own.
What would it take to warp a man's flesh so,
and what flies back into the night between the leaves?

Where Colors End,

Where shape begins,
without form myself
I have come here to speak for you,
to seek words as does darkness between the trees.
Make of me your lips.
There are many who have disappeared
in this instant between Charles Kuralt
and the stone cold buildings we walk among.
Open a beer. Put it down.
There is a cold circle on the table and on your palm.
Laughter is a ripple of molecules.
It is an echo of transference between the known
and the place that light travels to.
Perhaps the traveling never ends;
just gets softer, gentler, more elusive,
and becomes the desperate depth of darkness.

Come into me so that I may speak
as you would without the chandeliers,
as you would without the little pills on your nightstand.
I will be awake after the shadows are turned off.

Observing the Constellations in Grand Central Station

On a starry night beneath a dome that covers a station of unfilled trains
at one a.m. we can feel Vincent Van Gogh at Arles
and the madness that blows across him as he leans into the canvas
chiseling with his palette knife, grunting,
swirling his blue golden fingers across the sky
to obliterate the small fences that form our sanity.

So many things can be seen when put in a different range of colors.
In infrared, looking toward the distant stars,
galaxies are born where there was darkness.
Your lips press against the smoky rim of 50-year-old Scotch
and that madness filters between us. Fifty years
of grains growing as life grows and then dissipating into time.
Young lovers lying in the sun until their flesh is gone
and the golden fields are desert red and dry.

I think we are a Martian landscape
and the air has left us over countless generations.
The seas have gone dry or settled into the frozen soil of our dreams.
Our bones are left behind in the craters of asteroids.
The canals we shaped and drink from are a dream
set through myopic telescopes before we were born.
But you are there before me.

But it is the light I concentrate on.
The light in your eyes reflected from candles on the table.
The light in the grains grown dark and illuminated from within.
The light in your eyes and the pressure in my groin,
and the distant years that separate us from what should have been.
Choice is choice and a madman matters little in the scheme.

We talked of Arles and Mesopotamia, of Plato and of Aristotle,
You stayed behind, and I
was left to remember the beer dust sawdust on the floor
was as extensive as your mind on Saturday night
and the long train home we took in the morning
paid union men who sent their little girls to school
and punched tickets every day.

Asking Forgiveness

        tapping a white cane before him
     a man explores the corners of his universe
   as cold spring rain pours down his collar. A taxi
pulls over to pick up a woman waiting up ahead and a curtain of water washes over him.
                 He smells her perfume.
               It is drenched with memories.
              Beyond that it has no meaning,
               but he metronome-times it anyway.
        everything passing within the white arc
      means something…the hidden swirls of wind along the gutter
     most of us miss as they sweep a night's detritus about our feet. The postal box
    dented and rusting that a dog has peed on recently is real too.
The lamp post that spreads a light that does not reach his eyes snubs him aside.
                So unkempt man huddled
             against the elements is blind.
               The words he speaks are dark,
               and he speaks them to himself.
       a lot of balls it takes to walk the street
        at dawn when the sun is out, completely out, and it is night.
      You've seen him too, then? Rattling along Park Avenue
     coming out of a restaurant with his face pressed against the swinging door
    and a happy, dopey smile that wraps us all up in a paper bag blown into the wind
Last I heard, he was in St. Paul. Maybe Portland. Juneau is undoubtedly too far north
                Picture him like postcards
             written in Sanskrit and left in closets
              that he pops out of to his amazement.
             Like you, he talks to the darkness and hears the wind

Along Back Roads from Illinois to Pennsylvania

We spent that night in a motel room
so small you couldn't turn around without knocking the liquor off the table,
and we drank until we couldn't hear the rain outside.
But we were hard onto the highway
and all night we could hear trucks grinding their way through paper walls
until we imagined them as waves upon a shore
sweeping us along into the grayness of another day.

The next morning we stopped at Hawk Mountain Sanctuary
and after drinking from hand-picked imported coffee beans in a gift shop
climbed through low hanging clouds into the eastern flyway
where 20,000 raptors per month fly down from Canada
to wherever dreams of prey go when going over our country
in the guise of black vultures, ospreys, red tails, buteos, golden and bald eagles,
even little gray feathered birds twitching from leaf to leaf among the thickets,
spanning a continent of piney trees which roads have left behind.
I had my binoculars and camera, and you your notes;
and it was good.
It was good to see these birds which had been numbers on a computer screen,
had been tables inoculated onto a computer screen in my study in Illinois
separate from the fish that fled from marshy fields into their gullets in evening.
It was good to see them whole at last, moving out like heavy bombers
from the pellets of digested bone they dropped among the pines,
from the screaming flesh of small rabbits that suddenly found flight,
it was good to feel the strength of these birds and see the land from afar.

Now again, I know,
we will attempt to turn these taloned feathers
into dark marks upon white sheets of paper, present them in classrooms;
say the words out loud, trace the distance between wings, note the silhouettes.
I have a picture of a man squinting into the sun from Hawk Mountain
now among my data sheets.

After Sundown at Rye Beach

The fishing fields I dream are wild wide vales of long grasses
crossed by glass clear rills, rolling hillocks, wildflowers
and slowly swimming fish that eat the land with their eyes—
packing people, homes, and seasonal shift within their eyes.
And I, stalking them for years imagining them always salmon or trout,
I muse immutable alone at night across marshy autumnal grounds.
Boys bring their tin cans and dads down to the shore,
but these things neither catch nor weigh flash of scale on sun,
and gradually become as unassuming as barren boulders set random in the soil.

Together we are walking west along Long Island,
wading down city causeways to where the Sound is bordered by suburban bush.
Friday fishermen are casting to stripers from porches and amusement park promenades;
we wait for the tide to come in upon them in stubborn silence.
Boats leave from someone else's driveway and drift away offshore.

Tonight we have been back to the hills and streams of home,
and this time these are my kind of fish. I am at peace.
The streams flow down driveways and over lawns,
and the fish are no longer salmon or stripers, but are other things as well...
bass with big droopy heads floating above them like exotic goldfish,
fat harbor seals shaped like pillows swathed in black and white patches like guinea pigs,
giant chubs the size of sea turtles, and snouty things with piggy tails for noses.
The air is cool and misty, the men are wearing white straw boaters,
the women Easter bonnets, the children bland blue eyes.

You catch the biggest fish, jumping in and embracing it with your arms,
splashing and laughing. I hook fish this time too,
big and indecipherable. But I catch bushes mostly;
mostly I catch neighbors' bushes or screen doors. They come to help remove the barbs,
standing patiently, wondering how I caught my lures upon their lives,
probing my metal with their fingers in such silence
that I have to explain I never catch the fish.

Where the Farthest Galaxies Roar into Nothingness

I.

*blackness dropping into a hole
emits a universal B-flat hum.
All things
vibrate to it
clearly in frequency until something stops them
and they shut down, flying apart.*

As I lean toward you, cheap candles in plastic globes
light your eyes above dark mahogany;
cigarette smoke and years and CD music flow
across your gaze, your flesh still tense.

Everything I left unsaid in that room
has come to pass
or is becoming
except that I can no longer tell you,
can no longer press my fingers urgently against you.

Accelerate atomic particles to nearly the speed of light
(pour beer here)
*as we do in our laboratories every day; we are sending them into the future
because an object approaching the speed of light moves forward through
relative time.*
(ah…)

Focus on conflagration and chaos as the future;
if you find pattern in chaos there will be a future to share.
If there is a pattern in the black beyond the vacuum of space
out beyond time where the farthest galaxies roar into nothingness,
then there is an echo in your eyes

as you sit laughing with your friends drinking jokes into mythologies
struggling to get closer to the girl with too tight silks
roaring louder than any other man in the dimmed hall
as if it mattered that your penis would be within her sooner and longer than any other
    man's
and that your children born of your union and of our state
would be so controlled and so sheltered and so driven by your paycheck
that the one bright reflection of a candle's light in your eye this evening in a dark room
would have some manner of being that is worth it all because it is reflected
out there beyond the beginning of time.

II.

It doesn't matter if there is.
What matters is the entrance…the sawdust floor
the heavy smell of beer and wetness
       and of course the candles
     jukebox with flashing lights
the gleam of brass back chairs and polished oak
   your sweater white against your breasts your long blonde hair
when we were going anywhere
I didn't separate any part of you in my mind
there were not your so soft fingers your deep gray eyes your lips
certainly not your tight pink nipples nor your glorious round rump
your taut legs that could dance forever along my sides
these came very much later and though important
       these were separate only as I grew older
            or you more distant
because every part of me was focused on you
and in the beginning the words were in your voice.

It does not matter where you are now;
I will still pay the bill for any drink to touch your lips.

There is no science in this room
nor in the laughter neither male nor female
nor the distance with which the sidewalk weaves away
when we leave alone if we leave without each other.
                    again
having argued about art or who did what to whom
         who cheated where at what time
              is very extremely unimportant
                  now
 when I look back without any way of telling you,
when you may be no more than the glow of a candle in memory
you gave me thoughts that started all this into being
in a desolate space that I had not dreamed
nor had you;
this science and life thing this political thing this
series of things that people talk about in terms of money
this material thing is so much bigger
         but less important in driving us
               than that brief flicker in your eye
                        signifying that it was time to leave.

III.

Life was but a bar on Astor Place with sawdust and peanut shells
where we got away from everything,
yet it was the biggest thing we ever had.
I don't know how many girls I drank to there after you left,
nor how many men took you home with them.
The night is larger and lighter than either one of us.

Detonation of an atomic bomb propels matter beyond us
forward through time

>   *beyond   our universe*
> *into a future that is beyond fire beyond light beyond darkness.*
> *So does a cyclotron; Webster's should define it thus.*
> *(I have worked around them. I'm sorry that I bore you.)*
> *Certainly, there are no data stored there*
>   *no CDs to take it in no wireless worldwide web*
>   *no picture phones.*

But we didn't talk of that when we drank our beer and talked poetry.
                   Never.
We talked of nakedness, of walking into the coldness of politics or business
armed with ruthless and restless love. Your eyes were solar coronas
flaring outward from a fertile moon across infinite miles of total eclipse;
your life shining goldenly around the darkness,
for it is the darkness at your center that enlarges over your shutter,
and the nothing is but a cover for all our thoughts,
not the cold stone orb our physical universe provides.
Shadowed leaves on sidewalks lie in multifolded tiers.
I walk among them mouth open. What happens to the rest of my body
       is probably meaningless.

IV.

We do little things,
  any one among us,
in little groups…

small fish darting in schools
grabbing morsels from pebbles in tidal pools.
We're getting it wrong;
when things pop into existence—
subatomic particles suddenly appearing in laboratories
     in spaces all about us and then gone—

it isn't that they are popping into existence,
but are passing
are with us briefly and then gone
are the vanguards of something vast coming toward us
with all its complex interlocking structured particles with some of them
coming faster than others because
we can't get anywhere all at once none of us can.
Time is space and a particle moving through time
is a small bright flash in a tidal pool.
Trust the naturalists who walk the fields.

> *What was glowing in your eyes*
> *pulsing from your darker center all those years ago?*
> *What fueled the fire; ourselves or something other.*
> *It does not matter, for our bodies have been the means by which we carry on.*
> *After the nova, the expansion…and then everything collapses…*
> *light is drawn in, leaving coronal arches.*
> *The books you have read, the faces searched and loves ignored.*

Hungry Charlie's mouth was wide open
and I reached in and took you out
for one bright moment when the sun eclipsed behind our moon
and the maple leaves of Brooklyn layered two-tiered shadows
as they do only when once in a lifetime comes along.

V.

> There are two kinds of sciences, I like to think.
> One that is suspicious, incisive,
> cut into the infinitely small searching for failure.
> It believes in the honesty of deception.
> Its Achilles heel and Holy Grail are death.

There is another kind of science
that is expansive in the sense of water
percolating through stones until *they* become water.
It weighs the balances of the unbalanceable.

There is no third science
that determines whether any of this matters.

Best Not to Know a Town Too Well

You don't want to be on Clary Street in Biested Township
on May thirteenth, if what the locals say is true.
I've been there the morning of the day before
and have seen the orange police barricades
trashed one on top of another at each intersection
all along the cemetery fence
where the paved roads would go if not for the dead.
I've seen the banners out, the tense waiting on the faces
that morning before the town closes down
and visitors are turned away.
Tom Cowen, who was officer Cowen before the drinking,
told me how the winds were going to come up that night
sweeping the grass from graves and the stones from their mounds,
opening the marble statuary so that dark things that slide between fences
can come out into the night air and rattle around like keys in your pocket.
No telling what they come for each year, he said,
but the town folk will be back at their jobs the day after.
I used to work there; I should know, and every town's a little different.
It's best not to know a town too well, or why they built it there.

In the Beginning

When you get to the end of the road, how do you know?
The trees growing there are no more solid than your hands.
The guardrails may be stepped over. A deer path
tells your eyes it is too narrow for you;
plants are growing there between the footfalls,
but when you get to the end of the road life begins.

Published by Higganum Hill Books

2008

Acknowledgments

I want to thank the editors of the following magazines where some of these poems first appeared:

"Where We Lived" was in *After Hours*

"After a Woman Is Removed from a Roman Necropolis" appeared in *Bogg*

"Something There Is" was in *Confrontation*

"In Grief" appeared in *The Deronda Review*

"Looking into the Machinery" appeared in *Fifth Wednesday Journal*

"Evening, Yes, but a Man Is Still a Man" and "Pondfield Road" appeared in *Home Planet News*

"Lowered Expectations in the Lower 48" appeared in *The Ibettson Review* and in *Poetryfish*

"So You Say You've Got a Job?" first appeared in *The Iconoclast*

"Life at the Margins" was in *The Pedestal Magazine*

"Coping with Technology" appeared in *PoetrySky*

"Symphony" appeared in *Presa*

"Unsheathed and in Pain" appeared in *The Quirk*

"The Dark Machinery of Maybe" was in *Somerville News*

"What the Gardener Knows" and "Becoming Another" were in *Stone Table Review*

"The Graves Grow Bigger Between Generations" and "Tea Leaves an a Chamber Pot" both appeared in *Wilderness House Literary Review*

Crossing

It was evening when we came to the river
with a low moon over the desert
that we had lost in the mountains, forgotten,
what with the cold and the sweating
and the ranges barring the sky.
And when we found it again,
in the dry hills down by the river,
half withered, we had
the hot winds against us.

There were two palms by the landing;
the yuccas were flowering; there was
a light on the far shore, and tamarisks.
We waited a long time, in silence.
Then we heard the oars creaking
and afterwards, I remember,
the boatman called to us.
We did not look back at the mountains.

—J. Robert Oppenheimer,
Chief Scientist on
The Manhattan Project

A Silver Zipper

Merely meteoritic, this darkness
that started traveling before Earth formed
carrying no whiff of intelligence, nor sense of being,
nor breath of life, but having something that would
light up the darkness across a universe
when it entered our atmosphere.

Whatever is hidden burns brightest
when the time of counting shadows ends.
Your pocket-change melts back into your hands.
Your estate dances on the head of a pin.
Most of life is waiting for what comes in.
Most of what comes in was here before.

Beyond the buildings are estuarine islands
where a tall bird waits expectantly.

Tea Leaves in a Chamber Pot

This evening all across our nation
men are taking the bones from their arms
and rubbing them against each other for heat.
They are dropping the eyes of the dead
into their pockets, rattling them like change.
It is said that they see something coming.
Men are binding the night with their legs,
laying their penises across it like safety matches,
sitting in loose circles wondering
if they dare to strike the light will it flare
or will the shadows themselves swallow men
like a conflagration from the bowels of time.

Evening, Yes, but a Man Is Still a Man

When shadows grow from Chicago's alleys
and rattle garbage can lids with gusts of wind
that come in across the heartland,
an old man's attention flickers like a cigarette lighter.
He stubs the morning's sales beneath a worn boot heel,
and looks to stars that have not been seen for generations.
Babies are hung out to dry from fire escapes.
A truck becomes a German steelworkers' family
clearing their throats outside a vacant echoing oven in Detroit.
A broken hydrant leaks into the gutter, becomes a flood,
washes years from a plot where the pavement ends.

The man is a newspaper soaked into his own days,
where one page becomes glued onto another indelible
and indistinguishable from the stench of drunken nights.
The bottle to his lips has no name but darkness,
though it was filled from grains growing beneath the sun.
Call him stockbroker, and he will sell you a steer
with a wooden mallet buried between its eyes,
and he will follow you from city to city across our nation
offering up his family on every empty plate you come to.
Call him a tradesman, and he will trade every iron worker
for one closed out steel mill and a teenage soldier.
Tell him he is a product of the Rust Belt
and the infrastructure of every city will come uncoupled.

Do not try to sing his song on the radio.
Hunt for it instead in the loves he has left behind him.
Do not try to tell him what his interests are:
they can no longer be recognized for what they were.
Do not try to buy his wages or his time:
his is the Midwest voice newscasters dream of catching.
Tell him you're from Wall Street and you can offer a better living.
Tell him that, and he'll brick you in.

The Graves Grow Bigger Between Generations

Gonna' have a gravestone bigger than Carnegie,
he used to say. Became a mantra almost, every day
sitting with his lunch bucket amid the oily stench
of Liberty Refining Tower Number Three with
a bunch of roughneck roustabouts, oil paper
skittering around them in the wind each day
in a clearing along the banks of the Allegheny.

That's what I'm gonna do, he'd say,
and the other men would get so they'd just nod,
toss a chip of bark away, wait for the whistle to blow,
talk about the time a young girl went swimming
nude right there where they took their break one day.
How they never said anything until she was
neck deep to the stream, and then called out
so she ended up standing there and crying
while they challenged her until the whistle blew.

Like clockwork every day, marking out his misery
over a ham sandwich and a quick cup of cold coffee,
wiping his mouth on his sleeve in the stink of industry
watching the water roil by; he'd say Any of us
got more feelings about each other than he ever did,
him an' his high silk suits and fancy train cars
rolling black across the silver steel rails of Pennsylvania
lookin' like a coffin to me already, far as I can see.

Gonna' have something bigger to mark me when I go
than anything he can afford with all his meager money,
he was still saying after he went on and switched
to Bates Engineering. Same talk each day, but now
he was moving on to something bigger and he strode
the scaffolding they built across the river each day

with his lunch bucket and breathed the concrete dust
filling the air as they built the dam that would change us
in one sweeping huge arch of manmade stone,
would drown surrounding country homes, hold back floods,
generate electricity to power factories and light up homes,
bring television dramas to small blonde girls each evening,
tame the river and give the people something new to do.

Suma'bitch has a heart of stone, he'd say. But he was drinking by
that time of life, the way men do when stone begins to fill their veins,
and he wasn't as steady on his feet across the scaffolding
holding back the waters and the darkness,
so that when they poured the concrete and he fell in,
dropping from 179 feet into the concrete near where the water
held still he made one hell of an impact on society and on
each of the people who were with him on that day and each
person who drives through Warren or stops to cast a line;
and something within him does by God touch each blonde young girl
snuggling under her electric thermal blanket on winter nights
and brings the news to her each morning with the coffee
and with the interminable ads that go on and on.

Gonna' have it: a bigger gravestone, he said. And he got it all,
two miles wide and big enough to hold a town, a people,
a civilization in the woods even after the refineries failed,
with a drainage area of almost 2200 square miles, and
costing 108 million dollars, take that Mr. Carnegie! And
here I am, thinking that about his words, passing through
along the red brick roads where Grandma used to live,
her house backed against the river, across from the library
near the center of this empty town, the Carnegie, covered
with vines but still holding like a fortress, and with a map
room and dried purple flowers lighting up one corner of a desk

like every other Carnegie built across the small towns of America
standing near every abandoned downtown band shell in America.

Pitiful man. I'm going to have something even grander for
myself than even those of Rockefeller or Gates. His son stayed
on drier land helping to pave the roads beyond the dam,
sometimes pausing to look up at it or taking lunch in the park
at the end of that long road around the mountains, and he'd
look up, thinking well yes, it's pretty big. And you don't need
a name engraved on anything to prove what it was worth.
And he got run down by a cement hauler on a hot day.
One of how many highway workers and dam workers
disappearing into their work each year and leaving the little girls
lonely and crying in the sunlight because they loved them.
The graves grow ever bigger between generations,
I think as I roll on out of that time-forgotten town, my
wheels passing space where who knows how many
small blonde girls died suddenly in their automobiles
sometimes being marked by small white crosses and purple flowers
but mostly left without anything to mark them but the men who died.
A wall of cement and tarmac not two miles across, but
2800 miles from east to west and 1200 miles from north to south
and spread thin as the fabric of our lives and twined
in invisible threads of single lane highways through every town.

I swear I'm going to remember this, and forget the graves,
and forget the markers and forget the names, but I'm going to remember
the smell of furniture polish on old oak banisters, and the dust of books,
and the coolness of old stone buildings in sleepy towns on summer days.
I'm going to remember the too bright eyes of the small blonde girls
with their forced bright smiles in silent public rooms and archives
and I'm going to keep on rolling along across America unmarked,
taking the hand of each one and sweeping her off her feet,

making love with each one at the least expected time
and filling my heart with her smile and with her memory
because there is nothing larger than this that I can imagine:
the depth of shadowed rooms, a silent ray of light, purple flowers
and a woman's touch. The graves get ever bigger
from one generation unto the next.

Tracings

My fingernail placed against
the soft swell of your belly
begins a coming together
that departs from us over years.

Life at the Margins

Loosestrife leaves are the first to turn,
forming a bonfire of orange in evening
nestling among still purple blooms
at the very verge of marshland into grass.
Even before the flaming sumac
lifts its light torch, turning scar red
wounds that will not heal, this sifter of
pollutants that know the why of human waste
separating us from darker and more silent life
ignites in the last evening glow of September
setting fires that mark our progress among weeds.

I have come to love this mark of our imprudence
as I love the cattails that also mark our transgressions,
and the blue heron that wades among their blades.
We are a part of so much that is born of sun,
even as we roll away into the watch of space
devoid of hope. The shadows too are lighted.

I remember a string of shrimpers' boats
strung out across a black horizon, silvers
of latticed stars straining darkness with a white
roaring foam and a sea of salt separating us,
knowing there were heavy creatures before us
that had searched the depths of the world
to find flesh they might pack into their hides,
and of the small mollusks they sucked from rock
whose bones they tossed into the frigid swirl above them
in front of where our houses washed down to sand.

The wind blew cold almost all the time,
but I know that inside the shells that carried lights
upon the darkness of the horizon it was warm,
and food was caught from the cold and coffee
was served in battered china cups molded
and baked where cities came together to be stone.

Of Little Things That Carry Weight

In little packages of time, short circles on a man's wrist,
bleeding into but six months or moons across an ocean,
a new species of wasp was discovered in Scotland
burrowing under the bark of aspen trees.
Almost extinct okapi were found outside their former range.
A previously unknown species of primate emerged from Indonesia.
New kinds of cavefish and blind salamanders from the desert.
All these things in the past three months in the journal *Science*.

I'll bet that they are glad to know of themselves,
as are the predators that have fed upon them for millennia.
I'm glad they're classified. It gives men something to call
the things that hide underneath places none of us have looked.
It makes for something to write books of. It makes for catalogs.
It gives sportscasters and sitcom writers a chance to leave the stage.
It gives the journalists a break so that they don't have to analyze.

I read that chimps can learn to pass an oral language on
from one generation to another in a tribal unit,
and that they, like men, live in political units that hold the land
except when making incursions into other fields they can't maintain.
I've never seen a chimp do that in the wild, but I read they can.
I've seen many a man in power who cannot do either one.
There is something about power such men cannot understand.

It takes an ant to care for the community,
even the very smallest ant,
or even a termite at the heart of rotting wood
or a wasp beneath an aspen tree
or a fern growing in a shadowed glen,
a coral growing from the bones on which it feeds:
a bit too much for a man in power
in a virtual world he does not understand.

It behooves one to fear the ant,
though for all the weight it lifts per capita it won't build a human highway
nor drop a barrage of bombs that could eliminate life as we know it
among all the creatures we are uncovering in our notes each day.
It behooves one to fear because the weight of the very small when combined
is greater than all the men who ever lived in all the lands numbered in our books.
The farts termites give off in shuffling about their tasks each day give off
more methane than mankind's industry. I'm glad myself
to think of little things that carry weight.

Having Never Wanted to Own the Business,

I have come back from countless days of conference rooms
not knowing how to reduce the redundancy of numbers
beyond saying something soothing like ice on steel,
like armored tanks taking out the roads to madness.

My years are gone now, woven into grey wool, pressed
thin and shiny by the cigarettes, scotch, and dry-cleaning bills.
A man is 26 miles of intestine stretched above a desk,
running multiple times a day to the snack machine and urinals,
a sensory input in an electronic web of phone calls to the infinite.
My years are gone. I have come from countless halls.

I have come back to the page-torn poetry books I read and wrote
and to the fiery shriek of invisible angels celebrating
my return and the echoes of my now never empty room
and to the shared nights of readings, cryings, lovings,
amid the shingles of material poverty where soup bones boiled
all day and a can of beans was what we ate on a good day
and we drank each evening on what we could borrow
amid cigarettes and marijuana and loud music espresso machines
and made love in that until the sun rose and we had to hand in
our time machine cards that marked down our uselessness,
making ourselves a mockery of the machinery of diatribe.

Having never wanted to own the poetry, but only to talk with you,
or to take your clothes off and venture together into the street,
now as I come through the door built by someone else,
I find you still here, still waiting to make love, still…

Jack, ol' buddy, How ya doin', is what I wanted to hear;
and that's why I went into the business in the first place.
Just to hear someone say my name one time during the day,
say hey you're someone different that we care about.

That's what business is about. Their street gang who
don't believe in our women in their cool white gowns,
who smell of garlic and play trash music and chase whores
scoping in on our territory not even knowing our names.
We don't want much but you have to take your stand
with your own scorekeeper, accountant, referee, switchblade,
unsigned neutral contracts made out to the highest bidder.

I can tell you that having come back from countless halls.
I am a name on better than a thousand Rolodex from NY to Washington,
each one retired to rooms with shoeboxes of data cards and dust.
My eyes are the marble of office complexes and monuments.
Rodents scurry through my corridors with wireless whiskers
intent on gnawing their way to eternity on cockroach eggs.

And I come to you to plea. I come over dirty magazines
and scraps of yesterday, absolutely filled with dismay,
that those of us who are breaking away have broken away
the same way you are breaking away. With our lust hung up
but still coming unzipped at all the inappropriate times
and our belly buttons peeping through our clothes
speaking of the godly connection to flesh we were born of.

I come to you tired and heavy with the arguments of salesmen
who have died in unwashed alleys holding photos of their children.

Human Kindness

Every discovery worth its salt to the world
came from a man being cheated by his love.
You don't invent penicillin for a stranger,
and you don't take money for your time, not
when it's easier to fuck the one you want.
You don't build bombs or shape governments
or lie awake at night counting silver bullets
when salt isn't being rubbed into your wounds.
That's what getting older is all about, that and suits,
and developing a mind immune to too much liquor;
that and trying to impress a memory that moved away.

Symphony

A woman walks into a room laid with wooden planks.
       There are
                                three points
              between her and
   her lover.
There are   three points
         between her birth and
             her death.
There is a mirror
      on the wall
                    that sees one way
   until she turns.

        There are three points between her
     and a name that puts men to death in uniform.
She does not know this.   There is only one point
between her   and the man who will hold her hand at death.
A rosebud fills a table. The world is small. The floor polished.
        Dust floats across the mirror.

     She dances to a music no one else can see.

To Be Alive

Something goes out of girls somewhere
between 18 and 23 years of age, an
eagerness, or something else comes in,
a hostility and fear, or an inner strength
pushing against the world with their shoulders,
setting their faces beneath lowered brows.
Something light that leaves their eyes,
and I suspect it happens in boys too about
the same time. That's when we start
shipping them off in boxcars to the war
or fitting them into wallboard stalls with
columns of numbers around their necks
because what else are you going to do with
a universe when all its guts are emptied out.

These are airport thoughts. You can try
playing them out yourself next time you fly
about eight in the evening, end of a day's work,
they come down the airport runway like gray socks
no matter what they're wearing and they don't care.
One in fifty might be worth bedding whatever age
you think, and one in sixty men you might buy a drink.
You think I'm harsh, but try it out. Used to be one
in maybe ten or fifteen either way, didn't it? It's
not the biological clock, I can tell you that; it's
the look that says it's been hit with a blank white wall
repeatedly right between the eyes until you no longer feel.

It's the look of motherhood when the world comes
after your children with a big smile on its lips,
of trying to get from one job to another with time
to eat before turning in for the night, of worn fibers
and missed meetings with lovers who used to wait,

tightening against droned warnings of ticking packages
and of the secret police who will sweep them away.
It's a look that makes me catch the eye of one or another
each time and raise my eyebrow in almost invitation
just to catch the light in one face and turn it on again
so that we walk away from each other smiling,
shuffling a little lighter over the dark tunnels.

Touching one sometimes and seeing life,
myself I'd rather move more softly
more gently
myself
I too wish I knew what to do and how to cope,
and sometimes I think that in itself is enough
to be alive.

Coping with Technology

I alternate wallpapers on my computer screen,
letting my eyes follow the thought,
going from the constellation *Andromeda* in a sea of black
to the wattled orange face of a newly discovered bird in Indonesia,
a white disk, perhaps a camera flash, swirling in its pupil.

So You Say You Got a Job?

You better look busy, boy.
You were hired to do what machines can't do
other than take bathroom breaks and drink coffee.
You better make that phone ring
when I'm coming down the corridor.
You better write programs that confuse me
and make us think you're making money, boy.
I don't even want to think
what you're doing with your women and babies
when you go home and hit the bottle hit the babe
you're still on my disability and I don't want to know
whether you can pay the bills, because my strategic plan
already paid for the machines that keep us up at night
humming in their networked closets, warm
with their fresh coatings of plastic paint.

I'd wear a suit, if I were you.
No casual day here unless it means I pay you less.
Don't ever shake the bottom line, boy.
Your suit is made to swab sweat from your glands
and to cover the pimple on your ass. No man
is wanted to cause problems for our distribution.
You go inseminate someone else with your free time.
We've already got what I call accountability
and I'm watching your phone, emails, website visits,
and checking out your face each morning when you come in,
making sure you're looking rested and at ease.
We've got the company picnic coming up, you know.
Can you play soccer as hard as I can?
I've broken the bones of players on other teams.
We build loyalty here like we're fighting a war;
don't you forget or let down your guard.

One in three hundred employees hired will get a gold watch;
the rest will just get watched until health costs go up.
Who's your Daddy now, big boy?

You better hope we have enough crises to keep you on,
because repetition of what you do can be done cheaper, boy.
You'd better sweat those minutes that go by
without your negotiating a contract for your life with a customer.
You better hear and feel the leaking out of radium from your watch…
better feel those stress wrinkles burning into your forehead, boy.
There might be another job down the street, but the older you get
and the smarter you get, the less they'll want to pay you.
Who's your Daddy now, big boy?

Dark Machinery of Maybe

The long eastern snow has slowed,
leaving only at last scattered tracks,
bud-swelled branches scattered broken,
mailboxes filled with empty envelopes,
homes with no one left to light the lights,
a swirl of missed meaning and metaphor.

I do not have to travel far today:
the flights to Boston, London, and Sydney
are delayed in the dark machinery of maybe.
A cup of soup steeped with seeds from Beijing
brought inside with pine logs from Wisconsin
brings the miles together between my fingers.

Bartok plays shocked digital destinations magnetically
in a living room where my hands are warmed before a fire.

Communing with the Dead

A crushed aluminum beer can
is not the same as one of Hrothgar's casks
spilled across a banquet hall of ghosts.
No time where time is infinite.
No space where space is time.
We could no longer commune with the dead
at the beginning of the 21st century.

Transparency among Ghosts

A cormorant resting on an algaed piling.
A gaunt blue heron pacing the seats
of battered unused fishing skiffs
searching for scraps of yesterday,
then leaping confused to another craft
and another. The breeze stiffens.

With my own hand
I press the knife down severing
ligament, cutting thumb from fingers,
curling the bone into a cage,
removing the human connections,
and holding at the end of my arm a standing roast.
This does not prevent my flailing at the water
and turning sideways to the moon.

Sea oats, galardia, goldenrod,
sand slipping away beneath my heels
with wave rush the storm surge between my legs.
Broken fragments of the sun underfoot,
salt across windows on the calmest day
pelicans in heavy bomber formation.
The sand bears all these down,
and wind and water move the sand.
Everything crusted with the salt of inhuman industry.
The massive against the tiny.
And in our beach house, we watch television,
eat oranges from across the continent
and talk about dead generations.

An angler's line tautens
and he fights the darkness,
the bend of carbide and the screaming reel,

until the ocean begins to shape itself
into eyes, a fin, a cosmos of perception
that is spit out into a boat.
This it is to be a fisherman.

While we sit around a table
eating oysters, drinking beer,
the harbor dredging goes on.
The land shifts eastward
beneath our feet
and the eyes of darkness
never stop devouring themselves.
Each table holds one candle.
We are moths of particular arrogance.

a mouse's skull
clamshells
scrub pine
cedar
conch fragments

Has not the sun itself shaped the shells
I gather from these sands,
shaped them beneath the darkness;
has it not fed the pallid flesh
that built these coiled halls
and left them vacant?

A ghost crab diaphanous with
skin of dew drenched spiderweb,
stealing from grass root to root
grains of sand and salt upon it
and eyes of grain and salt.
All the rest transparency.

Lowered Expectations in the Lower 48

Dawn is the roaring maw of steel mill furnaces
waking and eating their way through hundreds of tons of darkness.
Evening is when twisted vines take root in parking lots
and eviction notices drop their seeds between abandoned cars.

There is no challenge I am not ready for,
but my allies will shift as the pages in the news.
I will hunt with the gaunt nosed urban coyote
down dream filled alleyways of processed food.

Do not look here for the resilient skin of democracy.
The blood on my lips is from gnawing at my paws to escape
or it is from the girls I lay among yesterday.
You cannot know or follow where it drips to earth.

Night is the sharp contraction of metal gone suddenly cold;
hard stone boxes emptied of the dark earth that was their fire;
the pockets of our suits and overalls emptied of keys and change;
a long cry of despair swelling from our communal memories.

Whatever Happened to Johnny Rebel?

Who is the Board of Directors, Johnny?
That's what the teachers should ask on each SAT American History test.
They're the ones who pushed the President to the front. He's a front
man, Johnny. Didn't your parents ever tell you that?
He didn't stand up to anyone; he's the heart of the machine;
he chopped the cherry tree and spit the pits in your face.
That's not acne, Johnny. It's American as cherry pie.

First thing you learn in business with your MBA
is to pay donations to each political party.
You buy guns from the biggest gun manufacturer;
you own stock in the mines that mine its barrels;
you pay dividends to people who don't shoot back.
You call it accountability. You're a team player, Johnny,
with a steel gray suit and a big zero on your back.

The Dirty Smelly Mess

of an artist's studio comes unglued
long after all the bright baubles congeal.
Unwashed underwear ferments in the corner.
Cold steam pipes bang against the night.
Cigarettes fill wine bottles of time.
Beneath a naked light bulb small white flowers
pasted onto cardboard sheets begin to sing
and all of man's soul turns to listen.

Poets

The enemies of our leaders are poets;
not good men necessarily, not at all,
but neither are they men who fire hell-fire missiles
into mud-bricked homes in the desert
nor who burn the jungles of the tropics
to eradicate the plants of dreams and nightmares;
not good men at all, and as much
tyrants as any man who has a god in his pocket.

The enemies of our leaders are poets.
Where men get up in the morning to work
and build words into dreams that give hope
and cut the flesh from their own hands
furrowing the earth until it bears seeds
until their screams divert resources
to the people among whom they live they find
the support of communication and of people
is much bigger than shock and awe.

The enemies of our leaders are poets
who listen to winds at night as they walk dark alleys,
who stop at lonely diners for a cup of coffee
before jotting down a few notes and going off
into the shuffle of their own tired footsteps;
who come together again in the workplace
speaking in tongues marketers do not understand,
and seducing women with eyes that do not waver.

The leaders cannot lead without the words
a culture creates within itself,
within its needs,
poets.

Who Carries the Message?

Do you understand what is at hand, America?
Your bedroom walls are filled with invisible ears.
Your meat is hewed from the arteries of mad cows.
Your water glows in the dark, and is dark by day.
Your children are put out of work to fight wars
for Congressmen who won't represent them.
Your paycheck cannot buy your future, America.
Who tells the tale? Who carries the message?

Do you understand what is at hand, America?
You are as replaceable as the bridges you build.
You are as faceless as electrons on election booth walls.
You are a suit in an unspeakable maze of indecision.
You are the genius who lives down the hall.
You are the madman who listens to history
while ignoring the bulls in the Wall Street China shop.
Your paycheck cannot buy your future, America.

Fortress

*

Your last paycheck
is an iron manhole cover.
A butterfly follows the wind.

*

Two dragonflies
are a gate into time.
An ocean itself has shores.

*

This watch has hands
that wrap about one twice.
A turtle scooping out sand.

*

The eye of a robin
can see across a continent.
My house has no doors.

*

A hawk above Manhattan
turning in the wind.
This desert has no end.

*

Your turn to wash dishes.
One more camel
comes into our tent.

*

A small farm pond reflects
each pinpoint of light
falling across our universe.

*

Dream catcher, your net is wide.
A mannequin melts into sand
in the sun of Millennium Park.

*

A year's telephone bills
are collapsed into your hand:
A pencil cut from your heart.

*

A falling coin fills
the parking meter's mind.
Human flesh is softer.

*

A microchip of Shakespeare
is nestled among grains of sand.
Why hunt for buried coins?

*

These young women among bottles:
silvery fish down an egret's throat,
urgently swimming into darkness.

*

I sponge blood from the top
of a stainless steel kitchen counter.
Pencil lines lead into evening.

*

This escalator in the subway:
a silver zipper on a long black dress
hanging in a closet that no one owns.

*

A herd of cows urges you to speak.
What if the bricks were to fall
and the empty panes of glass remain?

*

Black bags filled with violins.
Too many immigrants living
hollow-eyed in this tenement.

Learning to Breathe

For thirty years I have lived this way,
a stupid man, because there is coldness in you
that cannot be reached by the heat in my rage.

Maybe it is a coldness of candlelight in dining halls,
warming the polished wax of generations, giving
substance to the pewter vase against the mantel
with dimensions that come out only in shadows.
Maybe it is a coldness of having lost someone yourself
and knowing how to hold the patterns together even
when you have not learned to speak of them with words.

What we have always wanted most to hold onto
has always been that which has slipped from our lips.

Looking into the Machinery

Look into the machinery, I said,
the metal gears, covered in grease
with their teeth eating at each other.
Look into the spaces between them,
with the noxious fumes, the urine,
the unwashed flesh and sex,
look into the dark pressed sediment
rolling through space and time,
the spider's leg poised. Look
into the sweat, there is nothing *deus*
ex machina about this unless it is in
the gears turning where men work
together in tunnels beneath the moon
with electric headlamps, hammering
at the rock walls that enclose them.

Had to grow everything you could.
When we first came though, who woulda
traded anything you grew for metal made
in some small town back east, or ribbons,
bows, glass? Who woulda? Because you had to grow.
Not now, but even if you planted seed
it took all you had to harvest it yourself and
sometimes you had to shoot something small for meat.
Deer and buffalo stayed well away because
we shot them just for eating the grasses and
the seed before it grew into anything useful.
Of course the metal helped at last in the shape
of blades to haul along behind us or the horses.
Still, it was hard to harvest out the food until
the machinery came in from back east and
we were wondering what made a city grow

like that, why didn't we manage that here.
Takes a lot of folk I guess with time on their hands.

The machinery has life and the life
machinery ticking in the backlots
odd lots subplots of society, steeling
itself against the stropping of flesh.
Look into the darkness and there are eyes
and mouths and muscles straining,
giving up light for each other's dreams,
lurching drunkenly against each other,
laughing and dying in each others teeth.

We got the ore down from The Morningstar
right above the cabin and milled it—
more steel there from back east somewhere—
after Rich died in the cave-in, hit his
head trying to get out before the fuse
went off. We carried him out and paid
enough to get his widow back out east.
Lord knows she still comes back to visit,
but we got the ore milled down in Marysville
and bleached it out with arsenic and mercury.
Got a gold watch from that I did, and gave it
away to a woman 'cause I thought we had time.
Trees grow there now. And rocks, they grow.
I guess she pawned it in a shop or got it lost.

Passing through, that's what we're doing now
from one red-roofed saltbox to another, rolling
over the paved over seed beds we used to layout
in federally platted catalogs of fertile land laid
out about the size a man might grow with his own

and feed himself and his family god knew why
that's what we did each day, speaking only to
ourselves around the dinner table and then packing off.
God knows how we feed each other now, but its
clearly in the machine, down within its gears.

I remember meeting Mary down by the gate one day
maybe one hundred years ago after the dust blew through
and there wasn't anything growing then either, not any
more, but I handed her a piece of something golden warm
that had been across the country twice at least, and she
looked at me and then out across the dead landscape
and she said wasn't it beautiful and we walked back
to the old Ford, kicked it over at last, and went on
one more time.

Something There Is

I got into the funeral by accident while
talking with you while I turned the corner,
just missing a pigeon, finding myself
in a long line of sleek gray cars, my dry-cleaned
shirts piled up starched against the back seat,
their headlamps up against my bumper.
No way to turn aside at that point, so I hung up
the cell and moved implacably forward, listening.

We're waiting for you, it would say.
Mom, and Charlie, and your sisters.
That long-drawn two-note whistle meant "Come now!"
when I was growing up, dodging among shadows.
Each of your children would come running
because that whistle was unique to you. No
one else could perform it so clearly and unwavering;
gray as your eyes at the end of an office day
it could be heard throughout the neighborhood.

It comes back to me as I sit by my poet friend,
who, in dying slowly in his hospital bed at last,
looks up, reaches out his hand, and asks me to hold it
the way I held Charlie when he was run over. Charlie
had no pretense. He ate and slobbered and slept like a dog.
But I don't take your hand, poet. You have hands
and words. What if you don't want to let go;
what if you want to hang on and shake me,
until something falls out that you can take with you?

I just got into the funeral by accident.
I'm hunting for what it meant.
We're here for a reason, certainly,
as we carry our long trays of flowers through town.

I take what I am given unless it has hands.
The air stinks of sexual decay and hot asphalt.
When the phone rings again, I hear Dad's whistle,
two long notes across time and the line goes dead.

I can't find anything anymore, I tell him
        alone   in our time   alone
when I stare into slate gray rock cliffs of monuments
buried deep across the valley abutting our highway.
I am now, late in the day, of the gray rock monuments
and the valley is in my heart, stretched thin as the reception
of a flip-top cell phone in a tin can.
The messages might mean anything.

What the Gardener Knows

Late May, when the daffodils droop their leaves,
seed pods grow bulbous misshapen green
upon their stalks, but not in affluent suburbia.
There where white fingered housewives
pick over the beds, pulling weeds from lives,
the fruity pods are pinched off before they form.
All across America where men go to work
in the morning the work goes on unknown to poets.
Not noticed by accurate accountants, leering lawyers,
the women pinch growth back to build the bulbs,
to rebuild the roots that reach into their garden soil.
An accountable nation does not need to know,

because the bulbs grow each spring and spread
from one small clump to edge to edge within the bed,
their heads and seed picked clean as incest,
kept in control, stone sterile, protected in white fenced centers,
yet still reproducing in erotic flagrance on their own.
Strange, wild mementos from Wordsworth's dreams
reproducing either way, but this the way we like it best.
And with help each plant pleases only itself, grows hard,
beneath the surface only, alone in the dark, reproduces and goes on.
As the men come and go in suburbia only the gardener knows,
and the reproduction of ideas, the interdependencies of seed
that bring flexibility are choked off to build upon the known.

The Renter

sets off on a black bus from Omaha.
Rain is across her face and the farm fields.
Her eyes are heavy buckets of stars.
Machinery rocks against her buttocks.
Tolls are paid in advance of miles.
Dabs of sweat and oily skin remain
when she leaves in exhaustion and fear
drawing fluff from her sweater and
a crumpled paper soda straw holder,
a torn piece of gum wrapper, the
memory of memories in Omaha
and a flake of dandruff that remains
stuck down where the floor fuses into wall.
When the bus is hosed down
at the end of the month that cell of detritus
is pushed farther under by maintenance,
but will remain until the bus is buried
for scrap ten years later in Minnesota
with a lost piece of humanity dead inside.

Chicago appears as bright brick walls into sunlight,
and the number of people in the streets
indicate to her something important is going on,
and she is going to be there now. She sits
on the toilet in whatever terminal she arrived in
and leaves more of her background there as well.
It is a purging of red suns beyond harvest grain,
a purging of days spent watching the dust
swirl in from the western states, bringing age.
She rises and washes her hands, and leaves
fingerprints on paper towels to be thrown away.
Her left shoe dimples someone's urine on the floor
and she exchanges some more of her way of life.

She thinks of empty canisters and boxcars,
marvels at the candy in vending machines; going out
finds a home with a broken man from Detroit
she meets outside a bar that evening. She leaves
the imprint of her lips around his shaft, and he
leaves a dying of dreams into her womb that night.

We like the little things that contain memories,
so with a saved five bucks she buys a plastic radio,
white with gold painted dials, from a pawn shop
because it was filled with her past, and plants it
on the stained table by the foot of her bed,
sun catching off its dial each morning, angled just right
against the heavy hanging curtain shade. And a toaster,
there is a toaster with silver sides on the table as well,
with a dusky burned mark imprinted into that as well.
She polishes it each day she lives there, and she
walks the streets each day she lives there, and she gets
to know a lot of men by the stench of the clothes they wear
and then by the clothes they no longer wear, and she
distills herself and memories into them and they into her.

After a Woman Is Removed from a Rome Necropolis

Looking into an old skull
unearthed in Rome one can see the earth,
beneath shattered dome of cranium.
Nestled in the palm, calloused,
one can see the acropolis' towers
pockmarked with time through the eyes
when it is lifted from its shoe box.

Nothing remains of flesh, but a cave,
and bone itself a cup becomes stone.

Therefore, do not lock flesh away while it exists
beneath cloth and fashion, beneath jails and regulations,
beneath a merchant's watch applied in ritualistic parody,
when it is what we want eternally,
while it has a scent of its own
and animates not only itself
but the stone, the bone, and all we know.

For a Woman Minding the Store

You are stroking brass globes without edges
and fingering glass casements hunting for keys,
your fingers like flesh drum beats
urging your fertile eggs to go forth
in soft purple shadows with harsh, crisp shells...

but whatever is given for exchange
is given because it is not wanted
by you or by the institution that gives it.
You want the golden seeds that
crack open in the shadows of your den,
woman, I know that even as I am a man.

You want to be alone as a wolf at night
with tall spring grass flowing against your belly,
without being picked off by a sharpshooter.
You want to know the moon upon the waters
and feel that same swelling in your loins
while burrowing your muzzle into all that is soft

This is what the bright store mannequins know,
standing behind glass looking out into the street
after having their clothes changed, updated,
having had the dust mopped from clean faces,
watching the homeless men with shopping bags,
the poets going by with college textbooks
and beer-filled nights with bakery cakes,
watching the sleekest cars slow down to stare,
the black doors opening and women walking in,
the money money money picking up fingerprints
and DNA washed out into rain-filled gutters
negating and eliminating the golden seeds you need
that were once the seeds of September nights
stolen without malice from Midwestern fields.

Finishing Work,

I was going to go down to the pub and see if you dropped in
but my dog was sitting at the door, looking out
at that bright purple begonia tray we planted on the deck;
that alert stance but with a drooping tail asking if
I might somehow have time for him
but that's okay if I didn't.
And all things being as they are,
I didn't have to shave to go out with him,
so instead I took him over to the lake,
and for two hours we pushed our way through reeds,
sticking our rumps up in the air when we found
tunnels that might be worth exploring;
found a beaver house pressed up against the highway overpass,
followed deer trails that went nowhere. Just faded away.
We drank from the waters, found the silent places
where bass waited since we weren't hunting them.
He never said a sound in all that time.
He never asked if life was passing him by.
Dogs don't know about death, just about what's bigger.
The cupboard's always full, and I guess that's good enough
and tells where we've come to at this juncture.

Where We Lived

Your world has come into a tree
growing alongside our window
on rainy nights, rearranging the DNA
of furniture and long blonde hair
through its matrix of thirsty roots
with road salt and garage oil
inside its long twisting memory.
Beneath hard rugged bark slabs
just the smallest bit of you remains
with traces of the counter cleanser
and your scent when you pressed
your hands against the trunk in evening.

The dead and the living are an hourglass
funneling out in both directions.
All the lives that have been saved
progress outward in one hungry wave,
while those that have finished eating
roll backward in geometric time.
A thunderstorm rages at the fulcrum.
The hourglass becomes a butterfly
with one translucent wing swinging out
and then the other, one singed by sun,
the other curled into the coldness of night.

Willows are thirsty trees.
When developers build houses
along a marsh, they plant willows first.
When winter gusts split the trunk
after all these years I still think of you.
Running outside I hear your silence
and feel the earth with my hands,
starting at last to understand that this
may be the last time I come this close
to ordered principles I do not understand.

Becoming Another

"Baby fingers broken across the landscape.
that's what they look like," she said, watching
dry thunderheads come in from the northeast.
"Reaching up like they're going to get something."
She pursed her lips. "We used to sit here drinking
tea in the evening, just like you and I are doing.
Americans don't drink tea. Talk. You can talk.

It wasn't the same after Ricky moved away.
He took something out of the equipment with him,
so that it didn't shine as much and needed more oil.
We didn't hear the ticking in the barn anymore.
We slept heavier that summer in its humidity.
We divided our evenings into words like ice floes
between catching field mice and bringing in the cows.

You should have come to visit then.
I would have liked it, and he wouldn't know.
It might have saved a lot of empty years,
might have made the sunsets less desolate.
I might have carried a life into that world.

As it is, I can't say why he left.
He kept a postcard diary of sorts and I'd get notes:
Walking was the easiest way to get away.
Put space between yourself and the crime
without using wheels, without credit cards.
Hit the road that runs between macadam
and ignore the cities, the incendiary points of capital power.
Trust the women with long gray hair and slack eyes,
the gentle hands that would trap steel spiders on hot days.

Wafting Through Trees

There are those who would tell you what to say.
I will tell you only what I have observed.
There are those who teach you what to do,
and how to earn what they have come to know.
I teach you nothing, except that they do not
value anything so much as they value you
and they see you as an extension of themselves.
We are in a world of shadows that pass.
I care enough to tell you this, because
your arms are still open and your eyes soft,
still taking in light, and your hands can
shape what is around you in ways I don't understand.
And I want to understand for no other reason than
you don't feed me, support me, owe me or own me,
and there is no medium of exchange for the joy of music
wafting through trees on a summer evening as we walk.

A Prayer in the Teeth of Time

I blew an aqua blue bottle around you
to protect the flame inside,
but the glass separated us and light
not received by eyes goes dark into the heart
where it carries itself forever through time.

Where are we now when our love will leave no children?

Pondfield Road

What if technology allows you to stalk your life
as you would have lived it *if?*
What if you can google in by satellite imagery
to the house you would have lived in
and can see her latest car parked in the driveway,
or can count the number of tricycles not on the lawn,
would you ever grow apart from her? I'm interested
perpetually now in the color of her hair and
what kind of wine her husband drinks
when I zoom in on her door opening on the Web.

What if technology were to tie you to images
that are more than data but are tied to your heart
with the glue of an instant of failure in your past,
after all the memories of victory your mind carries?
I'm wondering what it might make your mind do.

Unsheathed and in Pain

Stalks once green are now dusty
spiking among grasses in a shallow glen.
The texture, pale blue foxglove limpid,
shaded until letting go, dropping into water.
Leaves curled, dried, gone dusty into August,

a whole field of foxglove
going into the margins at forest's edge;
purple of bleeding hearts against green money,
the spaces between individuals hot-curled
with expectation of breeze on a still afternoon.

It is this time of year girl's gowns drop down
petal upon petal after their support is dead.
Flesh fills the molding soil beneath their progeny.
Digitalis soaks the latticed fibers beneath greens and grey,
hearts beating harder now with each irregularity.

How many times did we strip off our clothes,
diving forward into the shallows;
how many years ago when our flesh was young,
and your nipples hard, my arms about you?
You are miles away now and your name is gone
into the ether of married Internet addresses; who
would have known a woman of your independence
would ever change her name and leave, curling
your arms about yourself. I grow heavy and sleepy
in the summer heat, keeping my shoes on now,
leaving anonymous prints that fill and swirl with mud,
losing direction at the meadow's verge.

I would tell you of mountains where my hands have bled,
scrabbling at rock, tearing at fallen trees to build bridges

over brooks where wild trout swim down from the clouds
and gooseberries raspberries blueberries grow free
along the hardly rutted road I built beside a cabin
where we would have lived had you remained;
of a vista across miles leading down to towns
 that are desert jewel boxes and the eyes of cats.

I'm sorry. Mostly, it is true, I write checks
to keep my options open now that you are gone;
sitting above a fire escape in a painted room.
as buses fill the streets below, the earth groans,
the bricks shake…old leaves and petals
and the ferns between them fossil fuel.

There are no mountain cats here.
The darkness of slag-stripped ore
does not watch over one's shoulders in the city.
Branches do not break in the night
under invisible feet. I know what it is
at last that has killed us here.

I cannot look you in the eye
and speak of anything else but your body
and the way you think of things.
When it is dark and the night deep
and the radium eyes on your bureau out
there are mountain cats prowling
with claws unsheathed.

I cannot look you in the eye at all.

In Grief

There are ghosts in the chandeliers
tricking light into hidden shapes and spectra
that are lost in white before light reaches me.
There are dark holes in the sofa by the lamp
where you used to read your books.
The dog sleeps alone on the landing now
as if trying to hold something together or apart.
I sent our children letters and they came,
carrying their return addresses with them.
The postman has gone. I am afraid,
and wonder which other room I might be sitting in
if I had opened other doors a long time ago.
I cannot bear the sorrow of knowing I have known you.

After Twenty-five Years

You are still the mother of my unborn children,
the keeper of their graves on winter nights.

It is impossible that I do not know whether you are alive,
but I closed a frosted door between us in a New York vestibule.

Your blind sensual longing
leads you to windows that cannot be viewed,
and I have gone far away with an empty heart
as dry leaves dispense our thoughts.

With Sunsets

Wild things are where they are unexpected.
My hair is gray with the passage of wind,
and I have come to show you these things
two steps from where the pavement cracks.

What I Take to My Grave

12:35 a.m., the lights on the home entertainment console
are a diagram of the choices I have made. Or they are eyes.
In an improper light they spell out Physical Comfort.
They give names to my children, now fuckers themselves.
They are lonely beacons to your memory, you
the urgent need who walks through my life each night.

Night Heron

When you have lived in the water long
do you feel its coolness on your lips?

If you grew drinking from cacti, slicing off the spines
with your teeth, would you walk to a lake for water?

Does the dark-striped night heron remember things
with his feet that no other thing dares think,
and are his feathers and beak built of dream?

We Are the Dawn People

In the years to come we are the Dawn People
and build our homes against the earth, snug
against the moist western mountains, where
sage mixes with dry grasses and cottonwood.
We lay our weathered wings against the sun
and bow down upon ourselves into each other's arms,
worshipping all that swirls about us and all that
is invisible but tearing at our roots, where we hold.
Some things are good, and some are not this way.
The aquifers from alpine fields come down to us
deep with their fields of deer and small blue asters.
The Chinooks come down as well, tearing at what
little shelter we have built about us to bear
the breath of life that is the earth itself caught
in a cosmos that extends beyond our labeled names.

At Breakfast with All the King's Men

long after Robert Penn Warren

Something slow is happening
    in the mind of a cow
        as it meanders around
  the bend in the stream ahead
and its eyes take us in and dismiss
the mists rising from this little rill
and the grasses growing green bellies
along banks where we turn no cash,
udderly content to wade the oxbows
burying its velvet nose in waters cold,
meandering their own way across fields
where small fish nip its milky belly
while it keeps separate its needs
stitched up tight in cowhide's fears,
green grasses growing meandering inside
the darkness and the pleasant stench
beneath and among sundown river sets,
and then the cool outside into the stream.

Watering the Lawn

A grackle stretches neck forward
from his perch on the white pine bough
then forward again black feathers glistening
and becoming prisms as they do in sun
dusting each in turn as each drop of water
falls between the open spaces beneath stars

where the stars are hidden in lightness,
he comes upon these sudden cloudbursts
very localized on even-numbered days
during drought season, nor is he the only one;
there are whole migrations of grass-birds
who seek out these mystical happenings:
a robin pulling worms at the edge of sun
as the worms come up to feast on aqua,
falling on lawn that is not native to our land,
meadowlarks seeking seeds to break loose,
hummingbirds to suddenly released pollen
on the purple plum blooming by the door,
the bees annoyed but hungry among clover.

Just for minutes it is there, and then moves on.
Another block of land down around the bend.
Or another day. Not the kind of roaring rains
that cause one to huddle deeper into nests,
just little ones that make rainbows on the skin.

Something New Is Hunting

Recently I've been finding dead animals around our home.
When I take our dog for walks in the evening.
For the first time in my fifty-seven years of life,
something seems to be hunting closer to the bone
and tearing at what is around us when it can't get in.

This evening a still-warm rabbit lay by the path
and our dog walked right by him before I tightened the leash.
My hands are almost as slow as my eyes in this light,
but the dog walked on along as if nothing like nourishment
however freshly laid out was lying there before him.
And yesterday there was a female mallard duck torn apart
with long orange legs reaching up into its open belly
disemboweled near where the school bus stops. He
didn't pause to look at that either, and that seems odd
for a carnivore, as if something unnatural laid it out.

The two geese in the grasses by the lake a month ago
with their wings torn out by something in the night
that came upon them quickly and left them uneaten;
their bodies lay there twisted for weeks. The dog and I
would pass near enough to glance but not go there.

For fifty-seven years I've walked the evening streets
and felt comfort in the wind of stars that others did not feel.
I have passed among the shadows beyond civilization
frequently and have known the balance of the universe.
But something new is hunting closer to the bone now,
tearing at the smaller things I shared the night with.

Poetry and Baseball and Pay-As-You-Go

I understand that boys watch baseball and old men
grow sterile watching boys run the bases on steroidal paychecks.
It's the same in any game when it's just a game and no one dies,
but how much is a society really willing to lay down
in salaries for entertainers to make its men go sterile?

Thirty million dollars a year is small potatoes on some diamonds,
but if you keep taking just a tad from each man, each bag of evil-smelling rags
you could fill up enough parking meters to stuff a city to its walls
with the chrome real men sweated over for most of their lives in
dark rocky mines and dark musty factories and dark were their lives.

Someone's got to put the bricks down and build walls.
Someone's got to pave the roads and bridges to tomorrow
with something that won't decay when it rains. Someone
has got to drive the trucks and fire the trains and weld the planes
that we're staggering under as we carry them across our land.

I understand the concept of the team and the nine players
and how each of them wears a number on his back and
runs around his prescribed base paths and catches flies, and
I understand the pitch that gets to you so fast you don't see it
and how you swing only to find the plate empty as your belly.

That's why I walk around amusement parks with my hands
knuckled deep into my pockets, astonished by the gapers
and even more by the overseers in their box seats and the
microphone announcers chanting out the obvious for all to see.
It's not like street yard baseball, this poetry thing anymore,
where you used to lean back with whatever piece of wood you found
lying around and hit each clunker of coal as far as it would go.

from Looking into the Machinery:
The Selected Longer Poems of Jared Smith

Published by Tamarack Editions

2010

A Trout in the Pick-up on Papago

                I.

"Like a tractor trailer out of water
is what them ol' bones are feeling like,
he said and I nodded and tapped the glass.
I mean you figure the pool he was born in
slipped away down the mountainside
almost before his gills drew breath, he said,
so I figured I'd see if we might keep him up
hold back give him a chance like democracy
but every time we tried we hit our heads on
rocks that the river kept on flowing through
while room after room, house after house kept
going on down the stream, and him crying
thinking how the hell am I going to learn anything
if it all keeps on sweeping by dissolving everything
and it's no wonder he doesn't have opposable thumbs
but just has to keep slipping along into things and
hoping they'll hold out until something better comes,
and of course it does until it doesn't or he doesn't know.
It seemed like the right thing to do…Patriotic, you know."

But I'm getting ahead, and we were 30 miles from Phoenix
along Papago Freeway Route 10 when I hung my thumb up
and he swung his wash-boarded pick-up truck over to let me in,
and there was a rainbow trout where the radio ought to be,
at least that's what he said, but there were only bones in
a Darwin fish perspective mounted there under glass
and they had so many chips and fragments sticking out I
figured they might have been fingers for all I knew, so

we tweaked the ribs to change the stations and turned
its eye on or off when the commercial messages got too much,
and pretty soon the roadway and the small towns and then
the sunset came rushing past us in our little bubble there.
"You wouldn't want to get out now," he said, and I knew
he was right and a lot can happen in a pick-up by the road.

II.

George, I might as well as call him George,
came from a small town outside of Hessie
in the Indian Peaks, late summer after finishing
a sandwich when I reached the plastic baggie
a chicken from Arkansas had been residing in
along with a pile of wheat from southern Kansas
under an undercut bank and it swam in, tipped
the scales so I could hold it up in the sun, look at it,
long enough to think it was important or ought to be,
and then folded over and squeezed the Ziploc cleat,
dropping it in my pocket where it looked around
awhile until it suffocated in the darkness I carry there.

Had it mounted in a veterinary shop in Old Orabi
so that it would get pregnant in the lands of little water
and multiply itself among the tourist shops. Got it framed
and convicted of promiscuous perversions and partnership,
things I knew that would break it up, but I kept a tight hold
on the leader all the time as I wound it in, and I told folks
that I caught it on the fly rather than on circumstance, and
I paid my dues, goddamn right, I paid the state DES,
I bought my stamps to send the abomination to Washington,

and they splintered everything that was wild within it
and sent it back right here on my dashboard radio so
that it tracks me every inch of the way across America.
Who woulda known it comes from little things in little towns.

III.

When I am hungry, I rise to the surface
and the universe settles a dusty miller
which I take into my bloodless lips;
the universe then settles around me.

The bones dry out over time, crumble
away but they always hold what built them.
They hold the sun and they hold the darkness
and every shade of color from in between.
Out of that I get direction indecipherable
in a dry land giving way to desert where
only towns and saguaros grow at night
and owls lie awake in their thorny burrows.

IV.

Winter is a time of entropy
where wind socks down mountain valleys
heaving boulders from frost-cracked perches,
spreading alluvial plains across the heart
white and then gone as wind boils tarmac.
If there were time I would say we wait it out,

and that energy arises as our earth draws
farther from the sun and the days grow warmer;
that energy is from old man sol, is where physics
reverse and organization builds across fields
and farms and streams where trout grow flesh
and come together in some cumbersome way
that includes us in our fiery streetwalkers clothes
and in our restaurants and you, oh you, also
coming together with me in suddenly not sterile rooms.
If there were time I would say we wait it out
and there are seasons enough for everything infinite
to reverse again and sweep us up into its season

Grassroots

poems by Jared Smith

Published by Wind Publications

2010

Acnowledgments

Big City Lit published "If You Want to Write," "One of Our Own," "Know in Your Absence," and "Monsoon"

Fifth Wednesday Journal published "Mining Coal in Marshall"

Gander published "American Hero" and "Knowing What Grows"

Green Fuse Poetic Arts Improv anthology published "What's in That Great Steel Belly?" and their *Poetry Saves* anthology published both "Perhaps That Too the Shadow" and "Flight 539"

Heavy Bear published "Why Real Men Don't Read Poetry Anymore" and "The Science of Expanded Understanding"

Home Planet News published "Remembering the Touch of Stars"

Ibbetson Street Press published "Among the Mystic Mountain Men"

The New York Quarterly published "Camelback," "Keeping Watch Over the Dead," and "Societal Psychosis"

The Pedestal Magazine published "*This Poem*"

The Same published "Do the Fish Drain Out?" and "Retaining an Empty Cell"

Statement: Journal of the Colorado Language Arts Society, published "What You Do When You Cannot Fly"

The Toronto Quarterly published "In the Rooms the Motels Match"

Wilderness House Review published "Once Beneath the Moon" and "The Majority of His Life He Could Reduce to Movie of the Week"

...this stripped and starving earth is not a grave.

—Martín Espada

This Poem

What can you write that cannot be photographed?
I want *this* poem to go along the parallel lines of force
you have carried from the factory floor in your eyes on leaving work,
the heavy beams that shape everything you see sitting here
reading these words and adding to them the images you've seen.
I would have the images of the signal fires of forgotten cities find fire
and reflect along the linear tunnels of time inside your mind and meld
with the lovers lost, the songs sung, the dreams dragged to dust,
because they too are singing the songs of you across all time
and this is bigger than we have known since data shrank itself to data.
Volumes of Homer, Shakespeare, Archimedes, Einstein, and Plotinus
and grunting guttural lovings and semen in the night are not data dots.

I want this poem to flicker in the electromagnetic spectrum of your mind,
reaching across our darkness like a candle in a sawdust barroom inside
a plastic globe encasing a flame that reflects only from your eyes and
then goes out across the universe as light rays do in never-ending time,
without echo, without ever coming back, but leaving a trail to follow
    between stars;
I want this poem to be of many facets that flicker unexpectedly in the mundane.
I want its awkwardness to jangle in your pockets so that you pull it out
and think about the twisted pieces of metal and see how they light up the dark...
this to be human thought expanding for eternity even as the insentient objects
of our first being in the Big Boom expanded across electromagnetic boundaries
with echoes still seen that have meaning far beyond our understanding.

Not One Homogenous

The Earth is not one homogenous whorl
whirling in its cold hardness. This we have come to know.
We know of the magnetic network latticed as angel wings
around our outer inner atmosphere, and other things ephemeral
speeding forever into the dignity of our outside of self.
We know the snow that falls from blue skies on cold days,
how each flake falls, rises, draws into each memory,
clings to the roots of each blade of grass, each cemented sand
scaled into the buildings that men build and raze again.

The earth is not one homogenous whorl
turning in the oblivion of Einstein's violin, its sounding box
thrumming with the echo of things long gone that glow. We
know… this we know, it comes to resonate within our bones,
and the mountains ringing continents are more than stones
stone dark within their un-breathing souls, they are swirled
with magma-begetting ores of iron, silver, jade, garnet
eyes within the rushing speed of things we do not see,
and of green that grows beneath the stone and feeds of these
melting upward in the darkness we have chosen not to see

The Earth is not one homogenous whorl,
but swirls of sediment and air and energy both dark and light
rebounding in communities across the universe, reflecting
with celestial speed the burning out of atoms and of what remains
in radio waves and human flesh and lovers lips upon a glass.

Knowing What Grows

Not the obliterations,
not the light leading into shadow,
nor the eviscerated bellies bleeding into mud,
nor the jagged holes in a skull which held
all that man loves and needs and fears...
these come soon enough to any of us
in the name of old age, disease, accidents.

It is the forced tearing of the fabric of those living,
the emptiness and building of bomb-proof souls
that is most terrible of all war's seeds,
seeds that cut across generations, deserts, oceans
and plant themselves sandpaper dry in immutable rock.
Why do we hasten the passing of those who pass
about us when there is not passage from this time?

Grassroots

Whenever office workers are standing around after work,
slouched against the bar on Friday evenings talking about
the way things work or who got paid or laid or laid off,
one name that almost never comes up is Joel Emmanuel Hägglung.

Nor do many teamsters, autoworkers, dock laborers, miners,
sitting around their lunch buckets, sweat soaking through their clothes,
turn to each other and say, That was a square guy who shot straight,
and without him my kids wouldn't have a chance of going to college.
Not many of them do that anymore when his name comes up.

Even poets, writers, opera singers, teachers seldom stare into the muse,
and say, when his name comes up, that's a name that puts to shame
the little ideas that you can use to lock a man's songs and soul into jail,
or that songs and letters are merely for entertainment in our time;
or even ask each other solemnly over the papers they are marking
like they still do in many countries of the world like Russia or Mexico or…
When was the last time an American poet and singer was executed
for singing songs that were written for men to sing while working,
and when was the last American poet really a laborer at heart?

Their eyebrows shift upward, shoulders shrug. What do you mean
to be a laborer, and what did he have a degree in and what school?
"Joel Emmanuel Hägglung"… must have been a small press man;
must have been before that… maybe back in the early Commie days.
And then someone who has pulled out a history book looks up,
and says with the air of someone having found something

Who was the last American poet shot to death for making love
and keeping his married lover's name his secret and dying for it
Or
Who was the last American singer to have his execution appealed
by an American President in office and by the not-so-blind Helen Keller?

Or
Who sang from America with so much power to the peoples of the world
that his ashes were mailed around the world in little envelopes and
stored for more than sixty years to be sprinkled at important ceremonies
for men who died trying to protect their families and educate America?
Or
Who was killed by the courts in Salt Lake City and cremated in Chicago
and is now fertilizing the soil and flowers of Colorado, and Pennsylvania,
and Ohio, and Sweden, and Nicaragua, and Australia?
Or
How do you define poetry if not by the human condition or communication
in ways that redefine our understanding of life with little words and
stronger actions that can set men free or lock their lives away?
Or
Why were a singer/poet's ashes mailed to every industrial nation in the world
and then forgotten except one envelope that was seized by the U.S. Postal Service,
was kept under a glass in a museum in Washington because our government feared
something that was not burned in that carbon dust prevailed and would
unlock the rights we all believed in as children, like Nothing stops the mail.
Why was that envelope set free and mailed out again so that fresh ashes could be
spilled in the suburbs growing on the edge of luxury condominiums in Colorado,
in a graveyard with a monument dedicated to machine-gunned miners from 1927—
12 years after the man had died, and 62 years before when the marker went up in 89?
What happened in that 75 years of industry that brought us to open the envelopes?

Most of the people who inhabit the upper classes, middle classes, lower classes
kind of shrug and do whatever it takes to show they're not too impressed by
some foreigner with a foreign name they can't pronounce. But in some back halls
in some dusty NPR or PBS studios, maybe at The Met, or in an old record shop
someone may put down their daily concerns and lean forward eyebrows raised to say
You're talking about Joe Hillström…I know about him because of Paul Robeson. Joe Hill,
the original hardworking hard-loving union organizer from the early 1900s when men died
   for being a whole lot less than that,

who wielded his words like diamond tipped chisels into songs to set men free in America,
the guy framed, encaged at last, and executed in his prime by the Utah copper bosses…

who came to America from Sweden and roamed the back-country labor camps,
chopping wood and mining ore from beneath the soil of America and organizing
the civil rights of any man or child regardless of their color or their country;
who was the first American folk song singer back before Woody Guthrie, long
long time before Bob Dylan, and in a different world where National Guard
troops mounted machine guns above western towns where labor laws were
being born and shot down into the towns at night killing women and children
just to keep the union organizers out of food and out of school. Well, it's
changed some now and we don't have to remember the name, I suppose, or
the tent towns that were burned in the night of our country's birth…Hell,
Joe Hill's best forgotten now unless you want to shake things. Of course,
I still wonder about a few things about the man and what was inside him
and maybe more, maybe a whole lot more about what we ever thought we
could do or what is inside a man that can't be locked away but keeps speaking.

It's important in some ways, though, that aren't contained within a name.
Names change. I can recite it out of mind. Joe Hill. Isn't that who
you're talking of? I can't imagine what it was they thought they kept
secret in little tin boxes or folded inside envelopes they sent out when
he died, surely whatever it was within him burned out except what
was on paper and written down, but someone believed him and kept that dust
through all the years between that time and ours while mines turned into malls
and the Columbine Mine in Colorado where six unarmed men were shot
by the National Guard that now protects our homes in Colorado is now
a parking lot where cars go to take their owners home not far from Lafayette,
where aerospace engineers mix with aging farmers and coal miners at the Café Mine.

I can't imagine it, but it must be a poem more than a song.
What is a song or a poem?
What forces it from the cavern of our minds.

What reverberates in our minds, and in our bones.
What does it take from us, and then bring back
and what comes back upon its melody.
I think this must be a part of what doesn't burn.
How many voices must one have to sing such a song
that wraps around a people not in one country
but all people in the serest, deadest land. It is
the music that we share that builds our understanding.

The lights go down over the bayou.
Water laps the roots of mangroves.
The Spanish moss encircles us.
A tree frog speaks from beneath a dock.
Another answers. A man knocks two
slabs of wood against each other. My eyes fill
and my bone dissolves. I hear Louis Armstrong and García Lorca
growing up in the impoverished ghettos, rolling their eyes
like billiard balls beneath the pirate ship moon,
and I wonder what makes a man to sing, to write.
You cannot put it in a performance hall.
It is something burning and suffocating
eternally through the years.

I can't imagine it burning there in the darkness and trying to get out in America
and in South America and in Europe and in Australia, fighting against ideologies
no man ever felt within his soul and standing up to them, burning holes in them
until some stranger made of shadows came to free whatever it was and let it
      blow to where some faded flower grows.
Perhaps, I think, it was not a man since all that is a man burns into the wind;
perhaps it was all that is within all men that comes on greater than all men,
that drives the electrons that drive the neurons that drive the history of all men,
that drives a sense of what it is to be a man—not a science, not an art, not labor,
not a song, not the pallid nothing of contemporary poetry—but *perhaps then*

some fading flower would come to life and bloom again
and that this would be the greatest and the final will when the banks and corporations and institutions of academic separation and world global financial trade away their modular clothes and religious wordings on their coinage and presidents come to admit that they too have one thing in common with every man and woman and child that lives to observe the world and learn from that which is larger,
Good luck to all…

Soaring on the Tectonic Waves of Time

A hawk folds itself into the updrafts atop Green Mountain,
its eyes now a part of the wind and the rock from which it came,
and in that instant it becomes itself the wind with a mind in time…
slow moving as it settles its way in circles down toward the earth again.
The light in its eye reflects the sage dry hills, the huckleberries' red blood,
the glass of family homes outside Boulder, the sun coming back. It is
a gliding between facets of time traveled across multiple universes.

These mountains are the slow-moving tectonic waves of time
tumbling over each other, wind whipping off the froth, sand shifting
and pulling away at the roots of whatever grows, but at a speed we
live almost outside of except for instants like these when we sit
on our porch watching out over the western ranges peak beyond peak
and shadows flow across evening canyons, shifting shapes so I rise
from the land, seeing from outside my body the rocks and trees grow small,
hovering with my shoulders against them turning back the tide not at all
but feeling the physics that set us all in motion in distant galaxies so long ago.

We start then with muses, as Hesiod wrote, telling of things that are,
that will be and that were with voices joined in harmony, and we partake
of shadow and of *eidos* in ways that are outside the neurons of our minds.
A mountain is a fabric and a wrinkle in the text of time, and is but one muse,
the city at its feet is another, in a concurrent folding of the fabric.

Living What the Mind Can Hold

When you live up close to the mountains
disaster comes at you quickly, without worry.
The floods, when they come, are instant washings
of trees, boulders, cars, mud, flesh, and then gone.
You rebuild instantly in a landscape shaped by nature;
you don't worry about the slow-building droughts
or the wearing away of cement-encased institutions
because you learn where the deepest rivers flow
and where the elk migrate among the seasons.
You learn the bitter acid tang of Oregon grapes.
You learn to keep a bit of land around you; you
learn to fill the hummingbird feeders in summer
because the bears will follow in their time, and
you never know when you'll need to find a bear.

Monsoon

The east winds are unsettling here, unnatural,
something against nature in the way they blow
cold and moisture in from the prairie states up
against the mountains. What more can nature
pile up against the shoulders of our continent;
enough, isn't it, that everything erodes away in
the normal passage of a man's life? The way the
jet stream always rushes east above us, it would
be natural if like a tired man the lower winds as
well stumbled down these pitch-forked heaps of
stone, just as usually they do. But stone is not
supposed to change as rapidly as these winds do
nor to let the wind sow rain into its crevices...
not here along the western flanks of our nation.

The sky is cornflower blue tonight,
mountains pasted against orange clouds.
No depth. But in this spring warmth
brought upon us Washington and Wall Street
are as far as a car can run on rum and corn.
Men with heart attacks building in their veins
are shipping coffins across the oceans
but here on the sere sands of home something
more sacred than all their dreams evanesces away.
I watch from my porch as distance falls flat with sun.

What would you have, poster child, filling your eyes.
A bucket of cornflakes with cream from the Midwest.
A trawler of fish from the mid Atlantic nights, eyes
flashing the distance of the big dipper at midnight,
casting spawn and milt across the Milky Way at dawn.
I think as we sit and sip our drinks I know your name,
but have been so wrong in so many things I dreamed upon.

Keeping Watch Over the Dead

They gather in remote areas
leaving nothing to chance,
bivouacking out beyond the trees,
silently, given their papers,
clustering together in groups of
tired and worn refugee families
where no one will disturb them.
But they talk, you know, you can
hear them when the wind blows,
and they are coming toward us
not one by one but by calling
others to the odor of their roots,
by their gathering of prairie seeds,
by the flowers that fill their smiles,
by the carving of the waters along
every town that grows into a city.

This is another way that cities come together
with their industry and magnetism
and energy and fire in the night,
with their hungry hollow walking
and their sleepless waking wailing,
with their majestic molten towers
and the betty crocker biscuit farmers
with talking silos at the breakfast table:
These things too that no longer talk
but creep forward carrying their stones.

Not that we lose track, not really
because each name and number
is kept on file a long long time…
back until the alphabets run out
and the matriarchal DNA sings

only in the loose branches of night
where the wind winnows leaves
on the coldest night of all; but still
someone somehow hasn't kept track
of how the seeds buried by tractors
keep coming back along the train tracks
down parallel metal corridors into cities,
and how butterflies themselves feed upon
the seeds and grasses and nectar
that once lay down beneath the ground.

How they come together from the centers
where people isolate their families,
come together for the cables
for the sitcoms from the front,
come together for the weather
and the trade of old ideals,
come together as a mass of electrons
glowing out into the desert of the night,
come together lighting up this globe in
little patches of the darkness of the soul.

Set up a reservation for these types
and what do you expect to happen
with all their dirty ways, rooting around.
Want to know what they're collecting,
what they're mining the earth for in
their little cubicles of earth factory time,
don't you?

Or how many of them there are.
Right now we outnumber the gathering ghosts
somehow after all these centuries where stillness

comes to still, still I wouldn't be counting on that
lasting too much longer. Probability
lays out its clotheslines with flesh,
but there's something beyond that
rancid and ripe flapping in the wind
advancing even while nailed down
and boxed and shipped and disemboweled.

They are coming for the news that sells the wheels
that collect; coming together all across the country
along the highways of our wars and peacetimes,
from Munich to Washington, from decade to year
and hotels motels no-tells ground the cables
on heavy tankers delivered from our past while
elections and electrons and data dots light it up.

I want to know what they say,
what the earth signals to itself
rushing outward in the cosmos
where we have no word for god
and yet our bones know somehow
where to go as the evenings gather.

Camelback

Electric light is perhaps the greatest illusion,
keeping us all on focus with what's around us,
I think watching cars descend down Camelback tonight,
each one a caravansary of the immediate: of NPR, of sports,
of Sirius radio with every band of music man has built
encased within a metal chassis made of punch card dreams.
I am the man behind the wheel on each turn, each sign
ignited in my headlights against the guardrails, I think,
sitting on my porch across the flatlands looking up that
I can see you settled sweetly into the upholstery, your
tanned legs and pouted lips illumined into shadows against
the windows that are so dark that everything reflects.

I don't know what goes on outside behind the guardrails
as I am speeding by, I think, with a whiskey in my hand, nor you.
Which begs the other question, perhaps, of what I type on my PC,
or of the electric starter that starts each car upon that hill, or
the furnace that heats our homes or radios or television news
or the computer chips that drive all things along in miniature.

We've never understood the way these gears interweave, I think,
and what chance to do so now when only the large and close are lit and seeable,
clicking the way down Camelback in the distance in the rising of the light.
A camel carries what it can of what it needs on desert nights, and light
is not something resembling a camel's weight but what it wants, I think
sitting on the deck outside our home with all the lights and television on,
hoping for communication that will change my life, searching
for Polaris from the stars of the Big Dipper and not knowing where it is
in an irrelative space measured by digital encryptions of electric light.

This is the West, I think. Take me back to doodlebugs, to candles
melted down and mixed with the flesh of man in holy cans of tin,
used to make only the shallowest dent of understanding, to light only

the most deliberate strokes of pen by men in search of understanding
when it meant something to stay up at night because it cost more than rent
to spend looking into the darkness, where one saw farther than the light on
Camelback. Come back, I think, to the time of log cabins in our mind,
when Lincoln sat in his log cabin of a nation and split rails not hairs,
writing on a shovel with burned out wood of the blind men of the *Iliad*,
traveling the world and all perversions to find out what was men.
and erasing it the next day to stay in context with what the message meant,
I think, I don't know, what goes on outside the light, but the clouds
over Camelback promise rain and lightning in the night. What we write
with coal in the darkness most enlightens us.

Do the Fish Drain Out?

Do the fish drain out when the ditch goes dry?
Do their eyes flash hard against the gemstone sand?

Through winter the irrigation ditch is kept dry,
autumn weeds profuse in their brownness filling,
twisting down into the nests of small red fox and rabbit,
a path that cougars take into the heart of suburbs,
a canyon of wildlife coursing perimeters of golf courses
across the flatlands just before the Flat Irons rise into the sky.

From Pittsburgh comes the heavy steel that builds the trucks
for carrying men in asbestos plastic overalls with axes and flame-
throwing Bunsen burners to clear the weeds away each spring,
to burn the brush and scorch the ground and seal the sands…
such trucks of steel from Pittsburgh, which come in to spawn
with iron from Indiana that grows in the shape of cogs and
wheels blocking up the lower edges and levees of each ditch,
waiting to be turned. *You never know*, the old man said to me,
what kind of animals are going to come up out of them each spring.

And each spring, each parade of the rubber men and each parade
of the steel and iron armies across the plane beneath the Flat Irons
is to wash the mountain snows full bore out into the plains each spring,
to scrape the ashes from each ditch and seed the arid land with grain;
and each of these waves of life is filled with fish from the mountains,
with their small eyes filled with snow-capped overhangs and air
so crystal clear you can hear the stardust fall upon the moonlight;
their mouths open, grabbing life from the soil themselves they come
to nest and spawn and breed among the reeds that line their banks.

A season, until the crops are grown and iron armies take them all away
to wait for what again, and the ditches go dry and the fishes perhaps
drain out, or do their eyes flash hard against the gemstone sand?

The Science of Expanded Understanding

The whole Front Range disappears from distance;
sometimes because of the curvature of the earth,
sometimes because of the dirty ways of industry,
but the nature of life and rock is thus invisibility.

And when the Continental Divide is neither there
nor the cold, cold rivers that give us life among
deep pools, then too there are no ranchers nor are
computers nor tabulators nor mappers able to re-
present the folds of consciousness separating us.

Nor are there farmers, nor hidden houses where
our unfound lovers can write messages of love,
nor is there a vocabulary that reaches inside us,
because each day it's in the nature of the beast to
need to reach out and traverse the distances, to
walk or drive or dream our way across our essence
without which any of this is meaningless and poetry
gives away to a dry science that has no meaning
and our bones are so caught up into the light of
expanding cosmos and so a part of time there is
no meaning, no poetry, no religion, no time, and
                    no expanding cosmos

Petroglyphs Above *Mesa Verde*

From the green table looking up into sand dry cliffs
you need the eyes of an eagle to see the schools
where words were chiseled rock on rock into stone.
A tourist or even a guide sees the animals encaged
with corn in mud-built cribs waiting for hard times,
but not the ancient ones who count the feathers
or note that at this site the circle is north-facing slope,
the one over there far older is facing south, or this
circle was drawn with ragged outline, that one smooth.
Two storage bins in that mural, one with a wild deer.
In that there is something that might be a fish or
something more likely in a dried out land like this.

It's clear that not one hand but many held the brush
that painted ochre on these walls inside our homes,
and that the arrangements were more than icons of desire
or ritualistic blankets woven of dryland sage and sedge.
In all time one takes the tools one has learned to use
to speak of other things one cannot control and say
to others if we were just to pluck another feather from
the wind or from the sere waste that stretches below
our outlook we could shape the way the wind blows.
Note I lay my brush this way when I speak. Now you.

There is indeed something terrible in the ancient ones
that lingers in the stone fortresses they build before
disappearing into the funnel of time they comprehend.
It may be the broken lettering of unfocused language
or of unfettered minds in the open terror of time here
settled in the backwash of gum wrappers and cigarettes,
but looking down on the highways far below us, where
muscles are not even strained at speeds beyond belief
it is incomprehensible how much space and time control

what it is we work with, running from our fingers to our minds generation upon generation losing names and gaining control of metal methodologies. I hear rain beginning to fall on the lower slopes, and see my footsteps by starlight on the rocky slopes.

Among the Mystic Mountain Men

I'm an urban fighter once skilled
with hard-edged things, wired
to the paychecks of accountants and
used to sending men into the ground
for precious metal or food grains or
permanently if the need is there
without raising my voice or doing
anything but pressing digits on a phone.

I was a thing of bricks in a mahogany
office of books and desks and sweat
with no windows except for those
looking out on other windows and
other men sweating animal fear behind
mahogany brick walls where women are
paychecks distributed by wire, but

I have been going west for thirty years
and earth has swelled from the heartland
as I have followed the setting sun, and as
the sun sets we become eagles and stolid
mountain peaks are more a home to us...

Ex-urban fighter, I now look out at land which
overlooks the ambitions and offices of warriors,
seeing the weak institutions we create among fields:
small against the plains and smaller against mountains.
Men give degrees for this and speak of dreams.
I do not have to take to be alive. I do not have to take
because I am an urban warrior, now in a pastoral land
and the sharp edges of mountains now cross my soul,
and drawing the mountains into oneself is understanding
and that is power over any man who speaks with threats

whether he comes with fighter planes or paper ballots
or with lies to buy food for a family's future. I, a
one-time urban fighter, know the weakness of my knives
and now the indomitable strength of lives.

A man who speaks
these languages speaks no words to anyone, is a tree
in a clearing growing old as the green foliage drops away.

American Hero

Coffee blurred highway baking down,
the all-news radio on, its streaming ads and
here I am another day of work breakfast in my hand
an egg and sausage trying to keep going a cup too hot
I'm watching the traffic, avoiding, breaking, stopping,
not able to catch the hot grease staining my shirt,
well that's what they get a grease ball for the day
that's what they get and how I am to greet customers
this day like so many others with a shrinking check. I
want to find another woman with a good job who likes me
or will put her purse down where I can get it...
arousal or anger, I'm not sure, but it fills my mind in traffic.

Why are the cars such bright colors, why the clothes,
why the flowers planted outside wind-worn homes. Why
do the keys jingle like Coney Island jewelry in our pockets
and the clocks make chunking noises when they count our names...
You want an identity, I've got one pre-shredded, bagged, and
it takes a lot to go through this every day the rest of your life.
I'm talking American Hero, lifelong soldier in a body bag
proud to keep on fighting for babies and wives and god.
An anthropologist would say there's violence building here.

What do we need, some kind of ombudsman to spread the word,
some kind of church built of human horrors, or maybe just walk out
in the middle of the day and take whatever we want from our offices
or drive school buses off across the farthest country roads. Maybe
there's still time to wake up in the evening and not take a drink
on the way home except with my buddies' home brew, and take
the wheels off this damned scrap of sunburned metal coinage,
stop driving in the same circles we grew up in and go out
to the dark alleys that are not lit by economists' ideas
and where food doesn't come in sculpted metal carts on rubber wheels.

The Eye of the Cyclops

in binary code is always open.
No man has hurled his spear into my eye.
No man is all men. And no man
today on a desecrated island rolls his stone
away from the cave that prophesies our demise.
I am an octopus on the sands of the Rocky Mountains.
My hands suck the stigmata of entire cultures.
Such things we sing from sharpened sticks alone.

If You Squeeze a People

If you squeeze a people in an arid land
the best among them will sit in the mountains
studying the reds and blues of flowers,
drawing their essences out for war paint
or wild and primitive mating rituals that pass
nothing on to children but life itself,
strip the bark from trees for medicines or
for working into silent crafts of the rivers,
will learn to weave the sere grasses of summer
into vessels that can be filled with harvests,
will call to the wolves, coyotes, and cougars
in the brotherhood of their moonlit fear. Blood
will be a color of the landscape after sun goes down,
and of the sky before and after everything congeals.

The best among them in the mountains will chant
around campfires worshipping memories and tossing
dried bits of dusty trees and shadows upon embers,
and their listeners will come…you cannot stop them
if you squeeze a people in an arid land where there
once was love and people knew how to sing this song,
they will come out upon the mountains and sing
in a harmony that bounces back from the native rock
sending shivers along the spines of those more civilized.
I see nothing bad in this…these tuning forks, these words,
vibrations across an empty space of consciousness where
nothing lasting is built except that which always changes.

I capture the mountain rivers in my hands in this way
while others may cup their palms and hope to save life
from being battered on its way downstream to the oceans.
All things are filled and moved trembling between stars
whether lost children in the desert, a scared fawn, a myth,

a stone knocked loose from the shape of stone, anything.
One becomes another over time, and one is richer then when
one asks another how best to use this time and earth we own and owe.
Perhaps it's not best to squeeze a people in an arid land,
because their decisions then might be formed in haste,
their blood poured out before its time, their reason for
sitting and discussing the patterns in the lands forgotten
before they ever have time to light the fires they would.

Societal Psychosis

A man must be as twisted as these mountains,
inflexibility and the crush of whatever sediment falls pushed up
and taking shape from patterns not imagined from forces
flashed in the molten center and pushed outward through veins,
hardening and twisting wherever the weakest arteries are found.
Here the granite, the garnets, the gold useless in darkness.
Would we think a child would be less twisted in our furnaces,
less weathered by the tin clocks laid out upon his trails?

What's in That Great Steel Belly?

Sometimes it takes the arms and legs of a lover
blowing apart while pushing a shopping cart
to make a man sit up and stop tinkering. It should
n't, but sometimes it has to get personal that way
before a man says Hey what's in that great steel belly
the legislators rolled into our town last night, and
what kind of monsters are going to come out of it?

What's important though is that it's going to be awhile
after the first neighborhood stores go up as funeral pyres
before the first man stands, stops sobbing and pulls back,
deciding that revenge can't fill his hairy belly no matter
where he lives and where he buys the wire that fires him.
Sometimes it takes the arms and legs of his lover
folding about him instead of raining down in pieces,
but it takes a long time in the eyes of a cow in a pasture
once he starts building bombs instead of spreading seed.

I envision an economy where we beat our swords into opium
pipes and alcohol vats instead of armored cars and tanks, and
eventually you have to trust each man to go the way he would…
those who want to slow down and plant a seed or light a candle
or get together with their buddies and build a ship can do
that as well, or can remind each other how they used to read
because after all even when a man is in a cold stone funk
he either gets bored and gets better or dies by himself
without taking any armies of men or countries with him.

I envision an economy where merchants make much more
even if they cannot dream by selling dreams to dreamers,
and where the merchant dreamers are dream catchers who
catch the limbs of lovers by candlelight, wrapping them
in their own erotic and endless meanings of eternities,
I envision an economy not of speed but of instance
where ships troll slowly and little enough is thrown away.

Wanna Be an Executive

Real executives don't keep pets.
They don't have cuddly poodles
that swarm about their feet or
snuggle up on their beds at night.
They have pristine wives instead
traded in on a regular basis who
think timid and healthy thoughts
and smell like hot wild animals
with eyes that open into nothing.

Perhaps That Too the Shadow

It's hard to see how an ant colony operates.
It's hard to see for a poet or scientist
what moves the herd. The herd is one.
It's hard to see for an ant how a man operates
or where he comes from or how to control
his impulse to shuffle through town with impunity
or how to bring him down. But ants are in council
somewhere there is no accountability,
are in council as one where there is no light
and little things can weigh heavily upon a man.
The sky too is dark tonight, the stars small.
Perhaps that too is the shadow of a man.

Retaining an Empty Cell

Evensong was her cell phone tone,
and hearing that was one way of knowing she was home.
The other of course just the ringing and her husky voice
saying I'm not home, but promising she would be soon.
Silent messages into the night coming home.
Even so, I've kept the phone now I'm alone,
and even now I pay the bill each month so she is close.
Only on this line in all the data dumps of the world
and empty streets can I hear her voice, and know it mine.
I've taken to calling vendors and asking them to call back,
then turning up the volume to hear her say she'll be home.
I've taken to turning her rings to vibrate
and pressing them against me in the night
while I call to her on another line.

Not Cutting Too Close to the Root

The For Sale sign goes up on my lawn tomorrow,
and I'm not sure what my hairy belly will think,
or how the lawnmower of my balls will react to that
probing question and excitement but I guess it's going
to be better than sitting in chairs and wondering why
the neighborhood's gotten more predictable since we
started watching the television news each evening and
stopped growing our own vegetables in the farm plot
after that one pale zucchini turned out to be a gourd—
man that was a bitter, poisonous fruit to taste—not that
I come easy but neither am I slow to learn and you
would think that we would have learned the world is
a safer and more stable place when we stay inside our own.

The Girl in the Coffee Shop

was different. Really. She
had a pair of tits that wouldn't quit
and a grandfather who was the
radio man on the Enola Gay.
She cried a lot in the evening.

In the Rooms the Motels Match

We are most powerful when most vulnerable,
closest when most distantly apart. We are
connected by the logo on a toothpaste tube, by
the plasma beams from sculpted worlds filmed far
away from the sets our fathers placed upon our walls.
Squeezing apart all these miles that are between us.
You bring the whiteness to your small fangs,
as I too keep mine from dropping out. And
the harried accountant's deepest sighs are keeping score
not of one man's wealth nor stockholders' boats nor
necessarily golden parachutes but of what holds us
within the perimeters of our childhood dreams. We
who sat behind dime store windows, display cases
encased listening in our odorless artistic intensities
are getting older now and are inevitably going away,
but we hold on to these tags that are ourselves in
some of the little ways that keep us all apart together.

We are most vulnerable in the fence posts of our childhood
You with desires of white clapboard house, shaded porch,
with rows of roses growing up along its picket fence and
Tom Sawyer with apple handing out deep buckets of whitewash.
I with Berber carpets and darker furniture and woods
filled with mildewed books and darker words. Or you
in some way that our grandparents saw these things before
they began carrying their days in cars across our land. In
the boom the motels come and go speaking of what makes it so.
I do not think that they will speak to you and me, but what
is within them surely will as long as light goes on. The wires
and desks and hands that remind us of what we started with,
what we planned. We can sit forever and talk about looking
into plastic screens, eye to eye across the miles where we live
with hard planned families which have ceased to be. It is
as if I hardly need to taste your lips nor touch your flesh,
and the wires are coming loose at last.

Cold As a Politician's Tit

Wind as cold as a politician's tit came in
moist, dank, and hard from the east last night,
one of those November monsoons filled with fear
designed to make you forget the flaming gold aspens
or the aspen trunks themselves logged up in the fireplace
sitting with your lover late afternoon after skiing at Breckenridge.

Hush little baby, don't you cry.
Daddy's going to give you room to die.
If the timing of that dying just won't do,
the market's going to leave it up to you.

Of course we coped, and the cannon crews got out
firing their rounds into the mountains bringing snow down
with rocks the size of avalanches over homes.
Trees gave up their roots, but the people somehow survived
and paid their tickets for another cattle crazy ride with god
on wings as cold as a politician's tit, the autumn winds bit
at our fingers until our wallets slipped beneath the ice.

If that market's not going to ring
Daddy's going to buy you a diamond ring
that will last longer than your bones
with GPS linked to cell phones

But women wear white ermines on such days, so who
when warmed with all that skin and with liquor to begin
taking the pain away would say that it was not a decent cause
we gathered there for with our morals not matched to our laws
and held an aspen institute to garner our ideas, our history
blowing west from the east on the wings of a politician's icy tit.

The women's ermines don't have shame,
nor family trees to strut their names.
They do it all with due diligence
and sell them off to other gents.

But still the harvest moon comes around here, every year,
and if there's one thing that that thought makes clear;
a man's a man for a' of that, and a' of that
a man's a man; a tit's a tit.
There's nothing coming after it
except a man's a man for a' of that.

People, Not So Much

Every single one of them has a nose
lying right in front of the jaws,
telling them whether to slip a tongue
or sink the teeth into a face.
And way down at the other end
most of them have some sort of stump
that tells one what the nose thought,
as if you'd need a reminder by then.

True of mountain lions, poodles, deer,
rhesus monkeys, alligators, bears,
and a whole lot of things with furry hair.
People not so much, though. Sometimes
you have to unwrap them and probe
because with people the teeth can lie,
and the nose may make that little stumpy thing
something a bit bigger and harder to handle,

which is something you'd like to know about
to know maybe if the ends justify the means.

Know in Your Absence

I had forgotten almost how to
touch your mind down here where
a freight train hangs my words
on cold tracks that sing with something
not my own nor yours but cars containing
factory floors and somehow songs that
touch you again here and here and
my fingers are tuned as memories.

Flight 539

Everyone on the plane is driving home alone
in their togetherness. The digital movie screens, ads, tickets…
It's a long, curved night around the moon.
Firelight, frost-touched cashmere sweaters, elegant
rolling amber liquors in a plethora of plastic packages.
Rise high sweet chariot! Joey's little girl got her first tooth
today. Linda's sister is getting married in the morning.
Paul's gonna' catch the next red-eye north.

Mementos

It's the knick-knacks on department store shelves that give it away.
I miss the way your hands used to curl about my thoughts each morning.
So much of life is our mementos being placed in orderly sequence and then sold.

Inside the Municipal Building

are sculptures of time,
immense courtyards of glass ascending
offices containing wires and desks
for secretarial elbows and folders,
gateways that beep at doorways of security
opening for the opening upraised arms
where the populace travels on Id cards.
There is much of Ego here above the masses.
Popes rise on air to upper floors
wafting on patents held in other fields
and oiled cables from foundry works.

Plans are shaped with the fingers and minds
of every man, Russian dolls inside each other
shellacked and impervious, a ripple in the universe
computer shelves and boxes where nothing is made of much
and silicon is sand upon a desert
which surrounds oases of our lives.

The Majority of His Life He Could Reduce to Movie of the Week

He scribbled many slogans inside his head
in that cerebral graffiti without paint
        "Desperation is simply life
                without the sales pitch."
                        "He hoped his misery was more
                              marketable than the next guy's."
                                  "Hey did you happen to see …"
but the slogans often disappeared just as birds do
strange for himself to quote himself to himself, while looking for
        inaccuracies in himself
was this enough of himself or did he need to get a few more of himselves
        in edgewise;
but as he began to understand, the quotation marks he attributed to
himself faded like crow's feet in a nervous mother's smile.
And the crow's feet became his oafish, Walgreen's stigmata feet
which each morning he anointed with Corn Huskers Lotion
mistaking the stinging for companionship
the cracks and fissures for experience,
pretending his calluses told stories
not even Dr. Scholl's on a good day,
would believe.

Each afternoon he went shooting
without a gun
knowing emotion like the spray of buckshot
had to nick a past love
or bleed into tv dinners,
sooner or later,
for the heart can be felled
with one smooth clean shot
from deep inside yourself.

He rode solipsistic shotgun
on the jet stream of vague recollections
took his own stupidity, wadded and shaped it into spitballs
that had no curve
but found their way to the backs of heads
who urged him into therapy
where he lip-synced such potential hits
as "How Does It Make You Feel"
how do you feel about that
does that feeling sound familiar
Still they never quite made it as explanations
or songs for that matter.
And when he examined it, scraped off the answers
he felt lighter than toast, the idiot myth.
Narcissus on the ice pond,
whose very reflection created a weight
about to give
way.

He wondered where were the Kewpie dolls
one was supposed to win with insight.
Why were realizations
                              as bare as branches.
Though grown children still live off of trust funds
could he live off the lone fat of his brain?

Half his thoughts tended to wear wigs,
the other half shed mascara tears
he would lick up faithfully
but sensitivity leaves blackened tongues
and a possible make-up overdose to boot.

He sought the women just leaving
because skin had its own distance
its own logic
impossible to figure or touch.
But imagination had its own skin
you could always touch
without figuring
so "go figure"
he told the hatchet-faced greeter at Wal-Mart.

The majority of his life
he could reduce down to Movie of the Week
bad dialogue. A movie that is never made but made up as you go along.
Lines you don't speak but speak through you.
Clichés you babble like the gaudiest of fountains
and your dignity lands you as the cherub facing East peeing on the lawns of suburbia.
"Do you choose solitude or does solitude choose you?"

What You Do When You Cannot Fly

One goose had a broken wing haunched
over its shoulder as it grew from its egg
almost, with death imprinted in its feathers,
slightly smaller than its sibling gaggle, but
always patrolled by two parental units,
two units who would never fly south again,
shuffling heavily even through late August
and eating its way never far from the pond.
Winter came and went but it remained
in the gusty feathers of misery and hope
if such a small and insignificant mind can
hope in the blinding whiteness of living, and
if the darkness at the center of its eyes can
see inside the same darkness that is ours then
surely the concrete tunnels that we built for
diversion of our waste were more a shelter
for life and the companionship of animals
and the caring of young through all seasons.
There now, I've said it, and I'm glad I've
laid it out where the darkness of your eyes
too can take it in and fold it like a hobo's
package as we trek across the coming America,
because geese are, like us, a smelly species
living in partnership through all their years,
and each one carries the burn of sunsets into night
pulled and twisted by things it cannot understand.

Why Real Men Don't Read Poetry Anymore

A lot of years go into reading the lines
between the lines M. L. Rosenthal said
every year as he taught the best of us how
Randall Jarrell wrote in the belly of war
and James Dickey in the Coca-Cola Corp.
and William Carlos Williams doctoring
and Wallace Stevens inking out insurance,
and he talked about scanning and all that
but also about how they caught the ear even
with their form and how you can't do that
unless you're out there talking to real men
about the things that can keep a man alive
when he gets so drawn out hungry he can't
hold himself up anymore or when he wants
a hot young woman to put her lips to him
for no other reason than he looks like what
she wants or he smells like the sound of money,
in any generation, in any literary period,
or she thinks he can outshoot any other man
because he's clearly killing men every day
and the gold pinstripe on his suit says that…
that's what real men talk about, and hear from
other men in every other walk of life you can
think of it any way you want, but when a man
spends his best years talking to children, even
the best children every year, he gets interested
in them…not just the tight skirts and bored eyes
but the same thing he hears coming back at him
every day of his life in that classroom where
people may be very smart but aren't around
the block enough times to offer much new to
the poet…so he keeps on spewing out the old
iambs and trochees and frailties and pain and
forgets there is a message comes before the form
and the message is spoken in language he doesn't
hear.

If You Want to Write

If you want to be noticed, write a poem with the effect
of being hired for a job after sixteen months laid off.
Write a poem that jingles in peoples' pockets.
Write a poem that Stephen Hawking reads.
Write a poem that takes apart the Atomic age
even as the ones Oppenheimer wrote put it together.
Write a poem that works harder for someone else
than for you and builds workingmen's unions.
Write a poem and fold it tight into an envelope
that will be the last thing a woman ever opens.

When You Stop Stroking the Machine

things don't change very much,
but the day I put *Poets & Writers* on my spam list
and opted out of all the retirement seminars lists
and canceled my subscription to *Consumer Reports*
and stopped the *Wall Street Journal* 'cause I moved to Colorado,
I got an aching feeling in my stomach, and no friends called
and my PC inbox stopped hugging me every time I turned on
and all my poet friends stopped asking for book blurbs, or
if they didn't maybe they just forgot to send any notes at all
most of them and those that did would pick up the phone
it being as cheap to call on their cell phones as not at all,
and all of a sudden I realized I was as popular as back in
the time when friends' book announcements came on Xeroxes
and the guys who called on the phone wanted to close a deal—
some of them running for president or financing a multinational,
so of course I helped them out because I was just writing poetry
and maybe if they closed a deal it might help some of us…
but there were just so many of them it filled every day and I
had to write by myself in the night when my family slept, so now
I think it's maybe just as good a time as any to cut out more spam
and get back toward living among the only people who can stand me
　anyway
and be back where the conversation turns to natural things and
nobody makes money ever because money doesn't mean an exchange
　of thought.

One of Our Own

People blinkin' out like fireflies on a bug zapper,
Charlie said as he rolled one of his own, a way of life
disappearing into the cosmos. Well, it happens time after time,
at least the way writers write about these things, he added;
but I don't know. Maybe I'm the first one to notice,
you know, the way language changes over time when
you write it down but it doesn't mean the same thing
a year from now when you pull it from your desk drawer;
and we've been among the best writers, the ones who paid
attention and dues and all the rest and listened in silent rooms
while other people around us made bug zappers and turned coins.
And I don't know that it hurt them zapping bugs,
and I don't know that the wheels of war make a hell of a difference,
just that it seems we're all one way and another drawn to light
that fries our hard drives down when we least expect it or see God.
You're one of our own, I say. *Good luck.*

The Making of Language

If I didn't have to be nice to children, I'd say
the road doesn't go on forever; heck, it hardly makes it
over the next hill when you carry the blacktop on your own back.
But that offends them and they've seen the great mirage already
driving westward looking out from their parents back-seat cars
shimmering where the heat meets the horizon in wavy lines...

so since I want to be paid I ask them how it feels to freeze
to the metal trees in their back yards when they stick out their tongues
to taste life in the middle of a January blizzard, and I say pull back
that image and look at yourself standing there bent over mouth open
eyes rolled back and baying at the storm clouds overhead and now
write it down in such a way that it makes dollar signs on paper that
can be cashed in the bank and taken home to feed your families.
It's easy, and anyone who can do that can write poetry,
and I drink myself sick on the way home.

Looking for the Foundations of Poetry

I'm looking at the home Webpage of Poetry Foundation
   dateline May 20, 2007,
and find nothing that is worth the time to sit at a keyboard
nor that makes me want to rebel against cultured media
nor that makes me feel an outlaw, nor makes me feel insider;
and find nothing that has any value to me as a person
   or as a member of society
nor any jingles that will reverberate in my head even
   at the very least
nor certainly any meditative calmness of mind that seeps
   out
anymore than as if I had just run a red light and hit a van
   filled with the bodies of small children.

Let's eviscerate:
the top left column is a "graphic poem," like a comic book
with pruney Dick Tracey faces and belly jellies over embryos
and a learned article about how poems are like comic books
that aren't funny but are graphic because the words get cut
into images
where they don't belong
like poets get up on stage and prance naked, but they don't,
I might add but I don't because blood obscures my eyes and I
can't imagine Auden or Eliot or Thomas or Wakoski or Buk
   or Kaufman or Ginsberg or Brautigan or
but then see that Graphic Poem #1 was cribbed from Wakoski
and I Buk the way Charles used to with my hole soul into beer
poured up out of some dark place deep in the bowels of society.

Then there's the blog link to click
and I click until some vacant image of a chick
sweetly opines how she can find the best poems online
before their authors are even old enough to write a book,

but it's coming, Look,
she says, Can I read this one. Can you? asks a fruity voice.
No, she can't: she mouths the words and they are empty sleds
with unwaxed runners running uphill over gravel winter roads.

Oh, Lord, it's entertaining,
but let's get to the meat of the matter: this
foundation is pushing poetry out its moneyed maw—hey
maw. hey paw, what's for dinner is whatever it wants to call
poetry
so I click next the podcast by a young editor and he says
until recently I never read much contemporary poetry.
And I think well why start now
with the sound of money.

Not Letting the Form Go On Another Generation

Today as the last hard snow melted away,
there were two-inch daffodil shoots green
emergent from the hard clay soil beneath,
but you could not see them. Another workday
where you sat once more in your starched sheath,
your breath too tight in the clothing I bequeathed.

Silicon chips. It comes to this from ruddy sunsets
driven across our continent while you were young;
from poems read to you in bed, from miles between,
I hoped that the factories' gleam would be what it seems
to me to be, irreducible from what is always sung,
by workers across generations met and never set.

But I see now we learned to confine it smaller still
into the little pleasures that bring us light and kill.

The Things That Happen

I too have had the little things that happen happen:
my braces stuck to the utensils of a young girl's mouth,
my tongue glued to an outside winter lamppost. I don't know
where we go from here…what separates us from the comic strips.

Things to Say in an Empty Room

I don't perform. I don't do it for the Man; I don't do it for you;
and I don't do it for an empty room of microphones
listening to the silence of everybody waiting to be free.
I don't do it for the host nor the emcee,
and I don't do it for my woman any longer than I want,
because I got a crazy thought one night…a light
that came on out of my glass of whiskey and lit up
with the reflections of windows no one looked out of
and the dull glaze of bricks getting mortared onto stone
and the sound of wind blowing aspens between stars.

I don't perform anymore, because I don't know what we're building
or why it seems worthwhile for some corporation to keep me inside,
and because I don't want to buy rings for women's fingers anymore.
I've got this short-sighted near vision sort of thing that comes from
looking out of Coke bottom glasses so long that indistinct is sweet
mass marketable nothingness that sits on shelves all day like men in
cartons coffins trade schools nestled packaged in their egg crate cups.

I don't perform, because I'm tone-deaf to the sirens wailing
and I don't see anything that can be destroyed that was not before,
and the sales are set and baited with sweaty suits I don't need
and I have sailed too long into empty lunch buckets with rusty hinges
and have then turned around proud and swaggered back into the daylight
with my finger raised and swinging my wallet in a roundhouse punch
  from the ground up because though my flesh is aging faster than the metal
   that they sell, by god I am alive still and the icons of industry are long dead.
And I know that every one of you will go away wondering what is it
that was said by that crazy grey-haired guy that night…well, let's
have sex, go down to the corner bar, write a poem, and cry
in each other's arms after the tab is paid and everyone goes home alone.

We're going home alone, my friends, and I don't perform
because it's too important and if I could talk to you any straighter
or you to me we wouldn't need to work in cardboard cubicles
or wash each other's dishes or take out each other's Glad trash bags
or sign time cards to account for time spent away from global trade.
Just you and me together at last, and that's when I do perform for real.

Mining Coal in Marshall

Hear it? There's someone walking over our heads again,
Bill used to say just before the whistle blew most days. I
don't know, though, because mostly I was just sweating
and the water filled my ears and my shoulders shook. Each
ligament cracked the ribs along our backs while we drilled,
dug, blasted. *I don't hear a thing,* I told him when I got
past gasping in each breath of that coal-blacked mountain air.
Someone going above our heads, he'd say, and I'd nod at last
convinced he was talking about the goons or mining boss,
but he didn't look focused like the guys around their whiskey
cursing or beating on their wives at the end of each day shift.
Not then, end of each day, when he looked to the tunnel roof
thirty yards down beneath the sandstone metamorphic overlay,
eyes following from one choked-off corner to another, and
he'd just stop sometimes if the shift foreman wasn't there and
he'd say that he heard some sort of music, some sort of
mechanical thing that had the sound of laughter in its hard soul.
Just the crushers breaking up the earth we bring up, I said,
right up until they closed down the mine that summer of 1929.

I'm taking my grandson and my dog out to the Mesa Trail this
afternoon, and maybe you'd like to come along as well when
the office lets you out if you have time to drive on over. I can
show you where Bill and I used to fill the ore cars by the gate
right across from where the water tower housed machine guns
manned by the National Guard at night. Right by that golden
stand of upper prairie grasses across from the abandoned school,
yes, where the horse barn has fallen apart these last five winters.
That's right on top of the shaft we almost made it out of that last
day right after the whistle blew, right there under Marshall, and
you can pick up a couple bottles of spring water across the street
before you come on down, but watch out for the bicycles, and the
cows that leave stuff lying around.

Preservation Hall, New Orleans, and Gregory Canyon Beyond Boulder, CO

The waves draw long and cold.
Lungs and gravid belly
the ocean promises, reminding
it will come even
while we walk the mountains
shells embedded in sandstone
metamorphosized above our heads
while the streetcar lights go out.
Roll over close your eyes inside
brick homes with wrought iron balconies,
courtyards of jazz along America's river.
We are here. Rising twisted as bacon
curling in a pan the radio's out
the media not reaching our log cabin
where the sun rises over Gregory Canyon,
autumn making its way among aspen, pine, juniper,
a huge entity of entities buried beneath our feet
reaching out and grasping sun
another year at a time each leaf
we are leaves each
a disc untouched but seen by man, falling
into coppered colors I black out on song and fall back
as the shells roll over me embedded deep in stone
music as the crickets in a bayou garden.
I know that space and distance
is abstraction and precious as Aunt Millie's tea service,
and I avoid that, but space
and distance are time enfolded in speed
and that speed unfolds across infinity.
I am a child still in love with broken notes.

Remembering the Touch of Stars

As evening comes upon us we see other worlds
more clearly. The houses beyond our balcony are small
no matter what their size. The lights upon the mountains
are large, whether car lights or house lights, enveloping
the space around their glass walls with heat and importance.
Stand here and we can see them across miles, though
in daylight they would not stand out from the stones, the grasses
we cannot see at all or scarcely remember in our talk.
The space between those lights and ours touches the stars
from which the fiery matter of our bones is wove.

Once, Beneath the Moon

Shelby, he said, learn to think with all the space
that is contained within the spherical orb of your eye,
and if you want a second opinion, use the other one.
Then, you puts your money in and takes your choice:
you lowers your monetary mechanical arm in and
takes home with you whatever gaudy thing grabs, and
hope to god it's bigger than whatever moment held it
so that it keeps on expanding beyond your body rags.

This is what's passing in the other direction
as you turn up the light, raising an eyebrow.
It is my way of checking out; saying so long, ciao,
I have copped my last feel. The grass
on a Colorado mountainside is the last
thing I will think of. My ashes will enter the food chain
and sure as life needs water will become a part of your children
but I won't remember your name while you are reading this.
I never knew for sure that you were going to pick it up.

Nobody can pay you enough for this
time you spend inside an institution when
trout are fanning in the fern-laid pool
with lowered brows and swollen lips
contemplating an endless stream of food,
I will be among them, along their gills,
inside their dappled, frothy universe
with no idea or feelings at all beyond our own.

The Enterprise Mine

The lady's high lace-up boot covered with mouse dirt
centered on the chessboard dining table was what got me,
facing west under the cracked window highlighted by a hot sun
while all the rest of that room was bleak as a working man
could be at the end of a long life looking out over the hills…
standard refrigerator next to a small box stove next to power
wheels and gears reaching down to a shaft below the cabin
maybe two feet and a one inch thick wall of board separating
the space where two men's heads must have slept the last night
some forty years ago I'd say by the buried cars outside,
had laid long looking into the night hearing machinery wheeze
from their fingers that last night on their blue-striped mattresses
and then gone away.

Where was she now, the lady who left that boot back in the '70s
centered in a hungry cabin just below timberline in a hollow
I had come to on this mountain I had climbed so many times
before without finding the old VW bus and the Ford Fairlanes
and the cut-out carburetors lying buried in fifty year old gold slag.
Twisted metal, I think, that and bullet holes buried in the spill.
It's a long, deep mine and what bright can come of that?
I don't know why anyone would bury cars with seatbelts atop
a mine in Colorado, and I don't know whether men or girls
were sitting in those cars when the bullets entered…I hope not,
I expect they were the shallow holes of young drinkers out
for target practice with their beer cans, but it's a darned long walk
for a man who's been drinking or wants to, and can a man however
else account for those tubes of metal being buried in the mine
and then go away.

Discovered and claimed and mined and sweated over by an
enterprising man, I muse, who clearly at some point dug himself too deep
during the years I was doing others' bidding at a wooden desk,

but what of the boot that still stands there on the table and the woman
whose leg tanned and strongly supple tied it to herself for warmth? Or
was it while I turned to my poetry after my wife and children slept
at the other end of a continent where the seaboard levels away into dark
and I kept myself awake all night trying to explain what I didn't see
happening between people who would somehow someday touch me
among the ripening Oregon grapes and sere switch grass, switching back
        and then going away
treading on boards that might break beneath my weight at any step.

Virtues of the Grassfire

The fire down Old Stage Road burned fast,
the way grassfires do with mountain winds behind them,
lighting canyon rock like a volcano coming back;
but it's in that speed that things survive if not caught
outside their burrows, if hunkered down in their dens
among the deep roots that permeate their lives, give meaning.
The fire blows past fast where it meets dry grass.
Hoses are no use, nor fire trucks out on the plains,
not until the flames draw up against the town itself.
Oh, we lost a house or two out there on the hills,
some artwork, paintings, a couple of songs as well,
blown away into the ages of wings that beat that night,
but the trees remain: the cottonwood, the piñon, spruce,
their trunks a bit blacked now, but they survive hardly
touched by the rage that shakes the grasses and moves on.
And the grasses too survive; I'm not sure what goes up
in that smoke that terrifies: certainly something does,
but the roots in the soil maintain their lives, dig deeper
and bloom again wildly when the spring rains come.

A man can make a stand in such storms at the end of town,
grab a shovel to clear brush away, hose down his fabricated home,
stop the fire with a blizzard of industry and camera crews.
That's all it takes: a man doesn't need deep roots for fire like this.
And it's just as well, because a man cannot come back like sage.

The bigger fires, though, we're lucky if they stay away.
The ones that get going in the national forest lands among pine
where the heat is greater and the flames roars two hundred feet high
and the trunks of trees are eaten away from inside and even the roots
of alpine grasses are heated over time beyond endurance.
These are the slow fires, the heavy ones that change a continent,

the ones that we band together to fight. We're lucky indeed to keep those fires away. They're enough to kill a man because they're slow and they sweep everything in their path. They come from a deeper drought, and I guess they have a purpose and a place, keeping man humble as they do, but they take a lot of life away for the sunsets that remain.

Seeking a Transrational Contemporary Postmodernism

an essay

Seeking a Transrational Contemporary Postmodernism

Our culture is in a state of simultaneously undergoing radical expansion and reduction in human knowledge. The sum total of our knowledge is increasing, while the *field* of knowledge possessed by any one individual is decreasing due to specialization. This is reflected not only in institutional settings, where teams of workplace professionals combine their islands of specialized knowledge through networked electronic systems, but in literature and poetry as well. Yet poets must strive to transcend these individualized islands of information in order to achieve meaningful artistic wholeness.

Information development and exchange is so fast—and frequently imperfect in its first iterations—that it requires two kinds of rational thought processes to develop it and make it emotionally meaningful. These thought processes combine, rather than divide, nonlinear creative rationality with a more linear rationality that is required in order to adequately represent a known base from which the new creative work arises. Such a combining of thought processes, reflective of the greater changes in the world about us, is a natural outgrowth of Postmodernism. I might call it Transrational Contemporary Postmodernism. If a poet is to capture the complexity of human experience in today's world, that poet has to reflect both kinds of rational processes by which our nation is evolving.

To achieve this, I seek to illuminate the linear and historical perceptions of a body of poetry at the same level that postmodernists have previously achieved in regard to physically sensual sound and imagery. This allows an intricate interweaving of thought and impression that brings forth the organic internal rhythms that are inherent to our lives as artists and as readers. One is not restricted in this way to being "an invisible eyeball," as Emerson claimed to be, nor to reveling only in the barbaric yawp of Whitman, though it all becomes part of the eclectic mix. One incorporates the transcultural intellectualism of Eliot and Pound, enlivens it with Albert Goldbarth; involves the imagism of Stein and Monroe with the mysticism of Robert Bly and W. S. Merwin; gives increased depth to the confessional agony of the artist as seen in Denise Levertov or Charles Bukowski; rolls it together with the sexual ecstasy of the Beats, the restrained balance of Galway Kinnell, the interior landscapes of Mark Strand; and achieves a new and more powerful eclectic balance that invokes and perturbs the whole spectrum of transrational experience. Contemporary poetics are designed for this: the organic line-breaks, internal rhythms and rhymes, and alternating cadences to match alternating frames of mind.

In this way, the postmodernist view of artistic development, which has been described as a circle—where perceptions and the means to invoke them are endlessly rediscovered by each culture—becomes perhaps more like a tightly wound spiral where each generation lays out its own broad expanse of artistic endeavor so that the next generation can draw the threads tight and keep at least a fringe expanding into the unknowable.

Alphabetical Index of Titles

index

4/26/72 and God / 48
Across a Continent / 35
After a Woman Is Removed from a Rome Necropolis / 488
After Midnight / 59
After Sundown at Rye Beach / 434
After Twenty-five Years / 499
The Alchemist's Stone / 384
Along Back Roads from Illinois to Pennsylvania / 433
The American Museum of Neutral History / 60
American Hero / 541
Among the Mystic Mountain Men / 539
And All the Day / 103
And the Beat in His Chest Goes On / 278
Andrea / 296
Animus / 38
Annelid / 76
Another Saturday Night with Cassandra / 283
Another Time / 100
An Apology / 294
An Arborist's Taxonomy / 412
Asking Forgiveness / 432
At Breakfast with All the King's Men / 504
At Christmas, Just Before Midnight / 397
At Evening / 286
At Home / 297
Autumn Is a Red Deer / 211
Autumnal / 83
Beach at Oceanside / 225
Because No Space Is Now Mine / 101
Becoming Another / 492
The Beehive / 45
Before the Fire / 298
Being Born of Bone / 402
Believing That You Understand / 266
Best Not to Know a Town Too Well / 441
Between Meetings / 281
The Blood of Wolves / 50
The Board Meets in November / 279
Brain Creature / 368
Camelback / 533
Cold as a Politician's Tit / 553
Coming of Age / 363
Coming on New Mexico / 81
Communing with the Dead / 468

Commuting / 234
The Company We Keep / 208
Controlled by Ghosts / 319
Coping with Technology / 464
The Corridor / 28
Dallas / 73
Dark Machinery of Maybe / 467
Dark Wing: / 151
Datamatatrons / 102
A Day in August / 215
Dead People / 401
Dead Stalk Watercolor / 56
Death by Drowning / 26
Departing from Portland / 61
Destination: Hunting / 41
The Dirty Smelly Mess / 473
Do the Fish Drain Out? / 535
The Dover Gas Garage / 33
Driving Small Town America / 327
Elegy to a Beetfield / 93
The Endless Chairs / 349
The Enterprise Mine / 579
Erie / 333
An Erosion / 331
An Essay on Illuminations / 196
Estuary / 24
Eternal / 51
Evening Along the Outer Banks / 329
Evening Coming in the East / 232
As Evening Draws / 207
Evening in the Heartland / 209
Evening, Yes, but a Man Is Still a Man / 449
Evening's Song / 47
Expectation of Six P.M. / 62
Exultance / 221
The Eye of the Cyclops / 542
Eyes, / 335
The Eyes on the Coin / 285
The Eyes Too Walls / 231
Face of the Phoenix / 228
Fast-Food Lunch: NY / 191
Father, / 382
Finding Love / 214
Finding Oneself in an American Fairy Tale / 323

Fine Bone China / 420
Finishing Work, / 490
Flight 539 / 557
For a Woman Dead in Grand Central / 241
For a Woman Minding the Store / 489
For My Daughter in Moonlight / 243
Fortress / 476
Fossil / 403
From the Rigging / 177
From Your Flesh / 240
Full Moon Above Main Street / 404
The Gates Are Set to Close / 418
Getting Ready to Move On / 307
The Girl in the Coffee Shop / 551
Give Our People / 199
The Glass Forest / 66
Grassroots / 522
The Graves Grow Bigger Between Generations / 450
Greenwich / 244
The Hand-off / 413
Having Never Wanted to Own the Business, / 458
Having Passed the Solstice / 336
He Who Says the Name of God Will Perish / 259
Helios / 425
Hibernation / 224
Hollowman / 365
Human Kindness / 460
I Wish That You Were Here in Spring / 290
If You Squeeze a People / 543
If You Want to Write / 565
If...but No / 201
Imagination and the Man / 337
Impossibly a Businessman / 198
In Age / 398
The Incident / 216
In Grief / 498
In Memory of Strain / 235
In Our Attraction to Electronic Media / 325
The Insomniac Groom / 42
The Intensity of Light / 414
The Interview / 226
In the Beginning / 442
In the Dark of the Station / 99
In the Parking Lot / 299

In the Plate Glass Window Factory / 261
In the Rooms the Motels Match / 552
In the Year of the Comets / 271
Information Superhighway of Death / 301
Inside the Municipal Building / 559
Invisible / 233
It Has Started / 288
It Is Time / 338
It Takes a Man / 213
Ka-ching! / 405
Keeping the Outlaw Alive / 178
Keeping Watch Over the Dead / 530
Know in Your Absence / 556
Knowing What Grows / 521
Lake Michigan / 310
The Last Nightmare / 52
The Last Snow Fell / 364
The Last Trip We Took Together / 292
The Last Wedding / 70
Learning to Breathe / 479
Leaves and Spit / 407
The Lessons of Millennia / 341
Letter to H. S. Mauberly / 27
Life at the Margins / 455
Lines Written in a Waiting Room / 253
Little Cowboy Geniuses / 419
The Little Things / 422
Living What the Mind Can Hold / 528
Looking Back on Having Left / 63
Looking for the Foundations of Poetry / 569
Looking into the Machinery / 480
Lowered Expectations in the Lower 48 / 471
The Majority of His Life He Could Reduce to Movie of the Week / 560
The Making of Language / 568
A Man Screaming / 189
A Marriage / 34
Masks and Carved Animals / 409
A Matter of Degrees / 393
Meditation on Old Movies / 65
Mementos / 558
A Memo Torn Along the Dotted Line / 282
The Mind / 200
Mining Coal in Marshall / 575
Model for a Romance / 230

Modern Man, Artificial Intelligence, and Humanity / 248
Monsoon / 529
Mood in Grays / 309
Morning Owls / 220
A Mountain in a Suitcase / 386
Nanotechnology Man / 427
Nationbuilding / 417
Night Heron / 502
Nobody Writes about Children / 212
Not Cutting Too Close to the Root / 550
Not Letting the Form Go on Another Generation / 571
Not One Homogenous / 520
Not the Lone Ranger's Horse / 262
Not Time / 421
Observing the Constellations in Grand Central Station / 430
Ode to a Goose / 272
Of Fire / 98
Of Little Things That Carry Weight / 456
Of Moons / 362
On Mr. Peabody's Estate / 268
On the Official 40th Anniversary of the Dignitaries at the U.N. / 247
Once, Beneath the Moon / 578
One of Our Own / 567
One / 227
The Only Man Who Lives / 95
Only One / 75
Our Last Walk / 293
Passage from Home / 308
The Paycheck / 242
Pebbles in a Stream / 267
The Penitent Voyeur / 239
People, Not So Much / 555
The Perfect Mirror / 357
Perhaps That Too the Shadow / 548
Petroglyphs Above *Mesa Verde* / 537
Picking Up the Empty Packages / 326
Poetry and Baseball and Pay-As-You-Go / 507
Poets / 474
Pondfield Road / 495
A Prayer in the Teeth of Time / 494
Preservation Hall, New Orleans, and Gregory Canyon Beyond Boulder, CO / 576
Promontory / 31
Proud Ilium, / 416
Putting the Passengers Off in Small Boats / 275

Putting Your Money In / 277
A Quantum Species / 324
Ramses Visits the Cradle of Democracy / 408
A Recurring Particular Day / 58
Reflecting on the Visions / 340
Remembering the Touch of Stars / 577
Remembering the Union Dead at My Door / 254
The Renter / 486
The Reservoir in Drought / 270
A Response to a Conversation with William Packard Where We Tried to Define Poetic Craft as Practiced by All Schools of Poets / 222
Retaining an Empty Cell / 549
Returning Home / 291
Rivers in the Ocean / 411
Roadhouse Restaurant & Grill / 428
Saturday Evening / 80
Saturday / 97
The Science of Expanded Understanding / 536
Searching the Horizon / 32
Seeking a Transrational Contemporary Postmodernism / 585
Seven Minutes Before the Bombs Drop / 321
Silence / 55
A Silence of Wings / 71
A Silver Zipper / 447
Sitting Dark in Life / 193
Snowball, Gregory Corso, and a Village Stoop / 399
So Far Descending / 194
So Much Growing / 342
So You Say You Got a Job? / 465
So, Here's, Then, to the People / 366
Soaring on the Tectonic Waves of Time / 527
Societal Psychosis / 545
Solitudes / 54
Some Primal Memory / 265
Something Natural Happening in an Office / 280
Something New Is Hunting / 506
Something There Is / 483
Song of the Blood / 107
Sound of Late Moonlight / 289
A Space Between Time / 359
The Spellweaver's Workshop / 67
Storm King Mountain / 380
The Street of the Little Sun / 84
Stroke! / 406

The Sun Finding Your Hands... / 287
Symmetries / 388
Symphony / 461
Tales of Silent Men / 284
Talking to My Son / 334
Tea Leaves in a Chamber Pot / 448
Then Gone / 263
There Is Something Soft in This / 49
They Did / 78
They've a Kind of Patronage / 229
The Things That Happen / 572
Things to Remember / 360
Things to Say in an Empty Room / 573
This Poem / 519
This Town Is Young / 195
This, Really, Is This / 202
A Time of Looking / 72
To Be Alive / 462
To Remember US By / 352
Tossing Jobs Around Like Manhole Covers / 350
The Tower / 46
Tracings / 454
Translucence / 400
Transparency among Ghosts / 469
Trout Fishing Along the Allagash / 358
A Trout in the Pick-Up on Papago / 511
The Turning Off of Lights / 77
Turtles / 300
—Twenty Years of Empty Spaces in the Rolodex— / 395
Underneath / 29
Unforgiving / 396
Unhinged at Last / 355
Unsheathed and in Pain / 496
Violins / 30
Virtues of the Grassfire / 581
Visions of a Pencil / 218
Wafting Through Trees / 493
Wait / 353
Walking the Perimeters / 256
Walking the Shore / 274
The Wall / 192
Wallpaper Memories / 410
Wanna Be an Executive / 547
Watching / 25

Watering the Lawn / 505
We Are the Dawn People / 503
We Are the Poets. We Live / 223
The Wedding Night / 44
What I Take to My Grave / 501
What Light? / 426
What Makes the Man Different / 205
What the Gardener Knows / 485
What You Do When You Cannot Fly / 563
What's in That Great Steel Belly? / 546
Whatever Happened to Johnny Rebel? / 472
When All Is Said / 351
When It's Time to Go / 354
When October Comes and the Wind Blows / 203
When You Stop Stroking the Machine / 566
Where Colors End, / 429
Where Nothing Gentle Survives / 79
Where the Farthest Galaxies Roar into Nothingness / 435
Where We Lived / 491
Where Wind Shakes Our Bones / 276
Who Carries the Message? / 475
Why Put Up with This Anymore? / 385
Why Real Men Don't Read Poetry Anymore / 564
The Wind in Winter / 206
With No Return Addresses / 424
With Sunsets / 500
Within the Garden / 57
Within the Islands of Solitude / 343
Witnessing the Writer Who Tried to Raise a Family; Dark Matter at the Beginning of the 21st Century / 345
The Wolf Shadow / 23
Wondering What It Takes / 264
The Word That Had Many Voices / 379
You Cannot Write a Poem / 237
The Young Success / 69
Your Room by Candlelight / 356

About the Author

Jared Smith is the author of nine previous volumes of poetry, dating from 1983, in addition to two CDs, and stage adaptations of his work in New York and Chicago. Actively involved in the literary and poetry scene for more than 40 years, he has served as an Editorial Board Member, Board Member, and Advisory Board Member of *The New York Quarterly*; as a Contributing Editor for *Home Planet News*; as Poetry Editor of *Trail & Timberline*; and several-time Guest Editor of *The Pedestal Magazine*, as well as past President of Poets & Patrons in Chicago; and host of three reading venues during the 1980s in New York's Greenwich Village; among other ventures in the arts.

His poetry is of the intellect, of the natural world about him, and the passions of life as well. It has been compared by critics to that of such diverse writers as Pablo Neruda, Philip Levine, Ted Kooser, Robert Frost, Ralph Waldo Emerson, Walt Whitman, and C.K. Williams, among others. His is a voice of the people, but distinctly different from what has been before. Perhaps it is hard to draw exact parallels, because his visions, passion, and insight come from both the world of literature and that of science and technology, where Jared spent many years in research, administration, and policy formation. After earning his degrees in poetry and literature from NYU, Jared spent thirty years in technology research and education, including appointments as a Special Appointee and Adviser to Argonne National Laboratory and technical and policy adviser to several White House Commissions during the Clinton Administration.

Jared now lives with his wife in the foothills of the Rocky Mountains, not far from Boulder, Colorado.

The New York Quarterly Foundation, Inc.
New York, New York

Poetry Magazine

Since 1969

Edgy, fresh, groundbreaking, eclectic—voices from all walks of life.

Definitely NOT your mama's poetry magazine!

The *New York Quarterly* has been defining the term contemporary American poetry since its first craft interview with W. H. Auden.

Interviews • Essays • and of course, lots of poems.

www.nyquarterly.org

No contest! That's correct, NYQ Books are NO CONTEST to other small presses because we do not support ourselves through contests. Our books are carefully selected by invitation only, so you know that NYQ Books are produced with the same editorial integrity as the magazine that has brought you the most eclectic contemporary American poetry since 1969.

Books

nyqbooks.org

poetry at the edge™

www.ingramcontent.com/pod-product-compliance
Lightning Source LLC
Chambersburg PA
CBHW021846230426
43671CB00006B/287